JESUS
AND HIS
STORY

JESUS
AND
HIS STORY

Ethelbert Stauffer

TRANSLATED FROM THE GERMAN BY

Richard and Clara Winston

ALFRED A. KNOPF   NEW YORK

1960

L. C. Catalog card number: 59-15321

© *Alfred A. Knopf*, Inc., 1959

THIS IS A BORZOI BOOK,

PUBLISHED BY ALFRED A. KNOPF, INC.

FIRST AMERICAN EDITION

Originally published in German as JESUS: *Gestalt und
Geschichte*. © A. Francke AG. Verlag Bern 1957.

To THE BUDAPESTI REFORMATUS THEOLOGIAI AKADEMIA

In respectful gratitude for conferral of the degree of
DOCTOR HONORIS CAUSA

PREFACE

T HIS BOOK has sprung from the endeavor to find a fresh way to approach the historical Jesus. It is not a summary of the material that may be found in many larger Lives of Jesus. Rather, it is intended as pioneer work.

It used to be thought that only the Fourth Gospel had any specific theological bias, and that the "Synoptic Gospels" —that is, the first three—were accounts of Jesus which antedated dogmatic theology. Then the dogmatic elements in the Synoptic Gospels were uncovered; and today we know that the theological and church-oriented bias in the traditions is much older than the Gospels themselves.

Twenty-five years ago a prominent Protestant theologian wrote: "The Passion of Jesus, as it unfolds before our eyes in the Gospels, must be counted among the most tremendous creations of religious fiction." [1] Today we must ask ourselves whether this same verdict does not apply to everything the

[1] Hans Lietzmann: *"Der Prozess Jesu," Sitzungsbericht der Preussischen Akademie der Wissenschaften, Philosophische-historische Klasse,* Vol. XXIII/XXIV (Berlin, 1931), p. 313.

Gospels have to say about Jesus. What is the meaning of "religious fiction"? What may still be considered historical truth? By what signs can a scholar separate, with any degree of certainty, the historical facts from the dogmatic bias?

The way out of this quandary is to open new sources entirely unaffected by Christian tendencies. The historian's task will then be to carefully evaluate such testimony and check it against the statements of the Christian witnesses.

To this end, we must first muster our "indirect" sources on Jesus—that is to say, the contemporary testimony on the conditions, events, and personalities that played a part in the story of Jesus. In such testimony there is no mention of Jesus himself. For the most part, the authors of these documents knew nothing whatsoever about the existence of Jesus. Consequently, these writings are quite free of religious fiction or dogmatic bias. But they provide abundant information on people and events that are only passingly mentioned in the Gospels, or are even only implicitly in the background. At every step there is the opportunity to check, to supplement, and perhaps to correct the narratives in the Gospels. The chronology of the life of Jesus, as set forth here, is drawn from the synchronization of these accounts with those of the Gospels—and chronology is essential, for upon it is based our picture of the world situation into which Jesus entered.

Virtually nothing is known about the childhood and youth of Jesus. I have made no attempt to fill this regrettable gap with legends. I have thought it useful, however, to say a few words about the historical environment in which Jesus grew up.

I have made a point of evaluating the Jewish legal provisions concerning heretics and the rules of trials. Without these, there is no grasping the legalistic basis of the charges against Jesus, especially as the Gospels deal with this matter but vaguely. And as soon as we attack this problem, we recognize the iron-clad logic that dominated the criminal proceedings against Jesus from the first secret tribunal to the great heresy trial. It becomes clear that everything followed clearly and consistently from the laws, and this may make us reflect a bit on the account given by the Gospels, and its reliability as source material. From this same material it is possible, moreover, to draw up a chronological framework for the course of events in the last years of Jesus' life. I may put it this way: when we train the rays of legal history upon the Gospels, we obtain a historical X-ray photograph. Upon it stands revealed the clear outline of the life of Jesus.

In addition to these indirect sources there are the direct statements concerning Jesus in ancient Jewish documents—texts in which Jesus is mentioned by name (or under a code name). Most of these texts are the work of the rabbinical authorities; a few spring from the movement that grew up around John the Baptist. There are not many; they are all very short, in many cases camouflaged and muddled; and in these texts, also, truth and fiction are closely intertwined. These Jewish mentions of Jesus have always been dismissed with scorn, much to the detriment of research. For in these brief notices lie concealed many an old tradition concerning Jesus, traditions perhaps reaching back to the days of Caiaphas, and at any rate back to the first and second centuries. These can be of immense aid to us in checking, clarifying, and evaluating the Gospel narratives. Naturally these Jewish accounts are at least as tendentious as the stories of Jesus in the Gospels. They are, we recognize, fresh instances of the campaign against Jesus which began during his lifetime and won its victory, of such importance to the history of the world, in his condemnation and crucifixion.

It is extremely painful to the believing Christian to read these texts. But we must remember that Jesus stood before the highest ecclesiastic tribunal of his people as a criminal heretic. Objectivity demands that the historian hear not only the friends of the defendant, the Christian Apostles and Evangelists, but the friends of the Great Sanhedrin as well, the rabbis and scribes. However devout a Christian, one must take these things into account if one wishes to be a just historian. And it will be well worth one's pain. For in the course of studying these texts, one will learn to distinguish between facts and their interpretation—a distinction important in all historical studies, but absolutely crucial in the study of Jesus. The dichotomy exists in both the Christian and the Jewish traditions concerning Jesus; only the bias is different. The same facts are employed in the one case to sustain faith in Christ, in the other to attack that faith.

The sharper the clash, the wider the gulf, the more vital does this alternation of testimony and counter-testimony become to the historical investigator. For if a confrontation of witnesses yields statements that agree on some points, then these points must represent facts accepted by both sides. This principle certainly holds true if the historical traditions of the two groups of witnesses are independent of each other. But it holds true almost as completely in cases where the traditions intersect. For it is highly significant that the witness for the prosecution admits that the witness for the defense is right on certain points; that he agrees with his opponents about certain common facts. But where the two sets of witnesses contradict each other, one side or the other, or both, must be distorting or fabricating the evidence, and it becomes the historian's task to trace the various revisions through the tradition and uncover the nature of the bias.

To this direct and indirect evidence concerning Jesus there has now been added a third category, a group of ancient texts which have long occupied me, and which, with the discovery of the Dead Sea scrolls, have become the center of an international controversy. These are the late-Judaistic Apocalyptic writings. These texts have no particular importance to a study of the *life* of Jesus, but they do have a great bearing on his *message*.

Preface

The spate of publications upon the newly discovered manuscripts has given the general public the impression that the scrolls contain everything Jesus ever said. Jesus, we are told, drew at least the key points of his doctrine from the traditional ideas of the Apocalyptists and devotees of the Torah gathered around the Dead Sea. But the historical fact that Jesus took a stand opposed to the Mosaic Torah, to scrupulosity regarding the Torah, and to the authorities of the Torah, would seem to attest to the contrary. Upon closer examination it appears that Jesus himself did not lean upon the Dead Sea school of thought. It was John the Baptist who was most strongly influenced by it, and then the Apostles and Evangelists—in different ways and to various degrees. Thus we obtain a wealth of material which throws great light on the Jesus tradition that prevailed among the Christians of Palestine and antedated the codification of the Gospels.

The preservation, decipherment, and publication of these texts is still proceeding. But it is already possible to make the following statements: many of the sayings of Jesus recorded in the Gospels, which have hitherto been considered authentic because they sounded characteristic of Palestinian Judaism, are more likely to have derived from the doctrinal traditions of the era preceding Jesus (the theology of the group around John the Baptist) or the era succeeding Jesus (the teachings of the Palestinian Christians). These sayings were incorporated into the very oldest traditions concerning Jesus in the course of a major effort to re-Judaicize his message. Jesus himself, however, was far less the child of his times and of his people than has hitherto been thought. He was far more solitary, more bellicose, more revolutionary than has generally been recognized. Judas was, after his fashion, a man who abided by the letter of the law and perhaps also by the instructions of his clerical authorities. But the execution of Jesus was wholly inevitable in any case, and, while it might have taken another form, was basically only a question of time.

So much for the new material on which this book is based. What can be achieved by the use of this material?

First of all, it enables us to form an entirely new, concrete, and dramatic picture of the beginnings of the Jesus tradition. We shall come to understand the Christian Gospels and the Jewish texts on Jesus as documents in a passionate controversy centering around the interpretation and the meaning of Jesus of Nazareth. Time and again the question has been raised: what was the actual function of the oldest traditions concerning Jesus? Did they serve for preaching, for liturgy, for the teaching of catechumens, for missionary work of the primitive church? Certainly for all of these. But the oldest and most important function of the traditions was polemical. They originated in the conflict over Jesus. For this conflict reached a pitch of violence even while Jesus still lived. It was revived with fresh passion after the epiphany, and flared up everywhere the message of Christ was proclaimed, in Jerusalem, Samaria, Galilee, Jamnia, Caesarea, Antioch, Rome, and later on, above all, in Ephesus. On either side in the great conflict there were a number of extremely stubborn, belligerent factions. On the one side there were the groups around Peter, James, Matthew, Luke, and John. On the other side stood the scribes, the anti-Roman partisans, the desert sects, the disciples of John the Baptist, and the Samaritans. In the course of these struggles the Christian and Jewish traditions of Jesus were shaped; out of these struggles emerged the Gospels and the rabbinical or Baptistic documents concerning Jesus.

At the beginning of all these struggles stood Jesus himself: "I came to cast fire upon the earth, and would that it were already kindled! I have a baptism to be baptized with; and how I am constrained until it is accomplished." [2]

[2] Luke 12, 49.

xii

Preface

It is evident that the figure of Jesus will appear in a new light when seen in terms of this conflict, and when we realize once and for all that both the Christian and Jewish documents on Jesus which we possess are all polemics.

The nineteenth-century ideal was a *biography* of Jesus —that is to say, a representation of the psychological development of Jesus, of his mind and his activities, rendered with narrative vividness, analytic insight, and plausibility. Whether this was a legitimate ideal is a moot question. At any rate, we know today that it was unattainable. What, then, may our ideal be, what ideal am I entitled to set up? I reply: a *history* of Jesus. By this term I mean something extremely modest. I mean a strict clarification of those facts which can be ascertained, possibly of a certain series of events, perhaps too of a number of causal relationships. I shall proceed along pragmatic lines, refraining from any psychologizing. Chronology will be my guide. I shall synchronize but not invent or speculate. This is what I mean by a historical viewpoint.

When I come to a point where presentation of facts and causal relationships stops and interpretation begins, I shall go no further. The Evangelists' interpretation of Jesus, the interpretation offered by the dogmas of the church, and even my personal interpretation of Jesus are barred from this book. However, the oldest and most important of all the interpretations of Jesus must be treated: Jesus' own interpretation of himself. For that necessarily belongs to the story, if only because it reached its historic climax in Jesus' self-witness before the Great Sanhedrin in Jerusalem.

No serious historian can or would wish to penetrate into Jesus' mental processes. Rather, I am concerned here solely with Jesus' witness to himself in the Gospels, in so far as this can be ascertained by the methods of philology. I proceed to examine critically the authentic self-affirmations of Jesus, and to determine their meaning within the history of re-

xiii

ligious ideas—neither more nor less than this. It will become evident that the historical phenomenon of Jesus was made manifest once again in all its uniqueness and gravity in his declaration before the Great Sanhedrin. This declaration can be set forth clearly, but it is not subject to argument. It can only be accepted or rejected.

NOTE

IN SCRIPTURAL REFERENCES, *the first Arabic number indicates the chapter, the second Arabic number the verse. John 4, 1.41 means: John, Chapter 4, verses 1 and 41.*

CONTENTS

I · PROBLEMS IN THE STORY

II · JESUS' ANCESTRY AND BIRTH

III · THE EARLY YEARS OF JESUS

xvii

CONTENTS

Contents

VIII · JESUS' WITNESS TO HIMSELF

JESUS
AND HIS
STORY

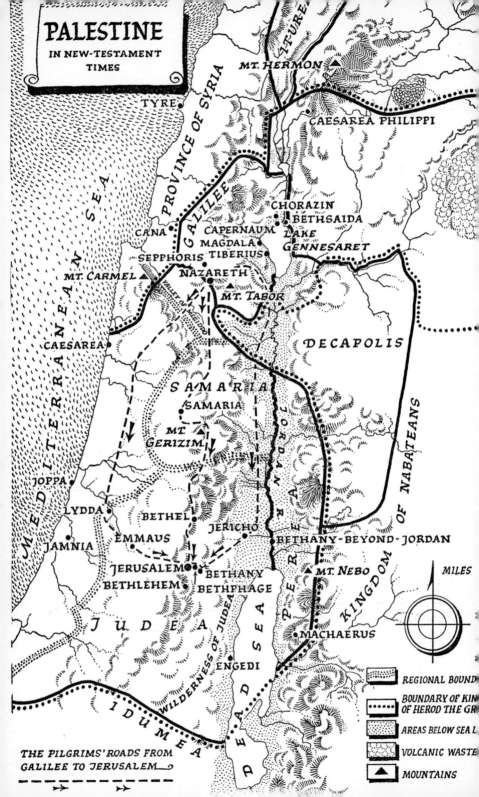

PALESTINE
IN NEW-TESTAMENT TIMES

MEDITERRANEAN SEA

TYRE

PROVINCE OF SYRIA

MT. HERMON

ITUREA

CAESAREA PHILIPPI

GALILEE

CHORAZIN
BETHSAIDA

CANA
CAPERNAUM
LAKE
MAGDALA
GENNESARET
SEPPHORIS
TIBERIUS

MT. CARMEL
NAZARETH

VALLEY OF MEGIDDO

MT. TABOR

DECAPOLIS

CAESAREA

SAMARIA

SAMARIA

MT.
GERIZIM

JORDAN RIVER

KINGDOM OF NABATEANS

JOPPA

LYDDA
BETHEL
JERICHO

JAMNIA
EMMAUS

BETHANY-BEYOND-JORDAN

PEREA

MT. NEBO

JERUSALEM
BETHLEHEM
BETHANY
BETHPHAGE

WILDERNESS OF JUDEA

JUDEA

MACHAERUS

KINGDOM OF THE

ENGEDI

DEAD SEA

IDUMEA

MILES

REGIONAL BOUND

BOUNDARY OF KIN
OF HEROD THE GR

AREAS BELOW SEA L

VOLCANIC WASTE

MOUNTAINS

THE PILGRIMS' ROADS FROM
GALILEE TO JERUSALEM

I

PROBLEMS
IN THE
STORY

➤➤➤-➤➤➤-➤➤ 1 ⫷⫷-⫷⫷⫷-⫷⫷

THE SOURCES ·

THE OLDEST SOURCES for the history of Jesus are the Petrine formulae in the Acts of the Apostles, which concisely trace Jesus' story from the arrest of John the Baptist to Easter, and the Epistles of Paul, which contain in particular some pre-Pauline phrases and items of tradition concerning the Passion story." The oldest Christian document on Jesus is, so far

method of establishing these?

3

as we know, the *Logia,* a collection of the sayings of Jesus which is now lost, but which can be largely reconstructed from the sayings present in both Matthew and Luke.[n] The most important sources are the Canonical Gospels. The three oldest Evangelists, the Synoptics (Mark, Matthew, Luke), on the whole adhered most faithfully to the language of Jesus. The Fourth Evangelist, John, clarified the chronology in the story of Jesus. A few Judao-Christian books about Jesus are of equal antiquity. These include an Aramaic version of Matthew, the Nazarene gospel, the Hebrew gospels, all of which, however, have come down to us only in fragments [1] and quotations by the Fathers of the Church. Then there are mentions of Jesus here and there, and numerous *Agrapha*— that is, scattered sayings of Jesus—which the Fathers of the Church cited from different, often unnamed sources. The pagan authors of the early days of the Roman Empire also supply a few items about Jesus.[n] The Jewish historian Flavius Josephus, a contemporary of Luke and John, provides some information on John the Baptist, Herod, Pilate, and James the Just, "brother of Jesus, the so-called Christ.[2] His account of Jesus has unfortunately been revised from the Christian point of view, and its original lineaments can no longer be retraced with any degree of certainty.[3] Far more questionable still are the accounts of Jesus provided by the "Slavic Josephus." The rabbinical tradition of Jesus is written in a polemic spirit— and is for that very reason indispensable to the historian who wishes to understand the opponents of Jesus. *Audiatur et altera pars*—the other side should be heard also. The fact that these sources supplement the accounts in the Gospels, providing additional details on such matters as the prosecution of Jesus, is of great importance. And though they dispute all his theological claims, they corroborate many historical points (for example, that Jesus was the son of Mary,

[1] For example, John 8, 1–11.   [2] *Antiquities,* 20, 9, 1.   [3] *Antiquities,* 18, 3, 3.

4

that he worked miracles, that he called himself the Son of Man, that he said "I am He," that the tomb was found empty). For the most part the older rabbinical statements about Jesus were written independently of the Gospels. A few of them date back to the lifetime of Jesus and to the early apostolic age.

In the Mandaean [4] texts of the Middle Ages a few time-honored fragments from the oldest community of Baptists are preserved. These, by their fanatical opposition to Jesus, convey some impression of the tensions between the disciples of John the Baptist and those of Jesus.

The tradition of Jesus reflected in Islamic literature occupies a large place in our body of source material. The Koran treats in detail of Jesus and Mary. Al Ghazzali, who gave Islamic dogma its classical form (around 1100), quotes some 115 *Agrapha,* more than any Christian Church Father. Some of these sayings of Jesus derive from an ancient Judao-Christian tradition. Otherwise the value of the Islamic tradition as historical source material is minor. The greater part of it is Oriental legend and proverbial wisdom.[n] For this very reason it provides an excellent study in the formal laws governing the Semitic tradition of logia.

Around 640 there were written, at the instance of Emperor Tai-Tsung, two Chinese Lives of Jesus. These are based upon Syrian tradition and contain a number of items about the group around John the Baptist, about Jesus' own statements concerning himself, and about the empty tomb, which in all probability derive from non-Christian sources. On the other hand, a Taoist account of Jesus, contained in a standard history of religion of the seventeenth century,[n] is valueless as source material.

In addition to the direct documents relating to Jesus there are the indirect sources, the Jewish and Greco-Roman ref-

---

[4] An ancient religious community. The religion of the Mandaeans is a kind of Gnosticism retaining many Jewish and Parsee elements.

erences to the period of the New Testament (historians, apocalyptics, books of ritual, legal treatises, inscriptions, papyri, coins, topographical monuments). These in many instances throw new light upon the accounts in the Gospels: on personalities, Jewish politics, Palestinian geography, jurisprudence, taxation, penal code, familial law, religious law, liturgy, expectation of the Messiah, astronomy, and astrology. A systematic evaluation of these contemporary sources will lead us out of the intellectual impasse in which we have found ourselves, enable us to go beyond "Lives" of Jesus based solely on the Bible or on imaginative techniques, and arrive at a pragmatic history of Jesus.

⇢⇢⇢-⇢⇢⇢-⇢⇢⇢ 2 ⇠⇠⇠-⇠⇠⇠-⇠⇠⇠

THE CHRONOLOGY

ACCORDING TO THE SYNOPTICS (who follow the pattern of the Petrine formulae), the public ministry of Jesus began after the arrest of John the Baptist[5] and lasted about one and a half years. In Mark 2, 23, it is spring (harvesttime); in Mark 14, 1, it is spring again (the Passover of death). The Fourth Gospel treats of about four years (between five Passover feasts), with the arrest of John the Baptist falling in the middle of this period.[6]

[5] Mark 1, 14.   [6] In John 1, 29. 41 ff., the situation during the Passover is assumed. In John 2, 13. 23, we hear of the second Passover. In John 3, 24, the Baptist is still active. In John 4, 35, it is winter. John does not mention the third Passover. In John 5, 1, it is autumn, the Feast of Tabernacles." In John 6, 4, the fourth Passover is impending. In John 7, 2, it is autumn again; in John 10, 22, winter once more, the Feast of Dedication at Jerusalem. In John 11, 55, we hear of the fifth Passover feast, the Passover of death.

6

There is no fitting the chronological structure of the Gospel of John within the narrow span of the Synoptic account. But it is possible to fit the Synoptic frame into John's structure. This is important as evidence for the correctness of the Johannine chronology. Jesus, therefore, devoted some four years to his ministry, first in the shadow of the Baptist and later in complete independence, working sometimes in the north, sometimes in the south, in Jerusalem and elsewhere. The Synoptics omit to tell of the ministry of Jesus under the aegis of the Baptist, and speak only of the last and decisive period of his activity, which did not begin until after the arrest of John the Baptist. The Fourth Evangelist corrects and integrates the Synoptic account [n] and treats of the entire period of Jesus' ministry, the early phase under the Baptist, and the concluding, climactic phase.

So much for the relative chronology. What about absolute chronology? How may we synchronize the story of Jesus with the history of his time?

According to Luke 2, 1, Jesus came into the world under the Emperor Augustus (27 B.C.–A.D. 14). The two major Evangelists agree [7] that Jesus was born under King Herod (37 B.C.–A.D. 4). The stories of the star of Bethlehem [8] and the census of Quirinius [9] both point to the year 7 B.C. Luke's statement that Jesus was about thirty years old at the time of his first public appearance [1] is useless for purposes of chronology. For in antiquity thirty was considered the age when a man stood at the peak of his powers, and Luke himself says that this ideal figure fitted Jesus only "approximately."

Luke gives us more precise information in the famous synchronism of Luke 3, 1 f.: the Baptist began his activity in the fifteenth year of the reign of Emperor Tiberius. Tiberius' fifteenth regnal year ran from January 1 to December 31, A.D. 28. The other data in the synchronism of Luke

[7] Matthew 2, 1; Luke 1, 5.   [8] Matthew 2, 2.   [9] Luke 2, 2.   [1] Luke 3, 23.

7

agree with this chronology. Therefore, the Baptist emerged for the first time in A.D. 28. According to the Petrine formulae, the Gospels, and all other sources, Jesus was crucified under Pilate (A.D. 26–36), and at the time of a Passover. Much data indicates that it was the first Passover after the execution of Tiberius' disgraced favorite, Lucius Aelius Sejanus, the Passover of A.D. 32. This assigns the period from the beginning of A.D. 28 to the spring of 32 for the public ministry of Jesus. Within this period there is room for all the feasts and dates mentioned in the Gospel of John, and for the dates fixed by the Synoptics as well, without any necessity for arbitrary rearrangements.

We arrive, then, at the following chronology: Spring of 28: Baptism of Jesus.[2] Passover of 29: cleansing of the Temple.[3] November 29: northward journey through Samaria.[4] December 29 to the autumn of 30: ten quiet months.[5] Autumn of 30: arrest of John the Baptist.[6] October 30: Feast of Tabernacles in Jerusalem.[7] Late autumn of 30: fresh beginning in Galilee.[8] Spring of 31: Passover in Galilee.[9] October 31: Feast of Tabernacles in Jerusalem.[1] Passover of 32: Passover of death.[2]

⋙⋙⋙ 3 ⋘⋘⋘

THE MIRACLES

THE GOSPELS REPORT miracles both great and numerous in the story of Jesus. The critical historian may neither accept these accounts without investigation, nor reject them

[2] Mark 1, 9 ff.; John 1, 32 f.   [3] John 2, 13 ff.   [4] John 4, 1 ff. 35.
[5] John 4, 54; 5, 1; cf. 4, 38.   [6] Mark 1, 14; cf. John 5, 35.   [7] John 5, 1.
[8] Mark 1, 14 ff.   [9] John 6, 4; Mark 2, 23.   [1] John 7, 14.   [2] Mark 11, 1 ff.; cf. John 12, 12 ff.

8

out of hand. Nor may he bring to bear upon his examination
a set of epistemological rules or philosophical axioms. In this
realm, above all, he must work solely with the legitimate,
classical methods of source-criticism. He must ask which
are the oldest, the most immediate, and the most impartial
sources.

The very old Petrine formulae speak of miracles of Jesus.[3]
So do all the four Gospels. But these are all Christian witnesses, perhaps *testimonia pro domo*. Jesus himself considered it of the greatest importance that his miracles should
be observed, checked, and confirmed by outsiders and opponents.[4] And in fact even his opponents were forced to con-
cede that Jesus worked miracles. According to Mark 3, 22,
the Sanhedrin in Jerusalem sent a commission of theologians
to Galilee to examine on the spot the question of miracles.
The conclusion they came to in their report was: he works
miracles with powers given him by the devil—but he works
miracles.[5] According to John 7, 12, Jesus was branded an
apostate preacher who had allied himself with the satanic
powers in order to mislead the people.[n] According to John
11, 47 f., Jesus was arrested and condemned as a deceiver of
the people precisely because of his miracles. All these charges
coincided precisely with the provisions against heretics.[6]

However, all this information is found in the New Testament. Do we also have firsthand Jewish evidence to sub-
stantiate the Gospel accounts of Jesus' miracle-working and
of his enemies' attacks upon these miracles?

There is indeed a great deal of such evidence. We shall
mention only the oldest items. Around A.D. 95 Rabbi Eliezer
ben Hyrcanus of Lydda speaks of Jesus' magic arts.[7] Around
110 we hear of a controversy among Palestinian Jews centering upon the question of whether it is permissible to be

---

[3] Acts 2, 22; 10, 38.   [4] Mark 1, 44; John 2, 8; 11, 42.   [5] Cf. Matthew
9, 34; John 8, 48.   [6] Appendix II, 52.   [7] Shabbath 104 b; Tosephta
Shabbath 11, 15.

healed in the name of Jesus.[8] Now, miraculous healings in the name of Jesus imply that Jesus himself performed such miracles. Around the same period (A.D. 95–110) we encounter the ritual denunciation: "Jesus practiced magic and led Israel astray."[9] There are various indications that this phraseology stems from the official records of the Great Sanhedrin of the year A.D. 32.[1] At any rate in this justification of the verdict, the authorities were once more pointing to the legal provisions governing the treatment of pseudo-prophetic miracle-workers.[2] All this fits in with the Gospel accounts of the miracles and prosecution of Jesus.[3]

At the moment we are not concerned with the interpretation of Jesus' miracles in these documents. Precisely because the sources are hostile, it is significant that the sheer fact of Jesus' working miracles is assumed and admitted throughout them.

This evidence in the sources cannot be discounted psychologically on the ground that in those days all stories of miracles were credulously accepted and uncritically spread about. For the Jews of antiquity were extremely realistic in regard to miracles, and at least the opponents of Jesus among them were highly critical. Had that not been so, the miracles of Jesus would not have been so vehemently discussed[4] and so gravely misinterpreted.[5]

Neither can we dismiss the matter of Jesus' miracles by contending that in those days miracles were ascribed to every prominent historical or religious personality. For that was not the case. The men of the New Testament considered John the Baptist, for example, as the greatest human being before Christ, and yet he was not regarded as a miracle-worker.[6] Josephus, too, attributes no miracles to the Baptist.[7]

---

[8] Aboda zara 27 b; Tosephta Hullin 2, 22 f.   [9] Sanhedrin 43 a; 107 b.
[1] Justin Martyr, *Dialogue* 69, 7; 108, 2; etc.   [2] Appendix II, 87 f.   [3] Mark 3, 22; Matthew 27, 63; John 9, 22 ff.; 11, 47 ff.   [4] John 10, 21.   [5] Mark 3, 22.   [6] John 10, 41.   [7] *Antiquities* 18, 5, 2.

3 · *The Miracles*

The Mandaeans hail the Baptist as a mythological savior and attack Jesus as his satanic adversary. But they, too, say a great deal about the (demon-inspired) miracles of Jesus, and not a word about any miracle wrought by John the Baptist. Islam has high regard for Jesus, still higher for Mohammed. But although many miracles are attributed to Jesus,[8] none are ascribed to Mohammed.

Analysis in terms of religious history also requires us to recognize the Gospel accounts of miracles as historically valid. The miracles recounted in the oldest traditions are miracles of revelation, in which the divine glory and the brotherly humanity of Jesus are made manifest. In this they are unique and differ sharply from the prestidigitation and wonder-working, the magic tricks, and the tales of demonic vengeance characterizing the other miracles that figure in contemporary accounts. They differ also from the fabulous miracles related in the post-apostolic traditions of Jesus. If we wish to study fictional miracles of Jesus, we need only read the Syriac or Islamic legends about him. In so doing we will sharpen our insight in preparation for a critical analysis of the Gospels and their accounts of miracles. For when we find that Jesus' miracle-working is historically unassailable, this does not mean the end of source-criticism. It means, rather, the beginning, for now every single tale of a miracle must be conscientiously examined.

Theologically speaking, historical demonstration that Jesus worked miracles "proves" nothing at all. The miracles of Jesus are signs that cannot and are not meant to prove anything—just as Jesus himself is a sign of God, not a proof of God; a sign, moreover, that will be "spoken against." [9] The miracles of Jesus are not incontrovertible. Even an eyewitness can challenge, mistake, misconstrue them, can close his mind to them, can condemn them as offensive and blasphemous—not in spite of the fact but because Jesus acted like

[8] Sura 5, 110, etc.   [9] Luke 2, 34.

II

God himself. Therefore the interpretation of Jesus' miracles by his opponents, the demonological construction we mentioned above, is a matter of considerable importance. It is as pertinent to the story of the miracles as shadow to light. Jesus' miracles created a crisis everywhere, marked the dividing-line. The Gospels repeatedly tell us of this dual reaction to the miracles of Jesus, and of the dual interpretation of the personality of Jesus.

II

JESUS' ANCESTRY AND BIRTH

➤➤➤➤➤➤ 1 ⫷⫷⫷⫷⫷⫷

THE HOUSE OF DAVID

IN THE NEW TESTAMENT Jesus is called the "Son of David." [n]
Luke uses a technical term of Jewish tribal law, declaring
that Joseph "was of the house and lineage of David." [n] This
is an item that we may not dismiss by saying that the descent
of the Messiah from the house of David was an inviolable
postulate of the Jewish creed, with the result that the Da-

vidic descent of Jesus had to become a dogma of Christology in the early church. Actually, there were groups among the Jews of Palestine who expected a Messiah from the house of David and other groups who hoped, for example, for a Messiah of the house of Aaron.[n] Nor can we discover any special bias on the part of the New Testament writers for a Davidic descent for Jesus. Jesus himself placed no value at all on his being a descendant of David, and neither Paul nor John drew any theological conclusions from it.[1] If the writers of the New Testament spoke of Davidic descent, they meant it as a simple historical statement which they considered was borne out by the facts.

But is it conceivable that Joseph, living a thousand years after David, should still possess a reliable family tradition regarding his descent from David? That is by no means impossible. Especially in the New Testament period we hear again and again of lists of generations kept by Jewish families and officially supervised. These lists were of the highest importance in legal matters concerning marriage, property, occupation, and religion. We hear in particular of the patriarchal houses and of their heads, of the common property of clans, and of the hereditary lands of the individual houses. We also hear a good many genealogical details regarding the house of David.[n] Evidently a family tradition of Davidic descent was nothing extraordinary in the days of Jesus. Apparently Joseph was one of those who had such a tradition.[n] For we learn that Domitian, in connection with his prosecution of the former Jewish royal dynasty, called to Rome two great-grandsons of Joseph (grand-nephews of Jesus) by the names of Zachariah and James, because they had been denounced to him as Davidites. The two "confessed" their Davidic origins without ifs or buts, but were released on the grounds that they were completely non-political. Under Trajan, however, the aged Bishop Simeon

[1] See Romans 1, 3; John 7, 41 f.

(cousin of Jesus and successor of James the Just) was condemned to death as a "Davidite and Christian." [n]

From this evidence it would seem that the Davidic descent of Jesus is historically established. Probably Joseph reckoned his descent from that Davidite who returned from Babylon in the days of Ezra.[2]

Establishing the Davidic descent of Jesus also answers the question of whether Jesus was a Jew. Joseph came of a family which though poor was proud of its ancestry, which for centuries and probably for a thousand years had guarded the purity of its blood with particular care. Jesus was a son of Israel, of the chosen and scorned people.[n]

2

THE SON OF MARY

IN BOTH the major Gospels (Matthew and Luke) Jesus is accounted the son of the Virgin Mary.[3] Is the miraculous birth of Jesus a historical fact? Or is it only a fable that first won acceptance in the late apostolic age, inspired by Isaiah 7, 14, and by the numerous legends of parthenogenesis which were rife in antiquity? "Parallels" in the history of religion are of no import in themselves against the authenticity of a historical account. But that only Matthew and Luke speak of the virgin birth gives rise to question. Nothing is said about it in the *Logia,* or in Mark and John.

However, this silence is only apparent. When the Fourth

Possible Origin

[2] Ezra 8, 2; Matthew 1, 12. 17; Luke 2, 4.   [3] Matthew 1, 20 ff.; Luke 1, 35.

Evangelist relates the story of the wedding at Cana, with Mary already counting upon Jesus' power to work miracles,[4] he appears to take it for granted that the mother knows from the beginning of the secret of her son. Still older and more impressive as evidence are two items from the *Logia* and the Gospel of Mark which concern the beginnings of the attacks upon Mary.

In the *Logia* we learn that Jesus was berated for being a "glutton and drunkard."[5] There must have been some grounds for this charge. For it fits in with all that we know about the attitude of Jesus and about the Pharisaical groups' reaction to it. Now, among Palestinian Jews this particular insult would be flung at a person born of an illegitimate connection who betrayed, by his mode of life and his religious conduct, the stain of his birth. This was the sense in which the Pharisees and their followers employed the phrase against Jesus. Their meaning was: he is a bastard.[n]

The First Evangelist gives us no background, and therefore has no occasion to deal with chronology in connection with the birth of Jesus. But in Mark 6, 3, we hear what Jesus' fellow countrymen in Nazareth thought about these matters: "Is not this the carpenter, the son of Mary and brother of James, and Joseph, and Judas, and Simon, and are not his sisters here with us? And they took offense at him."

This account, which appears only in Mark, does full justice to the situation.[n] The Jews had strict rules governing name-giving. A Jew was named after his father (Jochanan ben Sakkai, for example) even if his father had died before his birth. He was named after his mother only when the father was unknown.[6] The same custom prevailed among the Arabs, as well as in Egypt,[n] and, *mutatis mutandis,* still does in Western countries.

Therefore, the Jews mentioned in Mark 6, 4, were saying:

[4] John 2, 3.   [5] Matthew 11, 19; Luke 7, 34.   [6] Appendix II, 62.

16

Jesus is the son of Mary and only the son of Mary, not of Joseph. This, of course, was meant to defame him. The people of Nazareth had hitherto held their peace, out of consideration for the feelings of Jesus. But now when the man turned out to be an apostate who was making all kinds of blasphemous claims, they spoke out.[7] The intention was to drive the apostate from his native town by shaming him. For the present the dishonoring name sufficed: Jeshua ben Miriam.

After the death of Jesus the matter was spoken of more plainly. In a genealogical table dating from before A.D. 70 Jesus is listed as "the bastard of a wedded wife."[8] Evidently the Evangelist Matthew was familiar with such lists and was warring against them.[n] Later rabbis bluntly called Jesus the son of an adulteress.[n] They also claimed to know precisely the "unknown father's" name: Panthera. In old rabbinical texts we find frequent mention of Jesus ben Panthera, and the eclectic Platonist Celsus around 160 retails all sorts of gossipy anecdotes about Mary and the legionary Panthera.[n]

Among the Samaritans and Mandaeans also Jesus was referred to as the son of Mary, Jesus ben Miriam, with polemic intent.[n] We must ask ourselves whether these charges did not originate in the Palestinian community of the Baptist. For Luke, in 1, 41 ff., already seems aware of slander of Mary within that group, and takes issue with these slanders, just as Matthew 1, 3 ff., assumes and combats a similar movement in rabbinical circles.

The Islamic tradition of Jesus presents the exact opposite of these taunts against Mary. In the Koran we find Jesus referred to regularly as Isa ibn Maryam—Jesus, the son of Mary.[9] And Abdullah al-Baidawi, the classical commentator on the Koran, remarks with full understanding of the Semitic practice in nomenclature: the name of the mother is borne when the father is unknown. But this name and ex-

[7] Appendix II, 60, 61.   [8] Yebamoth 4, 13.   [9] Sura 3, 40, etc.

planation are here intended in a thoroughly positive sense. In Islam Jesus is regarded as the son of the Virgin Mary who was begotten by the creative Word of God.[1]

To sum up: Jesus was the son of Mary, not of Joseph. That is the historical fact, recognized alike by Christians and Jews, friends and adversaries. This fact is significant and ambiguous, like all facts in the history of Jesus. The Christians believed him to be begotten by an act of the Divine Creator. The Jews of antiquity spoke of Mary as an adulteress. Out of this struggle between interpretation and counter-interpretation—which, according to Mark 6, 3, and Matthew 11, 19, had already begun during the lifetime of Jesus—the account of the ancestry of Jesus in the major Gospels emerged. They lay stress on Joseph's having himself bowed to the miracle of God. He neither denounced nor abandoned Mary, but rather took her into his house as his lawful wife and legitimized the son of Mary by personally naming him. By this act Jesus was admitted in a formal, legal sense to the house of David.

Among the Jews of Palestine a betrothed bride was under the same strict obligation to fidelity as a wedded wife. If she proved unfaithful, the prospective husband could repudiate her or go to law. Stoning was the penalty for breach of faith on the part of a bride.[n] Completion of the wedding ceremonies was marked by fetching the bride home to the bridegroom's house.[n] If the husband gave a newborn child his name, he recognized the child as his own in blood, or at least in law, and accepted it into his family with all the legal consequences involved.[n]

[1] Sura 19, 16 ff.

⇶⇶⇶ 3 ⇷⇷⇷

BETHLEHEM

ACCORDING TO MATTHEW 2, 1 ff., and Luke 2, 4, Jesus was born in Bethlehem. Were the theologians at work here, seeking proofs from Scripture? For Bethlehem was the promised birthplace of the Messiah.[2] Therefore Jesus "had to have been born" in Bethlehem. But expectation of a Messiah out of Bethlehem was only one of many such anticipations in pre-Christian apocalyptics. In the age of Jesus there also existed a great many projections of the Messiah's coming in which Bethlehem played no part.[3] Thus, of the two Apostles who testify to Jesus's birth in Bethlehem, only Matthew has a certain interest in exploiting the Bethlehem tradition.[4] Luke is not at all concerned with this.

Against Bethlehem, there are the many passages in the Gospels which speak of Jesus of Nazareth, of the Nazarene, of Jesus the Galilean. But we must take these epithets in the same sense as Matthew and Luke, who were familiar with the phrases and use them [5] while at the same time taking the Bethlehem traditions for granted. They regard Bethlehem as ~~M & Luke~~ the birthplace, Nazareth as the residence. Nothing is more ordinary than this distinction between where a man is born and where he lives, and in the case of Jesus nothing was more natural. For Joseph was in the building trade, and even in ancient Palestine the workers in that trade moved from place to place.

[2] Micah 5, 1; Matthew 2, 5; John 7, 42.   [3] John 1, 20 ff.; 7, 27.
[4] Matthew 2, 5.   [5] Matthew 13, 54; Luke 24, 19; Acts 10, 38.

On the other hand, Jesus' Davidic descent is an argument in favor of Bethlehem. The house of David came to Jerusalem with Ezra.[6] Fanning out from Jerusalem, the returned exiles were resettled, each family in its own city,[7] their inheritances restored.[8] The family home of the Davidites was Bethlehem, the city of David.[9] There the homecoming members of the house of David established themselves again. In Nehemiah 7, 26, the "men of Bethlehem" are mentioned expressly. In Nehemiah 10, 35, the annual deliveries of wood for the use of the temple are assigned to the various patriarchal families who have settled around Jerusalem. In Ta'anith 4, 5, the house of David is specially named among the suppliers of wood. In John 7, 42, and elsewhere Bethlehem appears as the center of the Davidite clan. It is obvious that not all the descendants of the house of David could continue to reside permanently in Bethlehem. But Bethlehem did remain the center, in terms of property rights also. For Jewish laws of inheritance made a point of preserving unbroken the hereditary property of patriarchal houses.[n]

The decisive factor in favor of Bethlehem is once again the absence of discussion. Jewish writings never asserted that Jesus was born in Nazareth, nowhere denied his birth in Bethlehem. On the contrary, as Origen states, the Jews after the birth of Jesus were prone to pass over the prophecy that the Messiah would be born in Bethlehem.[n] To be sure, we find the rabbis discussing this point in a commentary to Micah 5, 1, the basis of which probably goes back to pre-Christian times; but in later commentaries they let fall only an occasional isolated remark about it. Origen's explanation appears logical: Jewish polemicists could not deny the birth of Jesus in Bethlehem and therefore expurgated any mention of Bethlehem in connection with the Messianic prophecies, in order not to foster belief in Jesus, the child of Bethlehem.

[6] Ezra 8, 2.   [7] Nehemiah 7, 26.   [8] Nehemiah 11, 3. 20.   [9] 1 Samuel 16, 4; Luke 2, 11.

20

That child came into the world in a temporary shelter, a stable.[1] Around Bethlehem there remain to this day numerous stables in caves, with mangers of packed clay. Even in apostolic times people were shown the "cave of the birth," and both the Judao-Christian gospels and the Palestinian Fathers of the Church frequently mention Jesus' birth in a stable in a cave at Bethlehem.[n]

➤➤➤-➤➤➤-➤➤➤ 4 ⫷⫷⫷-⫷⫷⫷-⫷⫷⫷

THE CENSUS

CONSIDERABLE DOUBT has been attached to Luke's account of the census,[2] the five chief points in question having been promulgated by David Friedrich Strauss in his *Das Leben Jesu* (1835). They are as follows: (1) There never was an imperial census during the time of Augustus. (2) An imperial census in the territory governed by King Herod was "extremely improbable." (3) The census of Quirinius could not have occurred during the time of King Herod, as Quirinius was never governor of the province of Syria during the King's lifetime. On the contrary, the Quirinine census took place about ten years after the death of King Herod. (4) Joseph's going to Bethlehem to enroll was contrary to Roman custom. (5) The registration of Mary was superfluous."[n]

At the time Strauss's book was published, these objections created a great uproar, and they have been reiterated ever since with only minor modifications,[n] even after their origi-

[1] Luke 2, 7.   [2] Luke 2, 1 ff.

nal source in Strauss had long been forgotten. They crop up still in much contemporary writing on the subject.

But since Strauss's book on Jesus more than 120 years have passed. In these four generations historical science has not stood still. Moreover, a wealth of inscriptions, papyri, and other original documents on ancient taxation laws has come to light. David Friedrich Strauss has been left far behind, and Luke's account of the census may now be considered in a wholly new light.

Strauss's criticism of Luke was based largely upon uncritical acceptance of Flavius Josephus. The past fifty years of research on the work of Josephus have taught us to be severely critical of his method and presentation. Josephus had an ax to grind; his historical journalism was intended as self-defense and self-aggrandizement. He wrote to glorify his people and to eulogize the Roman Emperor. He was an ardent sympathizer with the pro-Roman collaborationists among the Jews and an opponent of all the anti-Roman and anti-Herodian partisans of the Palestinian resistance movement. Crucial parts of Josephus' historical works, moreover, were casually patched together from older sources of uneven value; consequently they are replete with gaps and contradictions, are muddled and misleading. This is particularly true of his remarks on Augustus, Herod, Quirinius, and the census. Of course Josephus remains an invaluable source; but he is not to be read uncritically. His account must be studied point by point with the aid of the original documents that have turned up since Strauss's day, and must be corrected or reinterpreted.

Let us take each of the five arguments in detail.

Strauss's Point 1. Strauss conceives of an "imperial census" as a mode of taxation akin in many respects to a modern population census. That is, it starts on a set day at the same time in all parts of the Empire, is everywhere carried out in the same way, and after a few weeks or months comes to a halt everywhere. This was the preconception on which he based his quarrel with Luke. It reveals a misunderstanding of Augustan policies. In the summer of 30 B.C. Augustus conquered Egypt, a country where since the time of the pharaohs taxation had been developed to perfection. The model of Egypt was followed, with more or less significant local variations, in the taxation procedures of all the imperial provinces. In January 27 Augustus began his great imperial reform; that same year he initiated the census work in Gaul, which was to drag on for more than forty years.[n] Why so long? The situation in Gaul was quite different from that in Egypt. In Gaul a *descriptio prima,* a first registration, was to take place.[3] The proud Gallic chieftains and tribes desperately fought all attempts to take the census, and Augustus had to send his best generals to Gaul to crush the Gallic resistance movement in a series of bloody campaigns.

According to the theory of Roman imperial law, all real estate of a conquered country fell as a matter of principle to the Roman people. Taxation of this land accordingly formed the basis of the Roman system of taxation in the provinces. In Gaul as elsewhere, therefore, the fundamental task of the census-takers consisted of a comprehensive and precise survey of the land, a thorough classification of its potential revenue, and legal clarification of its private or collective ownership. A number of surveyors' reliefs, recently found in what had been Gaul, afford some idea of the immensely time-consuming precision with which the Roman surveyors worked. We can only marvel that Augustus made such "rapid" progress in Gaul.

In Syria the census-taking started later, and the fiscal situation was entirely different. For that land already had had experience with taxation practices. True, the tradition was not so ancient or conservative as that of Egypt, but still

[3] Cf. Luke 2, 2.

it extended back some two thousand years. Since 1933 there have come to light in the ancient royal city of Mari on the Euphrates approximately twenty-five thousand cuneiform tablets (today preserved in the Louvre) which consist for the most part of tax lists of the period around 1800 B.C. The further course of taxation policies in Syria has been illuminated by the rich documentary finds of Tell el-Amarna and Ras-Shamra (c. 1375 B.C.), by Herodotus' account of the Persian Empire, and by documents from the Hellenistic period. In Syria, then, the Romans could lean on existing practices.[n]

But there, too, widespread resistance was encountered. We hear of semi-savage mountain peoples who defended themselves with all their might against the first Roman attempts at a census, and as late as A.D. 300 dramatic incidents marked the effort to levy taxes in Syria. I shall quote a few sentences from the contemporary account of Lactantius, the "Christian Cicero": "The census-takers appeared everywhere, and produced tumult wherever they went. The fields were measured clod by clod; every grapevine and fruit tree counted, every head of livestock of every kind was listed, the exact number of people noted, and in the autonomous cities [in civitatibus] the urban and rural population were herded together until the market places were filled with the collected families. All came with their whole band of children and slaves. Everywhere was heard the screamings of those who were being interrogated with torture and beatings. Sons were forced to testify against their fathers, the trustiest slaves driven to bear witness against their masters, and wives against their husbands. When all other means had been exhausted, the victims were tortured until they gave evidence against themselves, and when pain had at last conquered, taxable property that did not exist was registered. Neither age nor illness won exemption. The ill and the infirm were dragged before the examiners; age was set down by estimate; the age of [tax-free] minors was raised while that of the old [who were likewise exempt] was lowered. The market places rang with lamentations. But the reports of the first census-takers were not yet sufficient. Others and still others were sent around to conduct still further examinations, as though there might be more to discover, and each time the levy was doubled. For whatever they did not find, they invented at will, so that their mission should not seem to have been in vain. Meanwhile men and livestock might perish, yet taxes had to be paid for the dead, so that neither life nor death should be free. Finally only beggars remained, from whom nothing more could be exacted. But in order that none might evade the tax by pretending inability to pay, a multitude of truly poverty-stricken wretches were put to death in defiance of every law of humanity." [n]

Augustus, of course, did not proceed so brutally. But the Augustan operation in Syria must have taken all the longer, as here what was being taken was the *prima descriptio Romana.*

We are well acquainted with the different stages of the taxation survey from numerous finds of Egyptian papyri,[n] and we have every reason to assume that Augustus applied the same procedure to Syria, with some adaptations for differing conditions.

The first stage was the *apographa,* a systematic listing of all taxable persons and property. For the register of persons, personal data were required. Everyone had to appear personally at the registry. Files were set up, descriptions entered, tax declarations were made and signed and sworn to with an oath to the Emperor. For the listing of property, a survey of the land and registration of ownership was essential. It is of this inital phase of the census that the Gospel of Luke speaks.[n]

The second and concluding phase of the protracted census, in Syria, Palestine, and elsewhere, was the *apotimesis,* the official assessment of taxes. It is this final phase which Flavius Josephus describes.[n]

Hitherto, both terms and both phases have frequently been confounded, and the result has been confusion. We must understand that the *apographa* constituted the starting-point, the *apotimesis* the conclusion of a long-drawn-out taxation procedure that lasted more than forty years in Gaul, and even in Egypt always extended over several years.

Strauss's Point 2. Here Strauss was led astray by Josephus' bombastic description of Herod. To understand correctly the legal position of Herod the Great, we must understand the adroit fiscal devices of Augustan imperial policy. We must also know something about the historical evolution of inter-locking sovereignties throughout Syria, concerning which we glean considerable information from a study of their coinages. I shall deal briefly with only three sample governments: the Nabataean kingdom of the Arab vassal kings in Petra, in the southeast of the Roman Empire; the Syrian city-state of Apamea on the Orontes; and the vassal kingdom of King Herod I.

The Nabataean kings in Petra had the right to mint their own silver coinage with Semitic inscriptions. They also assumed the right to settle questions of succession to the throne. Both these privileges were signs of a considerable measure of authority. But we find in Josephus several surprising items concerning their systems of taxation. Listing the leading men of Petra [4] around 9–6 B.C., Josephus mentions the imperial "slave" Fabatus, and speaks of this Fabatus twice as the chief imperial financial officer (*dioiketes*).[5] The man must therefore have been one of those numerous freedmen whom Augustus installed in high positions in the financial administrations of the provinces. From this one item it becomes apparent that Petra's entire system of taxation was

---

[4] *Antiquities* 17, 3, 2, 54.   [5] *Jewish War* 1, 29, 3, 575.

under the control of Augustus. This principle was maintained during the subsequent period of the Empire. Thus we hear of a Roman tax commissioner in the days of Vespasian who held sway in the Nabataean kingdom with the support of a Roman military detachment.[n] Naturally this does not exclude the co-operation of local rulers and authorities in all fiscal activities. The Egyptian taxation papyri offer many analogies to this practice.

The city-state of Apamea was allowed to mint only copper.[n] Nevertheless, we find it styling itself on its coins with the proud word *autonomos,* stressing with good reason its right to self-government. In New Testament times Apamea was one of the four most powerful city-states of Syria. We need only read Strabo to form some conception of the independence of this city in fiscal policy and taxation. The sizable towns of Larissa, Kasiana, Megara, Apollonia, and others were subject to taxation by Apamea. The priest-sovereigns of Emesa and the Ituraean kings of Chalcis on the Lebanon were allied to Apamea.[6] Yet, for all its power, this proud city could not evade Quirinius' census. We possess some interesting documentary proof of this. In the year 1674 the gravestone of an Augustan army officer turned up in Venice. The inscription on the stone mentioned certain taxation measures taken by Quirinius in Apamea. This inscription was copied at the time, and published in 1719. Meanwhile the original had disappeared, and for a long time the document was considered to be a forgery until in 1880 the lower half of the gravestone again came to light. Since then the authenticity of the marble slab has been universally recognized.[n]

The crucial words read: "On command of Quirinius I have carried out the census in Apamea, a city-state of one hundred and seventeen thousand citizens. Likewise I was

[6] Strabo 16, 2, 10, 752 f.

sent by Quirinius to march against the Ituraeans, and conquered their citadel on Lebanon mountain."[7] It is clear that Quirinius subjected the autonomous city-state of Apamea to the census, just as he did the vassal state of Nabataea. And it seems very probable that the campaign against the Ituraeans was connected with the work of the census. For we learn from Strabo that the Ituraean kings were allied to Apamea. These Semitic Ituraeans were a semi-nomadic, unruly, and marauding mountain folk, the kind of people who always offered the toughest resistance to the Roman census commissioners. Therefore Quirinius' census in Syria must have been accompanied in certain spots by as much bloodshed as the similar work in Gaul. In Apamea itself, and in other imperial cities, the work no doubt progressed more peacefully. But the foregoing quotation from Lactantius concerning the levies under Diocletian indicates how brutal the Romans could be when they met opposition.

Throughout his rule King Herod was allowed to mint only copper money. Therefore he was much worse off than Petra in respect to sovereignty, and no better off than Apamea. It is true that for a time he bore the titles Friend of Caesar and Ally of the Roman People,[8] and these dignities were possibly associated with a degree of authority in matters of taxation. But in the year 8 b.c. he was degraded to the rank of subject, in punishment for his autocratic conduct, and Augustus certainly did not restore him to favor as quickly and completely as the account of Flavius Josephus would have it. All these facts suggest that after 8 b.c. Herod was as restricted and dependent, in regard to the census, as were his proud neighbors in Petra and Apamea.[n] The only coin that was officially accepted for payment of taxes in the

---

[7] *Jussu Quirini censum egi Apamenæ civitatis millium hominum civium CXVII. Idem missu Quirini adversus Ituræos in Libano monte castellum eorum cepi.* [8] *Amicus Cæsaris et Socius Populi Romani.*

land of Israel, as throughout imperial territory, was the Roman denarius.[9]

Strauss's Point 3. We must thoroughly revise Strauss's ideas about the time consumed by a *descriptio prima,* and about Quirinius' official activities in the East. The Roman imperial government always preferred to place the management of Oriental affairs in the hands of a generalissimo. The first of such appointees was Cn. Pompeius Magnus, the second was Mark Antony, the third Marcus Vipsanius Agrippa, whom Augustus named vice-emperor of the Orient in 23 B.C. On January 1, 12 B.C., P. Sulpicius Quirinius became consul; on March 12 of the same year Agrippa died; and on August 1 Augustus released Consul Quirinius from the duties of his office, in all probability in order to send him directly to the Orient as temporary successor to Agrippa.

In any case, during the following years Quirinius appears to have been in charge of all campaigns and other affairs in the East. Two recently discovered inscriptions which sing his praises prove that the favor of this all-powerful man was eagerly sought after in Asia Minor. In Syria he governed sometimes alone—as had Agrippa before him—sometimes aided by an imperial provincial governor. From 9 to 6 B.C. the governor was C. Sentius Saturninus; from 6 to 4 B.C., P. Quintilius Varus. In 2 B.C. Gaius and Lucius Caesar, the two sons of Agrippa, who were also grandsons and adoptive sons of the Emperor, received the *toga virilis* and were declared future consuls and heirs to the throne. A gold coin was minted to celebrate this occasion. Lucius Caesar was sent to the West and died A.D. 2, at the age of eighteen, in Marseille. Gaius Caesar went to the Orient, where he was received by Quirinius and introduced to the duties of commander-in-chief of the East (*Orienti præpositus*). In A.D. 4 he died in Asia Minor at the age of twenty-three. Henceforth

[9] Matthew 22, 19 (note in Revised Standard Version).

the conduct of Oriental affairs lay once more in the experienced hands of Quirinius, until Emperor Tiberius in A.D. 17 sent his adoptive son Germanicus to the East, empowered to take supreme command over all the local governors. Two years later Germanicus died in Syria. But the imperial government continued to appoint new commanders or vice-emperors for the Orient.

It is evident that this division of power was in the nature of things, and Sulpicius Quirinius must be reckoned not only among the series of Syrian provincial governors, but also—and this chiefly—in the proud list of the Roman commanders-in-chief of the Orient. In this capacity he governed the Roman Orient like a vice-emperor from 12 B.C. to A.D. 16, with only a brief interruption (Gaius Caesar).[n] In this capacity he carried out the *prima descriptio* in the East. Thus, he was in a position to begin the work of the census in the days of King Herod, to continue it without regard to the temporary occupancy or vacancy of the post of Syrian governor, and finally to bring it to a peaceful conclusion.

Strauss's Point 4. The law of the Roman census stated: "Whoever has property in another city must deliver his tax declaration in that city. For land taxes must be paid to the community in whose territory the land is situated."[n] This provision necessarily lent a particular character to the census procedures in Palestine. For in that country ownership of property outside the community was not uncommon. The Romans were constantly encountering the family property of the "patriarchal houses," whose rights of possession were extremely difficult to disentangle. The part-owners who owed taxes were certainly not easy to locate.[n] In these cases the Romans' only course was to survey the existing property, assess its value, and then summon for registration all those who wished to claim total or partial rights of ownership in this property. Whoever turned up at the registries had to answer the prescribed questions. Then his rights of ownership were examined, his share in the property was clarified and its value estimated, and finally his property tax was fixed according to the size and value of his share. This was the very procedure the Romans followed in Palestine.[n]

Strauss's Point 5. When the census of citizens in Italy was taken, it was sufficient for the head of the household to appear at the registry office and give the necessary information about the members of his family. Had conditions been the same in Syria as in Italy, Mary's appearance at the registry would surely have been inappropriate. Quirinius' Syrian operation, however, was not a regular census, but a first survey. Above all, it was not a benevolent registration of the population, but a rigorous provincial taxation survey. In such circumstances personal appearance was a duty, for each individual had to be accounted for; personal declarations, signatures, and oaths were required; interrogation sometimes was by torture; evidence and counter-evidence was obtained. Women, too, were required to appear, and the bureaucrats of the tax office made no exception for illness or advanced pregnancy. We need only recall once more Lactantius' account of the Syrian provincial census.

It appears, then, that none of Strauss's arguments will bear examination. With some reservations we may now attempt to sketch the chronology of Quirinius' census as a whole. In the autumn of 12 B.C. Quirinius took charge of Oriental affairs and commenced the census in the Roman East. In 8 B.C. Herod the Great was demoted. In 7 B.C. the *apographa* in Palestine began.[n] At this time Joseph probably journeyed to Bethlehem with Mary. In A.D. 7 the work of the census was completed with the *apotimesis*. "In the thirty-seventh year after the emperor's victory at Actium, Quirinius brought the labors of the *apotimesis* to an end," Josephus writes.[1] He makes it sound like a sigh of relief after a long, wearing, hard-fought task. And indeed the first survey of

---

[1] *Antiquities,* 18, 2, 1.

Syria, the *prima Syriæ descriptio,* was completed within the short span of barely fourteen years—a respectable achievement, and one that reflects the energy and skill of Quirinius.

⇛⇛⇛ 5 ⇚⇚⇚

THE STAR

WHERE IS HE who has been born king of the Jews? For we have seen his star in the East, and have come to worship him." Thus the Magi from the East speak in Matthew 2, 2. Perhaps Paul in Galatians 4, 3 f., was also thinking of this appearance of the star. Thus, at any rate, he was understood by Ignatius of Antioch when he combined the motifs of Matthew 2 and Galatians 4 in one apocalyptic advent hymn to the Star of Bethlehem.[n]

As long ago as the seventeenth century, Kepler ascribed the star of Bethlehem to the unique orbit of the planet Jupiter in the year 7 B.C.[n] In the spring of that year there was a conjunction of Jupiter and Venus. In the summer and autumn of that year Jupiter encountered the planet Saturn in the Sign of the Fishes—this being the extremely rare Great Conjunction that takes place in this form only once every 794 years. According to the account in Matthew, the Magi noted only the beginning of the conjunction, only the appearance of Jupiter "out of the east." Upon this they based their astronomical and astrological forecast and thereupon set out for Palestine; when they reached Palestine they witnessed the crucial phenomenon in the heavens.[2] The rarity of that

[2] Matthew 2, 9 f.

32

conjunction of Jupiter could not have escaped the astronomers of antiquity. But was astronomical science in the days of Jesus sufficiently developed to forecast the orbits and conjunctions of the planets?

Two recent finds provide the answer to this question: the "Berlin Planetary Table" and the "Celestial Almanac" of the ancient observatory of Sippar,[n] the Greenwich of Babylonia. The Berlin Planetary Table is a list of forthcoming movements of the planets drawn up in the year 17 B.C., and extended to A.D. 10; it was copied on an Egyptian papyrus dating from A.D. 42. It proves that even then astronomers were able to calculate the positions of the planets decades in advance. The Celestial Almanac of Sippar is one of the most recent cuneiform tablets which have come down to us. It contains predictions of the positions of the planets for the year 7 B.C., probably drawn up at the beginning of that year. On this clay tablet all the principal motions and conjunctions of the year 7 were calculated in advance, precise to the month and day. The main subject of the tablet, however, was the impending conjunction of Jupiter and Saturn in the Fishes, annotations for which appear about five times, with exact dates. In sum, astronomers of the day knew accurately what events were to be expected in the firmament, and were looking forward with special eagerness to the rare conjunction of Jupiter in 7 B.C.

What opinions did contemporary astrologers hold concerning this phenomenon? Today we can answer this question also. Jupiter was regarded as the star of the ruler of the universe, and the constellation of the Fishes as the sign of the last days. In the East, Saturn was considered to be the planet of Palestine. If Jupiter encountered Saturn in the sign of the Fishes, it could only mean that the ruler of the last days would appear in Palestine.[n] Such were the passages that prompted the Magi of Matthew 2, 2, to go to Jerusalem.

Evidently, then, there is substance to the account in Matthew; it agrees excellently with the original documents of the period. The clay tablet of Sippar may be regarded as the astronomical pocket-almanac with which the wise men set out from the East, and it is understandable that their astrological deductions would cause a great stir in Herod's Jerusalem.[n]

Undoubtedly the unique orbit of Jupiter of the year 7 B.C. was also noticed and commented on in the western parts of the Roman Empire. We know that Augustus was deeply interested in astronomical phenomena, and it is evident from the Berlin Planetary Table that in Rome and Alexandria the movements in the heavens were followed with the closest attention. In the Roman Empire, Augustus was regarded as Jupiter in human form, and thus ruler of the *ultima ætas,* the last age. Venus was considered the star of the Julian family, and Saturn the symbol of the Golden Age. In these circumstances the extraordinary path of Jupiter in 7 B.C. could only be taken as referring to the career of the Emperor Augustus: surely this year would bring the glorious climax of his splendid career.

As a matter of fact, we possess a number of documents of the period which directly or indirectly confirm this deduction.[n] We may count among these the Augustan inscription at Philae, which I have discussed in detail elsewhere.[n] In the spring of 7 B.C. there took place the conjunction of Jupiter with Venus, which in Egypt was regarded as the star of Isis. On March 8 of that year an eminent Alexandrian erected a memorial tablet in the temple of Isis on the island of Philae in the Nile. The inscription upon the tablet of Philae hailed the Emperor as Zeus Eleutherios (that is, freedom-giving Jupiter).

Thus, the star of Bethlehem, too, is a historical fact. It, too, however, was a sign of God as ambiguous as all the other events in the story of Jesus. Whose coming was presaged by

34

the heavenly phenomena of the year 7 B.C.—Augustus' or
Jesus'?

>>>->>>->>> 6 <<<-<<<-<<<

THE MASSACRE
OF THE CHILDREN

IMMEDIATELY AFTER his account of the star, Matthew tells
the story of the massacre of the children in Bethlehem.
Now, a great many doubts have been raised concerning the
historical credibility of this story. We shall confine ourselves
to four principal points. (1) Only Matthew speaks of this.
(2) Can such mass murder ordered by Herod have lain
within the bounds of possibility? (3) Is it conceivable that
Augustus would have tolerated such an act without protest?
(4) The tale as told by Matthew displays a striking kinship
with traditional mythology and seems to follow a literary
pattern.

Point 1. We must here call attention to an item that has
not been noticed by commentators on the Gospels or historians of Herod's reign. In the *Assumption of Moses,* an apocalyptic document written by Palestinian Jews close to the
Qumran groups around A.D. 6–15, there is a passage dealing
with Herod I: "They [the Hasmonaeans] will be followed
by an arrogant king who will not be of a priestly clan, a
reckless and godless man. . . . He will exterminate their
chief men with the sword and bury their bodies in unknown

35

places, so that no man will know where they lie. He will slay the old and the young and show no mercy. Then terrible fear of him will come over the land. And he will rage among them with bloodthirsty commands, as was done in Egypt." [3]

What is this allusion to the young whom Herod would mercilessly kill? Our first thought is of his own three sons, whom Herod had executed. But why, then, the comparison to Egypt? [n] For Pharaoh killed not his own first-born, but the infants of the Hebrews. Not only the book of Exodus [4] tells this story; Jewish legend also dealt with it at length, and interpreted Pharaoh's bloodthirsty command as the Egyptian ruler's reaction to an oracle concerning the imminent birth of an Israelite savior-king and the downfall of the Egyptian dynasty. We find traces of this legend in the work of Philo of Alexandria, who lived at the time the *Assumption of Moses* was composed. [5] And Flavius Josephus tells us: "One of the sacred scribes—persons of considerable skill in accurately predicting the future—announced to the king that there would be born to the Israelites, at that time, one who would abase the sovereignty of the Egyptians and exalt the Israelites, were he reared to manhood, and would surpass all men in virtue and win everlasting renown. Alarmed thereat, the king, on the sage's advice, ordered that every male child born to the Israelites should be destroyed by being cast into the river." [6] In rabbinical tradition this legend was elaborated and embellished. [n] It is plain that the story of the Egyptian massacre of the innocents had seized the imagination of the people in the age of Jesus, and was recast in an entirely new form, being combined with the theme of oracular prophecy. The apocalyptic writers referred to it in the *Assumption of Moses* 6, 4. Herod was the new pharaoh. Therefore the pas-

---

[3] *Assumption of Moses* 6, 2 ff.   [4] 1, 15 ff.   [5] *Vita Mosis* 1, 8, 13. 32 and *passim*.   [6] *Antiquities* 2, 9, 2. Translation by H. St. J. Thackeray, Loeb Classical Library.

sage concerning the murder of the "young" can refer only to a massacre of children in the style of Pharaoh."

In Revelation 12, 1 ff., a recollection of Herod's massacre may also have been worked into the apocalyptic text. But the information in the *Assumption of Moses* is of far more value because it is at least eighty years older and certainly independent of all Christian traditions.

Point 2. In the history of Oriental potentates, massacres were commonplace, and Herod was one of the most bloodthirsty tyrants of antiquity. At the age of twenty-five he made a name for himself by having the Galilean partisan Hezekiah and his followers seized and summarily executed. He then pursued the members of the Galilean resistance, who lived by the hundreds with their wives and children in the mountains and caves of Galilee, and organized an enormous slaughter by having them smoked out with fires. In 37 B.C., with Roman aid, he entered Jerusalem as King of the Jews. He at once saw to it that the Romans beheaded (an unheard-of novelty in Roman law) his Hasmonaean predecessor and antagonist, Antigonus II, called Mattathias. He himself ordered the massacre of all friends of the Hasmonaeans at court and in the Great Sanhedrin. During the following years he eliminated the Hasmonaeans Aristobulus and Hyrcanus II, his own wife Mariamne, and Alexandra, and finally struck down the powerful clan of Bnay Baba, the last hope and support of the Hasmonaean party. About 25 B.C. Herod got wind of a conspiracy against him. He had the ringleaders tortured to death, and all their sympathizers with their wives and children killed. A succession of political murders followed. "Many were openly or secretly dragged off to the mountain citadel of Hyrcania and slaughtered there. In every place where people assembled, in the towns, on the main roads, men were on the watch to spy on them. . . . The great majority submitted, either out of servility or fear. But the independent souls who could not conceal their

37

hatred of the reign of terror, he got rid of by any means he could find." [7] Let us recall the prophecy in the *Assumption of Moses:* "He will exterminate their chief men with the sword and bury their bodies in unknown places, so that no man will know where they lie." We now see that this diatribe, though cast in apocalyptic language, is in the nature of a literal report.

In the year 7 B.C. Herod, with the sanction of Augustus, had Alexander and Aristobulus, his two sons by his Hasmonaean wife Mariamne, strangled on grounds of high treason. An oppositional army group of three hundred officers was simultaneously liquidated. That same year he engaged in a bitter struggle with six thousand Pharisees who refused to take the imperial oath (presumably the oath required by the census).[n] A number of the men in this group delivered a prophecy, which they claimed had been revealed to them by God, of the impending birth of the wonderful messianic king who would overthrow bloody Herod and bring about the Golden Age of the Last Days.[n] Herod's reply was a stupendous massacre among the Pharisees and the members of his own court. Even his handsome personal page, Carus, on whom all sorts of wild hopes seem to have been placed, fell victim to his rage. Three years later Herod was already fatally ill, but he still had the strength to suppress an attempted Pharisee coup by another blood bath, and to execute his son Antipater, once again with the Emperor's sanction. Moreover, he commanded all the leading men of the Jewish population of Palestine to assemble on pain of death in the hippodrome at Jericho. He had issued secret orders to have the place surrounded by soldiers. The citizens were to be kept prisoner there and shot down all at once by archers at the hour of his death, so that the King would not have to pass from this earth unaccompanied by lamentations for the

[7] Flavius Josephus: *Antiquities* 15, 10, 4.

dead. Then he died—and his men at once released the prisoners in the hippodrome.

In the life of such a ruler the slaughter of the innocents
of Bethlehem would be only a minor episode, the sort of
thing which happened frequently during the incessant struggle to hold power.

Point 3. Augustus, too, could act with brutality. He held
no brief for Julius Caesar's policy of conciliation, and returned to the dreaded proscription method of Sulla. He was
a lad of nineteen when he signed the Black Lists that condemned three hundred senators and two thousand Roman
patricians to death. As he grew older and felt his position
more secure, his temper became milder. But he never liked to
interfere in Asiatic problems and ways. And, unlike his great
predecessor Julius Caesar, Augustus had an aversion for the
Jews. He had never set foot in Jerusalem, and he commended
his nephew Gaius Caesar for likewise avoiding the capital of
the Jews during his travels in the Orient. Thus he was only
too glad to leave the treatment of this alien and troublesome
people to the Arab Herod. He was quite content to leave
Asia to the Asiatics. As we have seen, he gave his express
permission for Herod's murders of his nearest kin. Augustus
paid no more attention to the King's other killings in Palestine than did Tiberius to the bloody acts of terror committed
by Pilate.[8] Only once do we hear that Augustus commented
casually on Herod's policy of wholesale murder, and that remark speaks volumes. Around A.D. 450 the Roman eclectic
Macrobius wrote: "When Augustus learned that along with
the boys under two years of age who were strangled in Syria
by order of Herod, King of the Jews, the king's own son had
been killed, he remarked: 'It is better to be Herod's swine
(*hus*) than his son (*huios*).' " The chronology and content
of the passage are somewhat confused, so that it should not
be taken as an independent source of evidence for the massa-

[8] Luke 13, 1.

39

cre of the innocents at Bethlehem. But the bon mot rings true, revealing as it is of the Emperor's delight in Greek puns and his antipathy to all things Jewish. In the land of Israel, he was saying, the swine are better off than sons, for the swine are spared (because of dietary laws) but the sons are butchered. Anyone who passed over Herod's consistent policy of murder with such jokes is not likely to have been greatly troubled by the extermination of some Jewish children in a certain village of Bethlehem.

Point 4. The peril and miraculous deliverance of infants who will later become great men is a favorite theme in the world's literature. The tradition of Moses is well known. I need mention here only a few anecdotes of the childhood of Augustus. Julius Marathus, the emperor's Syrian freedman and private secretary, relates: "A few months before the birth of Augustus there was observed at Rome a prodigy which signified that nature would soon bear a king for the Roman people. Alarmed, the Senate resolved that no child born in that year should be raised to manhood. But those senators whose wives were with child saw to it that this decree of the Senate was not registered, which would have given it the force of law. For each of them secretly referred the promise to his own household." [9] On September 23 of that year (63 B.C.) Senator Gaius Octavius arrived at the meeting of the Senate somewhat belatedly, and excused himself by saying that a son of his had just been born. Senator Nigidius Figulus, an amateur astrologer, inquired the exact hour of the birth, immediately cast the horoscope, and then cried enthusiastically: "This day the master of the world has been born." [1] Dio Cassius, writing barely a century after Suetonius, has fused the two anecdotes in a self-contradictory manner: "When Nigidius learned the reason for the delay, he cried out: 'You have given us a master.' At this Octavius was affrighted and wished to destroy the infant. But Nigidius

[9] Suetonius: *Augustus* 94.   [1] Ibid.

40

restrained him, saying it would not be possible to do this to the boy." [2]

It is only natural that such tendencies toward stylization should have infiltrated the traditions around Jesus. In Matthew we also find a partiality for revelatory dreams, for appeals to Scripture, and so on. But Herod's massacre of the innocents is a historical fact, no matter what fable-making was at work. For there is mention of this very thing in the *Assumption of Moses* by a contemporary and pre-Christian author who, first, is an accurate chronicler and, secondly, is completely disinterested in the story of Jesus.

Thus we may venture, from the material in the *Assumption of Moses* 6, Matthew 2, Flavius Josephus, and the sources quoted above, to sketch with all due reservations the events of the year 7 B.C.

⇥≫⋙ 7 ⋘≪⇤

THE APOCALYPTIC YEAR

T HE YEAR 7 B.C. was a *fatalis annus,* a year of destiny. In the heavens the planet Jupiter entered the Great Conjunction, thus proclaiming the coming ruler of the final Golden Age. In Rome Augustus reached the climax of his career, and Tiberius held his great triumph *ad maiorem Augusti patris gloriam*—to the greater glory of Father Augustus. On the Nile the Emperor was being celebrated as Freedom-giving Jove. On the Euphrates the astrologers were setting out for Palestine to seek the promised king of peace. In the land of Israel, however, a tempest was brewing.

[2] *Romaika* 45, 1, 5.

Herod had been demoted several months before. Quirinius' census-takers were descending upon towns and villages, swords in their hands. The large clans were on the move. The bureaucracy ran wild, and the people fought back. The resistance movement grew.[3] Six thousand Pharisees refused to take the imperial oath to "freedom-giving" Jove. Herod, having so recently been demoted, was nervous, and did all in his power to satisfy the Roman tax commissioners. His nervousness increased when on all sides people began talking about signs in the heavens and divine revelations, of the imminent overthrow of all things, and of the advent of a new ruler of the world. In the face of these sinister portents, he resolved to exterminate all who might endanger him. In Samaria he had the two Hasmonaean princes killed, in Jerusalem the three hundred officers faithful to the Hasmonaeans, the page Carus, all suspect courtiers, and the oracular Pharisees. It was only natural and consistent for him also to strike in Bethlehem, the center for the house of David. For even if the Hasmonaeans were no more, the Davidites still remained, and would be more dangerous than ever.[n]

> *Justice is trampled underfoot,*
> *truth has perished.*
> *The reign of lies and malice has come.*
> *Nature is turned upside down;*
> *the measure of wickedness is full.*
> *But a cloud conceals*
> *the sufferings of men*
> *from the eyes of the evil-doers.*

Thus old Teron cried in the crooked, winding streets of Jerusalem, until Herod's henchmen silenced him forever.[n]
In that apocalyptic year Jesus came into the world—the son of David born in the ancient royal city of Bethlehem.

[3] Acts 5, 37.

THE
EARLY YEARS
OF
JESUS

→→→→→→ 1 ←←←←←←

THE HIDDEN YEARS

WE ARE TOLD very little about Jesus' youth from 7 B.C. to A.D. 27. Matthew speaks of the flight to Egypt, Luke of the twelve-year-old Jesus in the temple. Both stories throw an interesting light upon the political precariousness of Jesus' situation, and upon Joseph's political alertness. Joseph was not unacquainted with the ways of the world. He flees with

43

Mary and Jesus to Egypt, the favorite refuge of all Jewish exiles in antiquity.[1] Hearing there of the death of the old King, he returns, learns that Archelaus has meanwhile succeeded his father in Jerusalem and Judea, at once grows wary, and slips away to Galilee, the territory of Herod Antipas, old Herod's less vicious son.[2]

And so Jesus grew up in Nazareth, a small hill village on the northern edge of the plain of Megiddo whose inhabitants were in ill repute among pious circles in Galilee.[3]

In A.D. 6 Archelaus was deposed. At that time Jesus, according to our reckoning, was twelve years old. That year the cautious Joseph took young Jesus along on the Passover pilgrimage to Jerusalem for the first time.[4] Probably Joseph profited by the opportunity of this journey to settle some affairs connected with his taxes in Bethlehem, for the taxes were due just then.[5]

We know that Jesus learned Joseph's trade.[6] As we have mentioned, the carpenters of Palestine were itinerant craftsmen. There may be some connection between this fact and the Jewish tradition of Jesus' journeys in Egypt as a carpenter.[n]

The apocryphal legends of his childhood are of no value historically. To form a reliable picture of the world in which Jesus lived, outwardly and inwardly, during his early years, we must study the landscape of Palestine in his times, the political history of those years, the Old Testament, current Jewish apocalyptics, the Galilean tradition of Enoch and the anticipation of the Son of Man, and, above all, the whole complex of liturgy among the Palestinian Jews: private prayers, worship in the synagogue, and the temple ritual of the three great pilgrim festivals: the Feast of Tabernacles, Passover, and Pentecost.[n]

For the phraseology and rites of Jewish liturgy accompa-

[1] Matthew 2, 13 ff. [2] Matthew 2, 22 f. [3] John 1, 46. [4] Luke 2, 42.
[5] Cf. Flavius Josephus: *Antiquities* 18, 2, 1. [6] Mark 6, 3.

44

nied Jesus from the first to the last days of his life. He died
with the words of his forefathers' prayers upon his lips.[n]

⇝⇝⇝ 2 ⇜⇜⇜

HOME AND KIN

A s a Davidite, Joseph belonged to the tribe of Judah. Mary
was in all probability a Levite of the tribe of Aaron.[n]
The parents of Jesus were not prosperous.[n] The father seems
to have died before Jesus' first public appearance, for after
the story of the pilgrimage in Luke 2, 51, we hear no more
of him.[7] In Mark 6, 3, and Matthew 13, 55, four brothers of
Jesus are named: James, Joseph, Judas, and Simon. Sisters are
also mentioned, but their names and number are not given.

The New Testament always speaks without qualification
of Jesus' "brothers." But the term *adelphos* might equally
well mean full brother, stepbrother, or even cousin. Perhaps
in this case the meaning is stepbrother, for if James and his
brothers had been later sons of Mary, they would hardly
have been able to come forth against Jesus so authoritatively
as they attempt to do in Mark 3, 21. 32, or John 7, 3.[8]

In any case, Jesus was surrounded by a bustling family
life. His family also had a large group of relatives in the
south and north.[9] The relatives located in the south were
primarily Joseph's—for example, Cleopas, Joseph's brother,
and his son Simeon, both of whom lived in the same house
at Emmaus.[1] In the north there lived Salome, presumably

[7] Cf. John 2, 12. [8] Cf. Ethelbert Stauffer: *"Petrus und Jakobus in Jerusalem,"* *Festschrift Karrer* (1958). [9] Luke 2, 4. 44. [1] Luke 24, 18.

45

Mary's sister; she was the wife of Zebedee, who with his sons James and John ran a fishery on Lake Gennesaret.[n] Zebedee apparently belonged to the tribe of Levi; at any rate, his son John had unusually close connections with the family of the high priest of the same name in Jerusalem.[2] But Mary also had kinsfolk in the south. We know of the priest's daughter Elizabeth and her husband, the priest Zachariah, the parents of John the Baptist, who lived south of Jerusalem in the mountains of Judea.[3] And we hear of Mary's visiting for about three months her kinswoman Elizabeth.[4] Thus, Jesus grew up among a group of kindred who belonged to both the leading tribes of Israel and to the oldest families, who were scattered throughout the whole country and did not neglect their family relationships. Jesus unquestionably knew from childhood his young cousin John, who lived by Lake Gennesaret, as well as the parents of John the Baptist in the southern mountains.[n]

➤➤➤-➤➤➤-➤➤➤ 3 ᐊᐊᐊ-ᐊᐊᐊ-ᐊᐊᐊ

JESUS' NATIVE LAND

WHEN YOUNG JESUS climbed to the peak of the hill south of Nazareth,[5] he had at his back Sepphoris, the capital of the district, the old battle-stained headquarters of the Galilean guerilla chiefs Hezekiah and Judas. In 4 B.C. the town had been burned to ashes and evacuated, but Herod Antipas had soon rebuilt it and made it his official residence until A.D. 18. There this faithful vassal of the Romans held his gay

[2] John 18, 16.   [3] Luke 1, 5. 36. 39.   [4] Luke 1, 56.   [5] Luke 4, 29.

and amorous revels. To the northeast lay Lake Gennesaret,
and still farther north Caesarea Philippi, where Herod Philip
held court. Above it stood the temple of Herod I and, towering above all else, snow-covered Mount Hermon. To the east
lay Mount Tabor. "Tabor and Hermon joyously praise thy
name." [6] In the west could be seen Carmel, the mountain
where the priests of Baal had been slaughtered; beyond
stretched the Mediterranean. On the coast lay Caesarea, dominated by the towering temple, with its colossal statues of
Rome and Augustus. To the south Jesus looked down into
the plain of Megiddo, ancient battleground of the Near East.
Here Pharaoh Thutmose III (c. 1450) won the decisive battle
against Babylon. Here Deborah and Barak (c. 1250) stormed
down from Mount Tabor and fell victoriously upon the war
chariots of the Canaanites. Here Gideon, with the sword of
the Lord and a reckless band of men, conquered the Midian-
ites. Here Saul, a curse upon his head, ate his last meal in
the cave of the Witch of Endor; [7] here the next day he lost
the battle and his throne, and fell upon his sword (c. 1000).
"Ye mountains of Gilboa, let there be no dew or rain upon
you, nor upsurging of the deep! For there the shield of the
mighty was defiled, the shield of Saul, not anointed with oil"
—so the forefather of Jesus sang after his sorrowful victory.[8]
Here Ahab defeated the Aramaeans of Damascus; here Pharaoh Necho marched in the footsteps of Thutmose against
the Assyrian Empire, and Josiah came against him and died
(c. 600). Here, in this "place called Armageddon," the apocalyptic last battle would someday be fought between the
powers of good and evil.[9]

When in the spring Jesus trudged across the hills to visit
his cousins by the lake, he would spend several hours alone
in the wild mountains of Galilee, where the partisans had
their caves, and where his father felled timber for buildings.

[6] Psalms 89, 12. [7] 1 Samuel 28, 7 (Revised Standard Version calls her
a "medium"). [8] 2 Samuel 1, 21. [9] Daniel 11, 45; Revelation 16, 16.

Then the view widened out, and below him lay the blue Lake of Gennesaret, six hundred and fifty feet below sea level, embedded in a tropical landscape. On the shore oleanders flowered; a bright carpet of lilies covered the hillsides. And scattered among these slopes lay Tiberias, the gay new capital; lay the famous baths, sanatoria, and colonnades; lay the notorious red-light district of Magdala, and industrious Capernaum with its nets and fishing-boats. "Eretz Israel has seven lakes, but the Lake of Gennesaret is the lake chosen of God." [n]

Three roads led from Galilee to Jerusalem. The traveler might choose the coastal road, the ancient military highway of the pharaohs and kings, which turned southeastward into the mountains, passed by the graves of Samson and the Maccabees, and finally climbed among scattered farms from Emmaus to Jerusalem. Or else he might take the shortest road, leading over the ridges straight across Samaria. This went past Jacob's Well, past holy and unholy Mount Gerizim with its temple, to Bethel, the "frightful place" of patriarchal days. Here rose Gallows Hill, where Rizpah, the Biblical Antigone, kept the death watch by the seven who were hanged,[1] and Michmash, that ancient mountain fortress which played a part in Saul's struggles with the Philistines [2] and was to know a new moment of glory in the days of the Maccabaean wars. There Jonathan, the heroic, freedom-loving partisan, judged the people and drove the renegades out of Israel, while Jerusalem was ruled by collaborators of the Syrian king.[3] A few hours south of Bethel the pilgrims' road finally reached the "Hill of the Lookout," from which there opens out a view of Jerusalem itself. This was the famous point on the boundary of the Holy City where, according to Jewish tradition, Alexander the Great was once greeted by the high priest.

The majority of East Galilean pilgrims on their way to

[1] 2 Samuel 21, 10.   [2] 1 Samuel 13.   [3] 1 Maccabees 9, 73.

festivals in Jerusalem preferred the road along the Jordan River, which led through the barren valley of the Jordan and into the broad Jordanian plain and the world-famous palm groves of Cleopatra and Livia. On the other side the travelers caught sight of Mount Nebo, whence the dying Moses had beheld the Promised Land lying before him like a Garden of Eden. Then they reached the outworks of proud and sinister Jericho. There the view to the southeast lay open to the Dead Sea (the lowest spot on the surface of the earth) and the mountain ridges of the eastern bank of the Jordan. Beyond these lay concealed Herod's hill citadel of Machaerus, a place of atrocities and abominations. On the western shore of the Dead Sea, directly opposite Machaerus, lay the desert settlement of Engedi, in the times of Jesus the headquarters of the Essene order.

Jericho itself was the site of the three-thousand-year-old "tower" of Palestine, the Escorial of the earlier Herods and their little Versailles as well. Here, in the days after the death of Herod the Great, Simon the slave-king claimed a messianic crown and burned down the hated fortress that had dominated the surrounding countryside. With his band of runaway slaves he marched through the land until the Romans put a bloody end to the entire movement. In the time of Jesus, Jericho was the city of gay officers of the Roman occupation force and hardheaded tax-farmers.[4]

From Jericho a dreaded road led up through the wilderness of Judea. There robbers and predatory beasts menaced the traveler. There, too, was the cliff over which each year the scapegoat was driven to appease Azazel, the demon of the wilderness.[5]

Finally the traveler reached the Mount of Olives, with its pleasant villages of Bethphage and Bethany, and at last he saw Jerusalem before him—the towers of David and the walls of Herod, the Temple Mount and the smoke of the

[4] Luke 19, 2 ff.   [5] Leviticus 16, 10.

Eternal Fire, rising exactly above the Sacred Rock that sealed the underworld and formed the cornerstone of the structure of the universe. Here was the navel of the earth, the center of the nations of the world.[6] From the southern wall of the city you looked down into the sinister valley of Hinnom—the Gehenna of the New Testament—the hell to which the damned were consigned. Beyond rose the hill where Rachel wept for her children, and a little farther to the south lay Bethlehem, the city of David.

The people who inhabited this land along with Greeks and Romans and the abhorred Samaritans were a stern and austere folk. The fable of the gentle Galilean was never more than a fable. The Galileans, says Flavius Josephus, are of unbending nature from childhood; they do not know the meaning of fear and have a passion for freedom, upheaval, and rebellion.[7] The fishermen of Capernaum were an equally tough breed. For the blue lake was treacherous and beset by storms. The women of Nazareth and Magdala were famous for their beauty. In the age of Jesus, under the influence of war and the influx of foreigners, moral standards had deteriorated. But the mothers and daughters of Galilean guerilla chiefs knew how to die.

Between north and south there were a good many tensions. The devout in Jerusalem grumbled at the waywardness of their northern brethren in matters of religion. Galilee had been only tolerably Judaized since the days of Alexander Jannaeus; it was still cut off from Jerusalem by the barrier of Samaria, and the Galileans showed little interest in the new Torah movement, in scriptural learning, and Phariseeism. The great rabbi Johanan ben Zakkai lived in Galilee for eighteen years, and in all this time was consulted only twice regarding problems of the Torah. Whereupon he declared: "Galilee, Galilee, you hate the teaching, and you will end by falling prey to the bandit leaders." [8]

[6] Jubilees 8, 19.   [7] *Jewish War* 3, 3, 2; *Life* 17.

Jesus, however, loved the people of north and south with an equal love. It is not going too far if we venture to say: he loved this land, loved this people, with the love of God who chose, rejected, and pardoned Israel.

➤➤➤-➤➤➤-➤➤➤ 4 ⟨⟨⟨-⟨⟨⟨-⟨⟨⟨

JESUS THE STUDENT

SOON AFTER he became conscious of his native land, the son of an ancient Jewish household had his first encounter with the Torah.[8] His father took him upon his knee and taught him "Hear, O Israel," the Ten Commandments, and other fundamental passages of the Torah. In pious houses the family owned and could read their own scriptural scrolls.[n] This enabled the father to teach his small son his letters, and the reading of Scripture. This, we may imagine, was the practice in the household of Joseph. And when the boy grew older he could be sent to the "sexton's school," or to the village schools that had been established everywhere since the time of Simon ben Shatah (c. 75 B.C.). In these, too, the teaching centered around the Torah. Moreover, liturgical observances in the home and scriptural readings in the synagogue served to fix and extend a boy's knowledge of the sacred texts. As he matured, a thoughtful young man would be allowed to study the Bible scrolls on his own, at home and elsewhere.

We may be sure that Jesus did so during the quiet years he spent in Nazareth. For he not only spoke Aramaic and

[8] Proverbs 2, 1, ff.; Ecclesiasticus 14, 26.

Greek, which were the languages in ordinary use throughout his country, but also knew the holy language; he could read the Hebrew Bible, and read it aloud as well. He had a perfect knowledge of its contents, although he had never entered the academy for Torah studies in Jerusalem.[n]

The Torah stood in the foreground. But there were other Holy Scriptures at the time—above all, the Prophets and the Psalms. Jesus was at home in these also. In addition, in orthodox houses a great many other sacred writings were read which later were not incorporated into the official canon of Jamnia (c. A.D. 90). Jesus knew them all—far more of them than we know today. This is proved by the number of unverifiable "scriptural passages" that Jesus quoted—phrases, for example, out of unknown martyrological scriptures.[9] Even the familiar passages of the present canon were known to him in an older textual form that had not been subjected to the censorship the Scriptures were to undergo at Jamnia.

The newly discovered Qumran scrolls cast a welcome light upon this matter, for in many cases they corroborate pre-Christian phraseology that we had previously been unable to discover even in the pre-Christian Greek Bible known as the Septuagint. Conspicuous among such altered texts was Isaiah 53, the chapter dealing with the suffering servant of God. The version Jesus knew was, in crucial passages, that of the great Qumran scroll of Isaiah.

Jesus read the same "Bible" as his contemporaries in Palestine. But he read it with different eyes. He saw in it something more than prescripts, prohibitions, precepts, and warning anecdotes. Jesus found in it the living God who makes his sun shine upon good and evil alike and the rain fall upon the just and unjust, the God who loves freedom, life, beauty, greatness, ardor, abundance, prodigality, but also quietude, humbleness, and hidden splendor; the God who loves restless creativity and merciful loving-kindness. He dis-

[9] See Luke 11, 49 ff., and *passim*.

covered this God as one who belonged to him; he loved the glory of this God as an only son loves and understands his father. "And no one knows the Father except the Son, and any one to whom the Son chooses to reveal him." [1]

Jesus made still another discovery in his Bible. He found the great continuous strand of divine history which runs through all worlds and times, which determined the way of the people of God and the way of the Son, and he affirmed it all, from his first step into public life until his last step on the road to death. "Yea, Father, for such was thy gracious will." [2]

~>>>~>>>~>>> 5 <<<~<<<~<<<

REVERBERATIONS OF
WORLD EVENTS

JESUS EXPERIENCED the tragic denouement in the history of the world and the beginning of the political twilight of antiquity. He was born in the triumphal year *Romæ et Augusti,* of Rome and Augustus. When he was one year old, Tiberius went to Rhodes. When Jesus was two, Quintilius Varus sold the rebellious people of Sepphoris into slavery and crucified two thousand partisans before the gates of Jerusalem. In the following year Musa, the former Italian slave and now Queen of Parthia, succeeded—by murdering several members of her family—in placing her son Phraataces on the throne. Three years later this same Phraataces shook hands on an island in the Euphrates with Gaius Caesar, heir pre-

[1] Matthew 11, 27.   [2] Matthew 11, 26.

53

sumptive to the throne of Augustus. Within another three years Gaius Caesar was dead in Asia Minor and Phraataces in Ctesiphon.

When Jesus at the age of twelve first entered Jerusalem with the Passover pilgrims from Galilee, the occupation troops of the Roman procurator were marching through the streets of the city for the first time, and in the temple the new high priest, Annas, was officiating at his first service. When Jesus was fifteen, Quintilius Varus perished with his army in the Teutoburg Forest. Five years later Augustus died and Tiberius became emperor.

When Jesus was twenty, the anti-Semite Sejanus became prefect of the Pretorian Guard in Rome. In Jerusalem there at once began a great contest for the office of high priest, and three years later Joseph Caiaphas became high priest. When Jesus reached the age of thirty-one, Tiberius once again withdrew to his solitary debaucheries, and Sejanus became virtual ruler of Rome. Pilate was sent to Judea. A few months later Jesus made a Passover pilgrimage to Jerusalem and there witnessed the entry of the legionaries with their "idolatrous" imperial standards—while Caiaphas held his peace and the throngs of pilgrims went wild with resentment. Certainly Jesus had no lack of object lessons in current events.

It might seem that not much would be heard in Palestine, and particularly in the tiny village of Nazareth, of events in the remoter regions of the Empire. But that was not at all the case. For at Nazareth the road from Ptolemaïs (Accho) on the Mediterranean to Tiberias on Lake Gennesaret intersected the north-south artery that led to Jerusalem and on into Egypt. Three miles north of Nazareth lay Sepphoris, a Roman military colony and for many years Herod's capital.

But the chief thing was that the rulers possessed an apparatus which speedily transmitted official news and current ideas to the remotest corners and villages of the Empire. We refer to the coins of the realm, which were far more than a medium of exchange. By way of the coins the echo of world events reached Jesus, too. Jesus often spoke of money and coins; he knew exactly what pictures and legends they bore.[3] From mentions in the Gospels, from the dates of issue and duration of circulation of ancient coins, as well as from statistics regarding the sites of mints and from finds of coins, we can determine with considerable certainty which coins came Jesus' way."

When Joseph fled to Egypt with Mary and the child, a new series of bronze coins was just being issued. These coins bore the eagle, star, and crown of Isis, probably to celebrate the planetary conjunction of the spring of 7 B.C. But these coins did not circulate to any great extent beyond Egypt, and Jesus probably never saw them.

What coins circulated in Palestine? In the early days of the Empire the old silver pieces of the Seleucids were still current. There was one showing Antioch IV as Zeus, which bore the superscription: THE MANIFEST GOD (*Theos Epiphanes*). Another was of Demetrius, with an inscription below the head: THE SAVIOR (*Sōtèr*). There was an Alexander Balas inscribed: THE BENEFACTOR (*Euergetes*).

For the rest, however, the Roman denarius was the dominant coin, the official medium of exchange throughout the Empire. Unclipped denarii circulated for decades. In all probability, Palestinians still used denarii that commemorated the victory of Pompey by a head of the virgin Zion on one side and a picture of high priest Hyrcanus' act of homage on the other. Among Augustan coins were the famous denarii showing the zodiacal sign of the Emperor's birth, Capricorn. A special denarius was coined in honor of Crown Prince Gaius Caesar at the time of his campaign in the Orient. It showed the head of Augustus' grandson, and an incense candelabrum such as was used for worship of the Emperor. The denarius that was used for paying taxes [4] portrayed Tiberius

[3] Mark 12, 16.   [4] Matthew 22, 19.

as semi-divine son of the god Augustus and the goddess Livia. For some twenty years the Emperor supplied the Roman world with this coin.

In addition to the imperial coins, innumerable coins of eastern currencies circulated in Palestine. As relics of the era of Antony and Cleopatra, there were still Antiochian silver pieces bearing the portrait of the Queen of Egypt (long remembered and much hated by the Jews) done in the style of a cartoon. The inscription was curiously equivocal: QUEEN CLEOPATRA, THE NEW GODDESS (*Thea Neotera*). But this might also be translated differently, as QUEEN CLEOPATRA, THE YOUTHFUL GODDESS. Perhaps this spiteful and well-hidden implication was not entirely unintended. For never in the likeness of a queen of antiquity had the signs of premature old age been depicted as unsparingly as they were on this mocking Antiochian coin that glorified the aging Egyptian woman as a youthful goddess.

Copper coins were a reminder of the mournful year of 37 B.C., when Governor Sosius, on orders from Mark Antony, conquered Jerusalem for Herod. The coin bore the portrait of Antony and a trophy of victory (*tropaion*) above images of two Jewish prisoners of war—a coin even more humiliating than Pompey's denarius with the images of Zion and Hyrcanus. A few "eagles" of King Herod himself were still in circulation. Antiochian bronze coins bearing the name of Governor Quintilius Varus served as mementos of the man who in 4 B.C. sold the population of Sepphoris into slavery and crucified two thousand Jews before the gates of Jerusalem.

The North African copper coins, showing the vulture-like profile of Varus,[n] are not likely to have reached Palestine. But probably Arab caravans sometimes brought into the country the magnificent silver coins showing heads of Phraataces, the Parthian king, and his mother, Musa. Alongside the picture of the resolute Queen Mother was inscribed the former slave girl's sonorous title: QUEEN MUSA, HEAVENLY GODDESS (*Thea Urania*). In the ordinary commerce of Palestine the "silver pieces" from the eastern mints of the Empire played an important part. These were more or less incorporated into the customary local currency. There were Tiberian drachmas from Caesarea Cappadociae, bearing the official titles TIBERIUS CAESAR AUGUSTUS, SON OF THE DIVINE AUGUSTUS, and showing a full-length portrait of Augustus transfigured upon Argaeus, the Holy Mount. Even more common were the didrachmas of Tyre with the head of Hercules and the eagle, and the tetradrachmas of Antioch with portrait heads of Augustus or Tiberius and, on the reverse, the Hellenistic Zeus Nikephoros (Victory-bringing Jove).

Finally I shall mention only the most interesting of the copper coins struck by Herod Philip at Caesarea Philippi. The obverse shows the head of the reigning Emperor (first Augustus, then Tiberius), with the Emperor's name and the inscription: HE WHO DESERVES ADORATION. The reverse depicts the temple of Augustus at Caesarea Philippi. All these coins were dated. The first of them which has come down to us dates from A.D. 6, the year in which Archelaus was deposed. It is plain that Herod Philip wished to make an emphatic display of his loyalty in these critical times. Thenceforward these coins continued to be struck at short intervals until the death of Herod Philip in A.D. 34. After all, tokens of loyalty were always welcome, and the good will of the Roman Emperor counted for more than the temper of the Jewish subjects.

Evidently, then, Jesus' view of world politics was not so restricted as we might imagine. Possibly there were unworldly persons in Palestine who gave no thought to the meaning of these coins. But Jesus was not one of these. This is proved not only by the story of the tribute money, but also by his devastating comment about rulers who terrorize the people and would yet have themselves called "benefactors." [5] For this, as we have seen, was exactly the title borne by Alexander Balas on his silver coins.

Jesus said little about the petty rulers of Palestine and Syria. But he had a sharp eye, and his judgment of them was annihilating. When he heard of John the Baptist's death in Herod Antipas' dungeon, he said with bitterness: ". . . they did to him whatever they pleased. . . ." [6] When he himself was warned of Herod Antipas, he called him a "fox." [7] In his pastoral sayings he lavished equal indignation upon the secular and spiritual potentates who thought only of power and gain, of exploitation, trickery, and bloodshed. [8] When Pilate attempted to intimidate him, he said coolly: "You would have no power over me unless it had been given you from above." [9] They had all fallen down before Satan, worshipped the political diabolism of this world. [1] They all did as they pleased, did to him as they pleased also. But they did not really rule; they only gave the illusion of doing so. [2] He was a different kind of king, his kingdom was a different kingdom, and in this age his disciples had a different office from the small and great lords of this world. [3]

➤➤➤-➤➤➤-➤➤➤ 6 ᐸᐸᐸ-ᐸᐸᐸ-ᐸᐸᐸ

JESUS' PHYSICAL APPEARANCE

THE NEW TESTAMENT gives a physical description of John the Baptist, but none of Jesus. From this we may conclude that in appearance Jesus did not differ particularly

[5] Luke 22, 25.   [6] Mark 9, 13.   [7] Luke 13, 32.   [8] John 10, 1 ff.   [9] John 19, 11.   [1] Matthew 4, 9.   [2] Mark 10, 42.   [8] John 18, 37; Mark 10, 43 ff.

from other Palestinian Jews of his time. This conclusion is corroborated by the silence of his adversaries. The rabbis had very definite standards regarding the outward appearance of a proper Jew, especially a teacher. They could, if occasion demanded, scornfully and harshly decry any deviations from these standards. Evidently Jesus' person and dress supplied them with no material for criticism. This means that if we wish to form a picture of Jesus' appearance, we must sketch for ourselves a Palestinian Jew of the day, supplementing this with the few individual features we can gather from scattered and indirect evidence in the Gospels.

In rabbinical theory, the reflection of the divine presence could descend only upon a man of tall and powerful stature.[n] Evidently Jesus was able to meet this physical standard, for otherwise his adversaries would surely not have missed the chance to attack him on such grounds.[n] One confirmation of this suggestion is found in Luke's statement about young Jesus' satisfactory growth, and in John's account of Jesus' frequent journeys for the festivals and his rapid progress from place to place.[n] We may therefore conclude that Jesus had at least the average stature and physical strength of a Palestinian Jew.

The color of the Palestinian Jew of antiquity was light brown, the eyes usually brown. However, blue eyes were not rare.[n] The Gospels say nothing whatsoever about the color of his eyes. We do hear, however, that he could be taken to be in his forties when actually he was in his early thirties.[4] Ought we to conclude from this that Jesus did not have a youthful face, that he looked careworn and sorrowful?

The Palestinian Jews of antiquity were black-haired. Men wore their hair shoulder-length, parted in the middle, combed, and anointed with a thin, fine oil. Unkempt hair was looked upon with disfavor.[5] A beard and a mustache were also worn. Since the time of Alexander the Great men

[4] John 8, 57. [5] Numeri rabba 10.

59

had as a rule gone clean-shaven in the Hellenistic East; beardlessness also prevailed in the West from about 200 B.C. to A.D. 117. But the Jews continued steadfastly to wear beards, and particularly cherished full beards. A beardless Jew aroused the contempt of his fellow countrymen. Additional evidence accrues from the heads depicted on coins. Bacchius Judaeus on the triumphal coin of 54 B.C. and the Jewish prisoners on the coins of Sosius (37 B.C.) and Vespasian (A.D. 70) all wear shoulder-length hair and full beards. Jesus certainly adhered to the same style. He disliked untidy hair, even on fast days.[6] And he also wore a beard. Had he not, the rabbis would scarcely have remained silent on this critical point.[n]

The language of everyday use for Jesus was Aramaic, which he probably spoke with a Galilean accent. To Pilate he spoke Greek, and even as a small boy in the village he was no doubt able to communicate with the legionaries from Sepphoris in Latin. Probably he recited the liturgy and quoted the Bible in Hebrew. His voice must have had a unique resonance, and his manner of speech a unique gracefulness.[7]

His style of dress was inconspicuous, neither luxurious nor poor.[8] He wore a sleeveless undergarment with a belt,[9] the usual cloak,[1] sandals,[2] and on his journeyings carried a staff.[3] The only special detail we hear regarding his clothing was that his undergarment was seamless, woven in one piece like the *chiton* of the high priest.[n] Perhaps Jesus also wore a white cloth on his head, tied with a string and hanging down behind to the shoulders [n]—this typical Middle Eastern headgear was already popular in ancient Palestine. In those days many Galileans carried a sword tucked into their belts as protection against highway robbers and animals. Jesus

[6] Luke 7, 46; Matthew 6, 17.   [7] Luke 4, 22; John 7, 37; 11, 43; 20, 16.
[8] Luke 7, 25; John 19, 23.   [9] Mark 6, 8; John 19, 23.   [1] Luke 8, 44.
[2] Mark 1, 7; 6, 9.   [3] Mark 6, 8.

probably did not, but apparently some of his disciples did have swords. Jesus also seems not to have carried the customary money bag on his belt; Judas held the common purse for the disciples.

All this can be gathered from the customs of the time among Palestinian Jews and from hints in the Gospels. The representations of Christ in apocryphal tradition [n] and in the art of the early church were based upon dogmatic prototypes, and have no value as historical evidence.

❯❯❯❯❯❯❯❯❯ 7 ❮❮❮❮❮❮❮❮❮

THE LONG WAIT

JESUS WAS thirty-three years old when he received the baptism of John the Baptist. At the age of thirty-three a Palestinian Jew of those days was much "older" than a contemporary Westerner. Jesus was no longer a young hotspur when he came forth into public life for the first time. He was a mature man, a finished personality.

The men of the New Testament are unanimous in their testimony that his birth was a miracle. There had in the year of his birth been no lack of omens promising a great future for the child. Meanwhile, years and decades had passed. The story of his brief emergence at the age of twelve only serves to emphasize how little that was unusual had happened during the first three decades of his life. He had been a quiet child and a well-liked man, no more.[4] We may think of the story of Moses, who, after promising beginnings, herded

[4] Luke 2, 52.

sheep for decades.[5] In similar fashion Jesus worked at his trade for many years, and it was as though nothing had happened or was going to happen. These were not only years of quiet and maturation; they may also have been years of temptation, for Jesus and for his mother. Jewish apocalyptics frequently declared that the savior of the Last Days would live for a long time in concealment, either in a remote place or incognito among his own people, "misjudged and lowly."[n] In a sense Jesus fulfilled these conditions. For thirty years he lived in Nazareth, "quietly and unrecognized," among the members of his family, among fellow workmen and friends who shared his views, and no one paid any special attention to him. The excitement that had surrounded his birth had to remain concealed in order not to cast suspicion upon the grown man and bring down upon him the bloodhounds of Herod and the Romans. Jesus, too, held his peace. He could only wait. It was as if the millennial expectations of mankind and of all creation,[6] the ancient hopes of the people of Israel,[7] were concentrated and raised to their peak in those decades that Jesus of Nazareth spent in waiting.

[5] Exodus 3, 1; 7, 7.   [6] Romans 5, 12 ff.; 8, 19 ff.   [7] Luke 2, 25. 38.

IV

JESUS
AND THE
BAPTIST'S
MOVEMENT

›»›-›»›-›»› 1 ‹‹‹-‹‹‹-‹‹‹

JESUS IN THE CIRCLE
OF THE BAPTIST

A T THE BEGINNING of his mission Jesus was captivated by
the message of John the Baptist. During the early
weeks of this new movement—probably in February of
A.D. 28—he turned up at the Jordan and received the baptism
of repentance.[1] Then he withdrew into the desert for some

[1] Mark 1, 9.

time in order to fast and pray, following the example of John the Baptist and the members of his sect.[2] Only a few weeks later he set out for Jerusalem, presumably to celebrate the Passover there. Then we find him once more among the followers of the Baptist. Soon there formed around Jesus the Galilean a group made up of his own countrymen. Two Galilean disciples of the Baptist—John, the son of Zebedee, and Andrew—took the lead. Three pilgrims from Bethsaida and Cana joined this group about the same time. These were Peter, Philip, and Nathanael.[3] These, then, were the modest lines on which Jesus began his ministry as a disciple of the Baptist. The full story of this early period is mainly recorded by the Fourth Evangelist.[4] But the Synoptic Gospels also contain a number of preserved tales of this early activity; Mark, within the narrow compass of his Gospel, fits them in more or less fortuitously here and there.[a] Jewish traditions of Jesus, from Akiba to the *Toledoth Jeshu,* also appear to mention his early activity among the followers of the Baptist. Even the Mandaean tradition preserves a dim memory of these beginnings.[b]

With his small band of disciples Jesus went, in company with the majority of the pilgrims, back to his home in Galilee. He made a stop in Cana, and then, with his mother, his brothers, and his disciples, moved to Capernaum. His father does not seem to have been alive at this time; his sisters remained in Nazareth, where, presumably, they were married.[5] But Jesus did not linger long in Capernaum. Probably he soon returned to the Jordan with his disciples and merged for a time with the movement of the Baptist.

For the Passover feast of A.D. 29 Jesus once more made the pilgrimage to Jerusalem. On this occasion he drove the money-changers and merchants out of the temple.[6] Here we have an example of the Fourth Evangelist's quietly cor-

[2] Mark 1, 13; Luke 4, 1 ff.   [3] John 1, 35 ff.   [4] John 2 f.; see also John 3, 24.   [5] John 2, 12; Matthew 4, 13; Mark 6, 3.   [6] John 2, 13 ff.

recting the Synoptics who had had to date the purging of the temple in the last Passover because the framework of Mark's Gospel left no room for the passover of A.D. 29. John's statement that the temple took forty-six years to build [7] also points to A.D. 29. For the building of Herod's temple began in the spring of 736 *ab urbe condita* (from the founding of Rome). If we add to this forty-six years, we arrive at the spring of 782 *ab urbe condita,* which was A.D. 29.

After the Passover, Jesus remained for many months in the south, teaching, baptizing, and healing.[8] John the Baptist was meanwhile preaching along the middle Jordan.[9] It appears that at this time he also extended his range and wielded considerable influence among the Samaritans.

The distinctive sign of Jesus' period as an adherent of the Baptist was his work of baptizing.[1] Baptism as then practiced by him and his disciples evidently had nothing in common with the church sacrament of baptism mentioned in Matthew and Acts.[2] It was simple immersion without the gift of the Spirit, performed perhaps on Jesus' authority, but not yet "in the name of the Lord Jesus." [3] As long as Jesus adhered to this type of baptism he was considered by the public, and by the disciples of John as well, to be no more than the Baptist's favorite disciple, the most successful of his messengers.[4] In this sense the early period of Jesus' ministry is merely a chapter in the history of the Baptist's movement, not yet a part of Jesus' purely personal activity. Such, at any rate, was the view that Peter and Mark took of it. For that reason this period of Jesus' ministry was completely ignored in the Petrine formulae and the Gospel of Mark.

The Fourth Evangelist saw the matter quite differently. For John was writing at Ephesus, where the relationship between John the Baptist and Jesus was evidently still a great

[7] John 2, 20. [8] John 2, 23; 3, 2. 22 ff.; 4, 45; Luke 4, 44. [9] John 3, 23.
[1] John 3, 22. 26; 4, 1 f. [2] Matthew 28, 19 f.; Acts 2, 38. [3] Cf. Acts 19, 2 ff. [4] John 3, 26; Acts 18, 25.

source of controversy.[5] John makes it clear that Jesus himself deliberately remained in the shadow of the Baptist, wishing the essence of his own message to remain unrecognized at this time. "But Jesus did not trust himself to them." [6] Again and again he took care not to reveal his secret. That is the significance of the Evangelist's use of the imperfect tense.[n] Jesus for the present wished to remain *filius dei incognitus,* the unrecognized Son of God in the midst of men.[n]

His mother alone knew his secret.[7] And the disciples guessed it—ever since the miracle at Cana.[8] The dissident wing were loud in their condemnation of such rich banquets.[9] From the ranks of these came John the Baptist, the desert saint and "eunuch," who was opposed to wine, trained his disciples to fast, and called upon all the people to repent. And now here was John's favorite disciple, this same Jesus who had drawn his own first disciples from among the Baptist's followers, appearing with his apocalyptic retinue at a lavish wedding in Nathanael's native village; appearing, moreover, not to preach repentance and inveigh against marriage,[1] but to dine at the wedding table, join in the festivities, and contribute to the repast. This was a provocative act. It became one more sign, as ambiguous as all the signs of divinity in the story of Jesus. Many henceforth condemned Jesus as a "glutton and a drunkard." [2] The disciples, however, saw in this act of the Son a revelation of the Father's glory.[3] For the first time they recognized in the person of Jesus the God of the Old Testament [4] who loved abundance, beauty, prodigality, who had created the fruit of the vine in order to rejoice the hearts of men, who could be human with men and joyful among the joyous. The image of the Baptist

[5] See Acts 18, 25 ff.; 19, 3 ff.   [6] John 2, 24.   [7] John 2, 3 ff.   [8] John 2, 1 ff.   [9] *Assumption of Moses* 7, 4 ff.   [1] As later the Apostles did in the apocryphal Acts of the Apostles.   [2] Luke 7, 34.   [3] John 1, 14.   [4] Psalm 104.

66

faded; before the eyes of the disciples there arose the prespec-
tive of a new age, a new way of life.[n]

In these early days of his ministry Jesus met with much
response, but with much opposition also.[n] As yet he had not
come into conflict with the Torah.[n] Evidently the purging of
the temple had been taken for a fanatical demonstration on
the part of one of the Baptist's radical disciples. It was taken
for granted that the Baptist stood behind this act. For the
scheming "children of Annas" who ruled in the temple were
as hated as they were feared in Palestine.[5] The markets and
money-changers' booths that the commerce-minded high
priest maintained on Mount Zion to strengthen the temple
treasury were an offense to many.[n] And the fact that God
had not protected the temple's treasure from the avarice of
Pilate, as once before God had shielded it from the hands of
Heliodorus, must have seemed to many Jews a divine judgment upon the corruptness of the ruling priesthood.[n] Such
was the situation when Jesus drove the money-changers from
the temple. All genuinely religious people were on his side
—not only the opposition to the priests, but also the Pharisees
and the learned students of the Torah. He even had many
sympathizers in the ranks of the Great Sanhedrin.[6] For Jesus
was as concerned with preserving the holiness of the temple
as the most scrupulous Pharisee. Armed with a lash of reeds,
he stood guard to see that no one, under cover of the tumult,
carried any wares through the temple, not even through the
outer court where Annas' market stood.[7] Here was an absolutely rigorous application of the rabbinical precepts.[n] The
priests were naturally not very pleased by this sudden assault
on the part of the Baptist's followers.[8] But at the moment
they could take no action against Jesus without forfeiting the
last remnants of their own prestige.[9] For the time being, the

[5] Pesahim 57 a.   [6] John 3, 2; 7, 50; 19, 39.   [7] Mark 11, 16.   [8] John 2,
18; Mark 11, 27 ff.   [9] Mark 11, 32.

best they could do was to forge plans to destroy him at some future date.[1]

⇛⇛⇛ 2 ⇚⇚⇚

A STAY IN SAMARIA

THE POPULARITY Jesus enjoyed henceforth among the broad masses of the Jewish population was manifested in the increasing numbers who came to be baptized by him. This growth in his following could only intensify the priests' vexation with this fanatic. The priests now tried to establish closer contacts with the members of the Baptist's movement. They launched elaborate discussions of purification rituals, and provoked the Baptist's followers to question and resent the manner in which Jesus was administering baptism.[2] The Pharisees, for their part, had never sympathized strongly with John the Baptist, and now regarded Jesus—the man who kept the Sabbath so conscientiously, and so strictly enforced the ban on carrying things in the temple area—as an ally. They spoke with satisfaction of his remarkable successes in bringing the people to baptism.[3] For Jesus, this support from the Pharisees was a signal to retreat. He considered John the Baptist the greatest of all men born of women, a burning and shining lamp lit by God.[4] Jesus did not care to be used as a weapon against John, and the sympathy of his new-found Pharisaic friends made him uneasy. Abruptly, he

[1] Mark 11, 18; Luke 19, 47 ff.   [2] John 3, 25 ff.; cf. 1, 19 ff.   [3] John 4, 1; cf. 1, 24 f.   [4] Luke 7, 28; John 5, 35.

68

ceased his activities in Jerusalem and retired once more to Galilee.[5] He took the road through Samaria.

We can date this historic moment with some degree of certainty. John records: "There are yet four months, then comes the harvest."[6] The barley harvest was due in March, the wheat in April. Jesus spoke of white grainfields; hence, he was thinking of the barley harvest. Therefore, Jesus must have started on his northward journey through Samaria in November of A.D. 29.

The Fourth Evangelist says that Jesus "had to" pass through Samaria.[7] It would seem that he chose this road in order to escape as quickly as possible from the clutches of the priests.[8] In Samaria, on the other hand, he was eager to establish contact with the people, and succeeded. He associated with Samaritans, both men and women, and in particular with a Samaritan woman of doubtful reputation, without showing the slightest sign of prejudice.[9] As a Jew he believed that his people occupied a special position in the scheme of salvation.[1] But in Samaria he spoke bold words about the conflict between Zion and Gerizim,[2] and made a portentous declaration concerning his secret worth and mission.[3] Here in Samaria the enigmatic and significant "I am He" fell from his lips for the first time—those words which play so crucial a part in John's portrait of Christ.[4] Jesus accepted Samaritan hospitality at Shechem at the foot of Mount Gerizim.[n] Throughout Samaria he was honored and trusted.[5] Indeed, he even left his disciples behind in Samaria, and it appears that for the present they continued to preach the message of baptism there.[6] It may be that he once again became more closely associated with John the Baptist, who was at that time pursuing his ministry in Samaria.[n] When Jesus left Samaria, he bitterly "testified that a prophet has no honor in his own

---

[5] John 4, 3.   [6] John 4, 35.   [7] John 4, 4.   [8] Cf. John 4, 44.   [9] John 4, 7 ff. 27.   [1] John 4, 22.   [2] John 4, 21. 23 f.   [3] John 4, 10 ff.   [4] John 4, 26.   [5] John 4, 19 f. 28 ff. 39 ff.   [6] John 4, 2.

country." [7] In this context the meaning can only be: Jesus encountered a great deal of resistance among the people of Israel, but found a strong response to his message in Samaria. The leaders in Jerusalem were ready to reply, and later told him to his face: "You are a Samaritan." [8]

This is how the Fourth Evangelist represents the matter. Mark says not a word about Jesus' relations with the Samaritans, and quotes the saying about a prophet's honor in his own country in another connection where it scarcely seems to belong.[9] Matthew, too, does not say a good word about Samaria. In fact, he maintains that Jesus expressly forbade his disciples to undertake the mission to Samaria.[1]

It is quite otherwise with Luke, who, here as elsewhere, agrees closely with John. Luke tells us [2] that Jesus journeyed through Samaria and sought lodgings, but found none because the Samaritans learned that he was on a pilgrimage to Jerusalem. The purport of this, apparently, is that the Samaritans had previously been friends of Jesus and had readily offered him hospitality, but were now disappointed to find him deciding after all in favor of Zion and against Gerizim. They had expected other conduct from him. Now his Samarian followers began to fall away in droves.[3] The disciples wanted to retaliate, but Jesus forbade them. Instead he told them the story of the Good Samaritan,[4] in which the conduct of the Levite and the priest was condemned. Luke also relates the story of the grateful Samaritan,[5] the behavior of whose Jewish fellow lepers the Evangelist paints in such dark colors. In Acts 1, 8, moreover, Jesus specifically instructs his disciples to pursue their mission in Samaria; this stands in direct contrast to the prohibition in Matthew 10, 5. And in Acts 8, 5 ff., we read of the striking success of the mission in Samaria, and of the Apostle's encounter with the Samaritan Gnostic Simon Magus.

[7] John 4, 44.   [8] John 8, 48.   [9] Mark 6, 4.   [1] Matthew 10, 5.   [2] Luke 9, 52 ff.   [3] Cf. John 6, 66 ff.   [4] Luke 10, 33.   [5] Luke 17, 11 ff.

It is plain, then, that the primitive church was divided into two parties, one for and one against converting the Samaritans. Both parties claimed that they had received their orders from Jesus. Which was right? Matthew betrays the inveterate Jewish dislike of the Samaritans, who were regarded as no better, and in fact far worse, than the pagans. This was a Jewish or Judao-Christian attitude, but it was not that of Jesus.[11] Elsewhere Matthew and Mark have nothing further to say on the Samaritan problem; they maintain a sullen silence. Luke and John, however, relate a wealth of specific details which fit admirably into our picture of Jesus and the times. Certainly we must ascribe the core of the parable of the Good Samaritan to Jesus himself. This suggests that the pro-Samaritans in the primitive church were in the right when they referred their policy to Jesus, and that the beginnings of the "Samaritan mission" may actually be traced back to the early period of Jesus' ministry. This contention is supported by everything we know about the remarkable interrelations and reciprocal effects in Samaria of the tradition of the Baptist, the work of Jesus, and the Gnosticism of Simon Magus.

⇛⇛⇛ 3 ⇚⇚⇚

THE QUIET MONTHS

JESUS PRESUMABLY RETURNED to his carpentry. This Galilean disciple of the Baptist ceased to be the focus of attention, and we hear no more of him until the autumn of A.D. 30, ten months later. We do not even know where and when he celebrated the Passover feast. This was the great gap in Jesus' public activity, the long pause that separated his activity under the shadow of John [6] from his later ministry.

Concerning these quiet months that intervened between the events described in John 4, 53 ff., and 5, 1 ff., nothing is expressly said in any of the Gospels, and we never are directly informed what happened to, and went on within and around, Jesus during that period.[n] This is scarcely surprising when we consider that the Gospels tell us virtually nothing about the first three decades of Jesus' life. But it is necessary to take note of this gap in his public ministry in order to arrive at a relative and absolute chronology of his story, into which we may fit all the authenticated details of his life and times.

There were a good many events during those months which were to prove of importance for his further history. In A.D. 30 the all-powerful anti-Semite Sejanus was making his final preparations for a "total solution of the Jewish problem," to use the notorious Nazi phrase. Pilate was a creature of Sejanus, and as military governor of Jerusalem he would be a key figure in the projected campaign of annihilation. In the spring of A.D. 30 Pilate issued his coins with the augur's crook of the divine emperor; these were intended to outrage the Jews, and did. That same year the Great Sanhedrin was deprived of its jurisdiction over capital crimes and had to cease meeting in the sacred Hall of Hewn Stone in the temple court. They moved to the market of Annas on the temple mount.[7] That same year Rabbi Johanan ben Zakkai prophesied the downfall of the temple. And around this time Rabbi Zadok, in Jerusalem, began his forty-year fast in behalf of the Holy City.[n]

Sejanus also had his hand in the political game in Galilee, whose ruler was a willing tool of the all-powerful Roman.[8]

[6] John 1–4. [7] Shabbath 15 a. [8] See Flavius Josephus: *Antiquities* 18, 7, 2.

But only the diplomats knew of this. The public was chiefly interested in the matrimonial scandal in which that ruler, Herod Antipas, was involved.

$$\text{≫»-≫»-≫» 4 ≪-≪≪-≪≪}$$

THE ARREST OF
JOHN THE BAPTIST

EROD THE TETRARCH, who had been reproved by him [i.e., John the Baptist] for Herodias, his brother's wife, and for all the evil things that Herod had done, added this to them all, that he shut up John in prison." [9]

Apparently Jesus first heard of the imprisonment of John when he arrived in Jerusalem for "the feast." [1] When Jewish texts, especially in theological writings, speak simply of the "feast," the Feast of Tabernacles is meant.[n] Therefore the arrest of John probably took place shortly before the Feast of Tabernacles of A.D. 30. Perhaps it occurred when Herod Antipas was making a pious pilgrimage to participate in the Day of Atonement and the Feast of Tabernacles of that year.

Around the same time that John the Baptist was arrested for his extremist adherence to the Torah, his former favorite disciple Jesus was making his official break with the Torah. We do not know the psychological background of this event. The great turning-point must have been reached and passed during the quiet months in Galilee. We can only observe the tangible results.

[9] Luke 3, 19 f.   [1] John 5, 1.

On the Sabbath during the week of the Feast of Taber-nacles Jesus came to the famous porches of Bethesda where the diseased and disabled lay waiting for a rippling of the healing waters of the pool. (The remains of the porticos have recently been excavated.) Here Jesus cured a lame man and bade him carry home his pallet—on the Sabbath! The heal-ing itself was no violation of the Sabbath, but the order to carry away the pallet was open incitement to breach of the Sabbath and apostasy. The penalty for this was death.[2] The Great Sanhedrin immediately took action.[3] Jesus defended himself on the grounds of his purely personal and unique allegiance to God, which he regarded as higher than alle-giance to the Torah. In the eyes of the Great Sanhedrin this was sheer blasphemy.[4] Finally, referring back to the ministry of John the Baptist, Jesus attacked the Great Sanhedrin's atti-tude toward the Baptist's movement.[5] This, too, was a crime punishable by death.[6]

On this occasion Jesus escaped his judges somehow. But when he left Jerusalem, he left behind two implacable ene-mies: the higher priesthood, with their Sadducean adherents, and the rabbinate, with its following of Pharisees. He had earlier incurred the enmity of the priesthood by his purging of the temple; now he had antagonized the rabbinate by breach of the Sabbath. These two power groups had formed an alliance in the course of the Sanhedrin's proceedings, and now combined in a charge of blasphemy against Jesus. For the present, Jesus could no longer venture to appear in Jeru-salem. It remained to be seen whether he would be left un-molested in Galilee.

[2] Appendix II, 30.   [3] John 5, 10 ff.   [4] John 5, 17 f.; Appendix II, 1 and 18.   [5] John 5, 35.   [6] Appendix II, 6, 7.

>>>->>>->>> 5 <<<-<<<-<<<

JESUS' BREAK
WITH THE TORAH

THE HEALING of the disabled man at the pool of Bethesda led to the first datable conflict between Jesus and the orthodox adherents of the Torah. This break is of the highest importance for an understanding of the subsequent events, as well as of the spiritual evolution of Jesus.

Jesus first emerged from the Baptist's followers, and John the Baptist himself from the Qumran movement. The members of the Qumran sect practiced the most rigorous observation of the precepts of the Torah. To them the Torah was the absolute manifestation of the will of God, final codification of the divine revelation, the measure of all things in life and in thought. John the Baptist had grown up in this spirit, and until his death clung fast to this intense orthodoxy. Jesus also had partaken of this spirit. His own baptism, his baptizing of others, and other aspects of his ministry indicate that as long as he had been under the influence of John he had remained unconditionally faithful to the Torah. Probably Jesus had never been so strict an interpreter of the Torah as the Qumran sectarians were—or as the Gospel of Matthew made him out to be. In the oldest and best traditions of Jesus all the special aspects of the Qumran sect's pieties are lacking.[1] But he was a devout Jew of the Torah, as such devoutness was understood by the members of the Baptist's movement. The miracle of the wine at Cana shows

75

that he was not completely in harmony with the movement, even at that time. But the purification of the temple proves that in spite of all his differences he could still act in the spirit of a radical disciple of John the Baptist.[7]

Now, in the climactic period of Jesus' ministry, which began with the healing on the Sabbath, all these old attitudes underwent a change. Now Jesus proclaimed new tidings of God, a new religion that in principle was no longer bound by the Torah and therefore departed fundamentally from the creed of the Baptist's movement and had nothing whatsoever to do with the rigidities of the Qumran sect.

Consequently, from the point of view of scientific religious history and source-criticism, it is utterly improper to regard Jesus as a camp-follower of the Qumran sect. His ideas stood in the sharpest possible opposition to the Qumran sectarians, to their interpretation of the Torah and their extreme piety. Moreover, he now assumed a posture of antagonism toward the Baptist's movement, which in turn was wroth with him. Feeling was acutely bitter on both sides, for all that the Evangelists try to make light of it. The very fact that Jesus during the climactic period of his ministry no longer performed or had his disciples perform John's kind of baptism proves that a new era had dawned. Jesus did not reject John's baptism, but abandoned it.[8] The tradition of the Baptist's movement records some extremely harsh words that were said about Jesus. And the Christian tradition did not succeed in totally burying the evidence of grave tensions between Jesus and John the Baptist.

This spiritual metamorphosis in Jesus gave rise to practical changes also. At the point recorded in John 5—that is to say, precisely at the beginning of Jesus' new and fateful activity, which coincided with his first break with the Torah— there began the legal prosecution that ended in his condem-

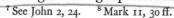

[7] See John 2, 24.   [8] Mark 11, 30 ff.

76

nation and execution. Jesus was prosecuted as a violator of the Torah and a preacher of apostasy. If we study the provisions against heresy in the ancient legal sources, we are overwhelmed by the exact correspondence between these and the prosecution of Jesus as it is described in the Gospels. Thus, by availing ourselves of Jewish legal documents we obtain a wholly new basis for evaluating the historicity of the Gospels. We also find valuable data for an objective reconstruction of the story of Jesus. That story is revealed, in the light of Jewish law, as the dramatic unfolding of an inevitable conflict that had to end in a verdict of death. Only in that light can we understand the separate stages and measures, the accelerating and retarding factors in this juridical drama. We understand Jesus' early conviction that death would be his lot; we understand the attitude of Judas, the fears of Jesus' mother, his kindred, his disciples, and sympathizers; and we understand as well the rigid consistency of the Great Sanhedrin.

The old adage that holds for the judge applies as well to the historian: *audiatur et altera pars*—the other side must be given a hearing too. It is high time for a historical reconstruction of the prosecution and condemnation of Jesus which aspires, at least, to objectivity. Not only the attitude of Jesus, but also the logic and motivations of Caiaphas must be examined. The key factor for such a project is an evaluation of Jesus' position after the arrest of John the Baptist, and of his conflict with the Torah. And a key tool of research must be knowledge of the provisions against heresy which dictated each successive phase in the prosecution of Jesus.

The destruction of Jesus was the business of the Great Sanhedrin in Jerusalem, which had authority to deal with all capital crimes against the laws of religion [9] and which was then presided over by High Priest Caiaphas, a non-Zadokite.

[9] Appendix II, 64.

IV · JESUS AND THE BAPTIST'S MOVEMENT

The Qumran sect denounced the man and his entire court as illegal. They were powerless exiles and had nothing to do with the trial of Jesus. Yet we may be sure that, had they held power, they would have condemned Jesus to death at least as swiftly and mercilessly as Caiaphas did.[n]

V

THE
GALILEAN
MINISTRY

⇛⇛⇛ 1 ⇚⇚⇚

WINTER IN GALILEE

N ow after John was arrested, Jesus came into Galilee, preaching the gospel of God, and saying, 'The time is fulfilled, and the Kingdom of God is at hand; repent, and believe in the gospel.' " Thus Mark begins his account of the great ministry of Jesus in Galilee." This must have been in the late autumn of A.D. 30. Jesus began his activity in Capernaum.[1] For Capernaum was where he lived, and for a good many months the synagogue at Capernaum remained the focus of his ministry. We hear [2] of how Jesus fetched the four fishermen, Simon, Andrew, James, and John, away from their nets right at the start of the best fishing season, which began in November. This was not his first meeting with these men; but it was a new summons after their parting in November of A.D. 29, and this time the call was irrevocable.

he had called the disciples before

We no longer hear of Jesus or the disciples practicing baptism. His emancipation from the movement of the Baptist was now complete.

Mark [3] relates how Jesus cured a leper and sent him off to the priestly health authority in Jerusalem "for a proof to the people." [4] Mark then [5] immediately proceeds to describe the clashes with certain scribes and Pharisees, most of whom had probably been sent from Jerusalem to collect evidence against Jesus.[6] The first dispute concerned the problems of forgiveness of sins and blasphemy.[7] Furthermore, the scribes criticized his dining with "tax collectors and sinners." [8] Others were distressed to see that the disciples of Jesus did not fast, whereas the Pharisees and the followers of John the Baptist made much of fasting. The days of fasting, the days of concord with the Pharisees and John's followers, were over now. Now the time had come for nuptial joys, Jesus said significantly.[9]

The number of his disciples increased rapidly. In the hilly country near Capernaum Jesus performed the solemn ceremony of choosing and appointing the "Twelve Apostles." At the head of the list stood Simon, upon whom Jesus now (if not earlier) conferred the nickname of Peter; [1] in so

---

[1] Mark 1, 21; Matthew 4, 13.   [2] Mark 1, 16 ff.   [3] Mark 1, 41 ff.
[4] Mark 1, 44.   [5] Mark 2, 1 ff.   [6] Appendix II, 34.   [7] Mark 2, 7; cf.
Appendix II, 18.   [8] Mark 2, 16.   [9] Mark 2, 19.   [1] From the Greek word for *rock*.

doing, Jesus was giving him his special role in the later history of the group of disciples.

At the end of the list was Judas, who came from Kerioth in southern Judea and was apparently the only non-Galilean among the Twelve Apostles. He was appointed to hold the communal purse.[2]

The events related in Mark 4 f. are all said to have taken place by Lake Gennesaret. Probably all of them may be ascribed to December of A.D. 30, for December was the time of sowing and the season of storms.[n] The question that John the Baptist sent from his prison—"Are you he who is to come, or shall we look for another?"[3]—may be dated in January of A.D. 31. Jesus replied by referring to his miracles ("The blind receive their sight, the lame walk"), and added meaningfully: "Blessed is he who takes no offense at me."

A few days or weeks later John the Baptist was beheaded at the mountain citadel of Machaerus, upon the demand of Herodias. "They did to him whatever they pleased," Jesus commented. The death of John was a sample of the fate of God's saints in this world, and an omen of things to come.[4]

At the beginning of February the collection of the temple dues took place.[5] At the time Peter was still in Capernaum. The sending forth of the Twelve Apostles probably took place shortly thereafter, and they returned about the middle of March.[6] The new movement had reached its zenith.

[2] John 12, 6.   [3] Luke 7, 18 ff.   [4] Mark 6, 19 ff.; 9, 13.   [5] Matthew 17, 24 ff.   [6] Mark 6, 6 ff. 30 ff.

>>>->>>->>> 2 <<<-<<<-<<<

GALILEAN PASSOVER

PASSOVER TIME was drawing near.[7] But at the moment Jesus could not venture to go to Jerusalem, where he would be putting himself into the power of his mortal enemies.[8] In Galilee the Great Sanhedrin could not strike at him so directly as in Judea. And the ruler of Galilee, Herod Antipas, was at the moment not at all in the mood to take action against Jesus.[n] In other words, for the present Jesus was relatively safe in Galilee. Therefore, this time he celebrated the Passover with his disciples and fellow countrymen in his native Galilee, first by giving an apocalyptic feast [n] to the five thousand by Lake Gennesaret, and then, at Capernaum, by reciting a Passover liturgy among his disciples. No sacrifice accompanied this liturgy, nor did it take place in a temple. In part the liturgy Jesus adopted followed the traditional Passover ritual of the Galileans "who had stayed at home." [n] Nevertheless, the Galilean Passover meal in the spring of A.D. 31 represented a revolution in ritual, and in this sense set a precedent for the Last Supper on Maundy Thursday of A.D. 32, which likewise took place outside the temple and omitted sacrifice.

Among the Jews of Palestine the notion prevailed that the coming Last Days would culminate in an apocalyptic feast. Israel would assemble once again in the ancient order observed by the Israelites who had camped in the desert, and the Anointed of God would shower them with blessings and

[7] John 6, 4.   [8] Cf. John 7, 1.

82

food. Among the Dead Sea scrolls a fragment of an actual seating-plan for the messianic meal of the Last Days has come to light. To properly understand the Gospel accounts of the apocalyptic banquet and the miracle of the loaves and fishes by Lake Gennesaret, we must be familiar with these and similar expectations concerning the Last Days.[n]

This act of Jesus obviously made a tremendous impression upon all who witnessed it, for it is related five times in the Synoptic tradition,[n] and is almost the only event of this climactic period in Galilee to be reported by the Fourth Evangelist.[9] John appears to have woven into his account anticipations of the novel Passover feast that took place in the year 31.[1] The *Logia* also apparently preserved significant sayings spoken during the days of that Passover.[2] The best traditions concerning those days were probably contained in the Judao-Christian gospels, through which, it would seem, bits found their way into the Koran. For in the Koran[3] we read of a table laden with celestial food, of a feast day, a sign from God, and a dividing of the elect from the damned. According to statements of the oldest commentaries on the Koran, and of Islamic Lives of Jesus, these ideas derived not from the Church's celebration of the Eucharist, but from the Passover described in John 6, 4.

The Passover was the appointed time for the coming of the Messiah who would establish the Kingdom of Israel. Since A.D. 30 the imperial government's anti-Semitic policies had aggravated the despair of the Palestinian Jews and given fresh impetus to their hopes of the Messiah. By the Passover of 31 a storm was brewing in any case, and the effect of the miracle of the loaves and fishes was almost inevitable. Jesus' fellow countrymen wanted to proclaim him the Messiah.[4] The people of Galilee had always sympathized with the resistance movement.[5] While the Galileans gathered expect-

[9] John 6, 1 ff. [1] John 6, 32 ff. 52 ff. [2] Matthew 11, 25 ff. and *passim*.
[3] Sura 5, 112 ff. [4] John 6, 15. [5] Acts 5, 37.

83

antly around Jesus at the lake, those Galileans who had gone to Jerusalem on pilgrimage evidently attempted an armed uprising in the name of the Messiah. For we hear of a bloody massacre, on orders from Pilate, of the Galileans assembled on the temple mount.[6] The political tensions in southern Palestine were growing daily more unendurable. An accident at the Tower of Siloam, which claimed eighteen victims, also spread alarm. Jesus regarded these events as omens of still greater catastrophes. "Unless you repent you will all likewise perish." [7]

⇥⇥⇥ 3 ⇤⇤⇤

THE OPPOSITION GATHERS

PASSOVER OF THE YEAR 31 marks the culminating point in Jesus' Galilean ministry.[8] The descending curve began at once.[9] Jesus had not come to Jerusalem for the Passover feast, much to the disappointment of his adversaries.[1] Thereupon a new swarm of emissaries from the Sanhedrin arrived in Galilee. There were signs of intensified counter-propaganda. Curses were called down upon the head of the blasphemer.[n]

Jesus lingered a short while longer in the vicinty of Capernaum.[2] In April the wheatfields turn yellow. His disciples caused offense by plucking ears of wheat on the Sabbath.[n] Jesus was requested to warn them against this violation of the Sabbath.[3] But he refused to do so, thereby making him-

[6] Luke 13, 1.   [7] Luke 13, 3 ff.   [8] John 6, 14 f.   [9] John 6, 60 ff.   [1] Cf. John 7, 1. 11; 11, 56.   [2] John 6, 59.   [3] Appendix II, 2.

self guilty of misleading the people.[4] And by the nature of his arguments he also incurred condemnation for blasphemy,[5] as he had done before.[6] On that same Sabbath two agents [7] watched Jesus at the synagogue of Capernaum, waiting (in vain) for the apostate preacher personally to violate the Sabbath. They also attempted to have Jesus arrested by Herod's police.[8] But in this they failed, for Herod practiced a benevolent restraint.[9] Shortly afterward the legal aspects of the case became more acute for all concerned.

Jesus was an apostate preacher, and the people were still thronging to him in hordes, from Capernaum, from all of Galilee and Palestine, and even from Jerusalem.[1] Would Capernaum be declared a "seduced city"? [2] This could be done only by official emissaries from the Great Sanhedrin.[3] The lawyers from Jerusalem were already arriving in Capernaum to look into Jesus' miracles on the spot.[4] They delivered themselves of an official opinion, to wit: his exorcisms are a fact; but his preaching of apostasy is likewise a fact; therefore he is a pseudo-prophet and his miracles are demonic miracles.[5] As we have already seen, this legal opinion was cited in original rabbinic documents (see page 9 f.). The men from Jerusalem could not arrest Jesus in Galilee unless the ruler of that country chose to help them.[6] Without a verdict from the Great Sanhedrin they could not even pronounce the formal ban upon Jesus.[7] But their legal opinion carried with it the threat of this ban, or of a death sentence.

The situation was certainly threatening enough for Jesus, for his relatives and disciples, for all who wished to remain loyal to him. At this point his friends hit upon the desperate idea of declaring him mentally not responsible for his actions.[8] In this way they hoped to save him and his kinsmen

---

[4] Appendix II, 30. [5] Appendix II, 18. [6] John 5, 9 ff. [7] Appendix II, 33. [8] Mark 3, 1 ff. [9] Cf. Mark 6, 14 ff.; Luke 9, 9. [1] Mark 3, 7. 20. [2] Appendix II, 42. [3] Appendix II, 43. [4] Mark 3, 22 f. [5] Appendix II, 52, 54. [6] Appendix II, 107. [7] Appendix II, 65. [8] Mark 3, 21.

and followers as well. This well-meant attempt at rescue failed completely.[9] The people of Capernaum took shelter in mass defection from the outlawed preacher. The movement to desert Jesus spread widely among his disciples.[1] Jesus left Capernaum.[2] Those disciples who had remained faithful accompanied him, and a number of Galilean women also joined the fleeing band.[n] Apparently Jesus first sought refuge in Nazareth.[3] There, after all, he had grown up, and there his sisters still lived. After a promising reception, the opposition to him swiftly won the upper hand. Nowhere else, in fact, did the evil tales of the emissaries from Jerusalem take effect so strongly as they did here. Jesus was reviled as a bastard and apostate (see page 17), and as a sorry sorcerer who could no longer even help himself.[4] Indeed, he barely escaped the zealots who wished to stone him as a pseudo-prophet.[5]

All the historical and legal circumstances suggest that the difficulties in Nazareth ought not to be consigned to Jesus' early period, as it is given in Luke,[6] but rather, as it is given in Mark,[7] to his late period in Galilee.[n] His mother and brothers had long since ceased to live in Nazareth.[8] Jesus had already wrought many miracles, especially in Capernaum.[9] His enemies hurled the old proverb "Physician, heal thine own limp" at him;[1] did it not perfectly fit this notorious pseudo-sorcerer who could save himself only by ignominious flight?[2] This scorn at the miracle-worker's "helplessness" is reiterated time and again in the polemics against Jesus.[n] We find it also in Julian.[n] The scene described in Luke 4, 29, was once again an attempt at stoning on the part of the zealots. The ancient process of stoning began with the culprit's being pushed over a cliff.[3] South of Nazareth there is a famous

---

[9] Mark 3, 31 ff.   [1] John 6, 66 ff.   [2] Cf. Matthew 11, 23 f.   [3] Mark 6, 1 ff.   [4] Luke 4, 23.   [5] Luke 4, 29.   [6] Luke 4, 16 ff.   [7] Mark 6, 1 ff.
[8] Mark 6, 3; cf. John 2, 12.   [9] Luke 4, 23; cf. Matthew 11, 23.   [1] Luke 4, 23 (see Genesis rabba 23).   [2] Luke 4, 30.   [3] Sanhedrin 6, 4 and *passim*.

precipice, the "Rock of Precipitation," which rises above the plain of Megiddo. There, according to the Judao-Christian gospel tradition, the people wanted to push Jesus over the edge.[n] To sum up, the episode preserved in Matthew 6, 1 ff., and Luke 4, 16, resembles a snapshot taken during a critical moment in the late period of Jesus' ministry in Galilee.

During the rest of the summer we find Jesus now in southern Galilee,[4] now in the vicinity of Tyre and Sidon,[5] now again by the lake and in Trans-Jordan.[6] He healed two sick men, but forbade them to speak of it.[7] He wanted to create as little stir as possible; he was a fugitive. "Foxes have holes, and birds of the air have nests; but the Son of man has nowhere to lay his head," he declared.[8] Meanwhile, the efforts to drive him into a corner were becoming more systematic. Everywhere emissaries of the Great Sanhedrin confronted him. They entangled him in a basic controversy over ritualistic hand-washing and the validity of the Halakah— that is, the oral rabbinical exegesis of the Torah.[9] They demanded "incontestable" signs.[1] Jesus' replies and diatribes were becoming increasingly forceful, his predictions ever gloomier.[n] He called woe upon the cities by the lake, Capernaum, Chorazin, and Bethsaida.[2] He warned the disciples against the propagandists who wished to poison their hearts, the Pharisaic emissaries of the Great Sanhedrin, and also against the secret agents of Herod Antipas.[3] For the government of Galilee seemed on the point of taking serious measures against Jesus, more serious than any it had been willing to take the year before, at any rate.[4] Jesus fled across the northern border into the territory of Herod Philip.[n]

On the Day of Atonement (A.D. 31) Jesus was at Caesarea Philippi, at the foot of the Hermon range. There he asked his disciples what they thought about him. Peter replied by

[4] Luke 7, 11 ff. [5] Mark 7, 24. 31. [6] Mark 7, 31; 8, 22. [7] Mark 7, 36; 8, 26. [8] Luke 9, 58. [9] Mark 7, 1 ff. [1] Mark 8, 11 ff. [2] Luke 10, 13 ff. [3] Mark 8, 15. [4] Mark 3, 6.

hailing him as the Messiah. Jesus, however, reproved him and spoke of the sufferings the Son of Man must endure for the redemption of the world.[5] Then he returned to Capernaum. His brothers were at this time just preparing to leave for Jerusalem to celebrate the Feast of Tabernacles there, and wanted to take him along. To their surprise, however, he chose to remain in the north. His decisions and actions at this period seemed to be dictated more and more by some transcendental law.[6] After the departure of his brothers he went to Mount Tabor, accompanied by his disciples. On the evening before the week of the Feast of Tabernacles he appeared before his disciples in the snow-white garment of the Son of Man. Peter wished to start setting up the tabernacles immediately. But again Jesus spoke of the coming Passion of the Son of Man.[7] Then he set out by the shortest pilgrims' road toward Jerusalem.[n] In the middle of the week of Tabernacles he suddenly appeared at the temple and "taught."[8]

[5] Mark 8, 27 ff.   [6] John 7, 2 ff.   [7] Mark 9, 2 ff.   [8] John 7, 14.

VI

THE
LAST WINTER
IN
JUDEA

─➤➤➤─➤➤➤─➤➤➤ 1 ◄◄◄─◄◄◄─◄◄◄

JESUS AT THE FEAST
OF TABERNACLES

THE TENSIONS IN JERUSALEM had evidently mounted greatly during the past twelve months. Friendly voices were hushed, hostile voices loud. Jesus was called a misleader of the people, a man possessed by devils. Questions were asked about his early training and his competence to teach. People made fun of his origins, which were well known; it was assumed that a true Messiah would have come upon the scene more mysteriously. People wondered why the Sanhedrin had not arrested him long before.[9] But no one dared to lay hands upon him, although his speeches were becoming ever more daring.

Jesus loved the liturgy of his people, and always took part in it. But since the Passover of 31 he had begun to invest the old feasts with new meanings, in terms of his tidings of salvation. On the seventh day, the day on which the famous water ceremony was celebrated with the greatest solemnity,[1] he appeared in the forecourt of the temple and cried loudly to the crowd at their worship: "If any one thirst, let him come to me and drink. He who believes in me, as the Scripture has said, 'Out of his heart shall flow rivers of living water.'"[2] As had happened once before during the Passover time, the messianic hopes of the anti-priesthood party awoke once again.[n] The masses, too, began to murmur of the coming Messiah.[3]

On the seventh and last night of the week of Tabernacles the traditionally joyous celebration had reached its height.[4] In the morning the scribes and Pharisees brought an adulteress before Jesus. She had been caught in her sin that very night. In a single sentence Jesus comdemned her Pharisaic accusers and pardoned the sinner on divine authority. So the tale is related in a Judao-Christian tradition which belongs among the best of the traditions concerning Jesus and which ancient annotators have placed, with understanding of the logic of the situation, immediately after John's account of the seventh day of the Feast of Tabernacles.[5] By this flouting of the moral code Jesus created additional enemies for himself in the Great Sanhedrin.

The eighth day was considered an additional half-holiday. On this day, in a portico off the women's courtyard, Jesus

[9] John 7, 26. 30. 32.   [1] Sukka 4, 9 f.   [2] John 7, 37 f.   [3] John 7, 41; cf. John 6, 15.   [4] Sukka 5, 1 ff.   [5] John 7, 53; 8, 1–8, 11.

made the tremendous statement: "I am the light of the world."[6] His identification of himself with the Festival of Lights was as obvious as it was bold. Yet Jesus became even bolder now.[7] In speaking of himself he used the formula of the divine revelation: "I am He," which originated in the Old Testament, but which since the days of Hillel had also played a crucial part in the liturgy and theology of the Feast of Tabernacles.[n] Not content with this, he called for a confession of faith in this "I am He" as the prerequisite for the forgiveness of sins, that very forgiveness of sins which was praised in the liturgical thanksgivings of the Festival of Lights as the merciful act of the living God.[8]

These words of Jesus at the Feast of Tabernacles, like everything else he said, provoked crisis and division among his audience.[9] The officers of the Great Sanhedrin, who had been sent out to arrest him, returned empty-handed.[1] Now it was decided to declare him in absentia a heretical "Samaritan," and thus exclude him from the Jewish religious community.[n] The charge was obviously directed principally against his theophanic "I am He." For during these same years Simon Magus, the Samarian Gnostic and practitioner of black magic, had been creating a sensation with self-glorifying phrases of many kinds.[n]

The motion of excommunication failed due to the opposition of Nicodemus, who pointed out that it was a violation of legal procedure.[2] But the condemning epithet "Samaritan" spread, and critical voices also increased among the common people. More and more frequently the opinion was expressed that Jesus was possessed by a devil.[n] All these charges were later reflected in the rabbinical texts: Jesus was called a magician, a deceiver, a madman,[3] a heretic, a Samaritan, an idolator, a polytheist.[n]

But the conflict hardened, sharpened. "Before ever a day

[6] John 8, 12.   [7] John 8, 21 ff.   [8] Tosephta Sukka 4, 1 ff.   [9] John 7, 31 ff. 40 ff.   [1] John 7, 45.   [2] John 7, 51.   [3] Cf. Mark 3, 21.

was, I am He," God said in Isaiah.[4] And Jesus declared: "Truly, truly, I say to you, before Abraham was, I am."[5] Then the other Jews understood what Jesus wanted to say, and what outrageous claim he was making.[6] The zealots, who trailed at the heels of this blasphemer, reached for stones, intending to make away with him on the spot. "But Jesus hid himself, and went out of the temple."[7]

➤➤➤-➤➤➤-➤➤➤ 2 ⫷⫷-⫷⫷⫷-⫷⫷⫷

THE

FIRST EXCOMMUNICATION

ONCE MORE the Fourth Gospel relates a conflict over the Sabbath.[8] On a Sabbath Jesus healed a man of congenital blindness. This time he did not heal him by a word of command, as he had done with the lame man at the pool of Bethesda[9] and the man with the withered hand at Capernaum.[1] He healed by therapeutic manipulation (the making of a clay poultice), which was forbidden on the Sabbath unless the patient was in acute peril of death.[2] "This man is not from God, for he does not keep the sabbath."[3] The Sanhedrin held a long meeting and at last came to the unanimous decision to excommunicate anyone who, in spite of previous formal warning, declared his faith in Jesus. The healed

---

[4] Isaiah 43, 13. Revised Standard Version gives: "I am God, and also henceforth I am He." [5] John 8, 58. [6] Appendix II, 18. [7] John 8, 59. [8] John 9, 1 ff. [9] John 5, 8. [1] Mark 3, 5. [2] Shabbath 22, 6. [3] John 9, 16.

blind man was called before the tribunal and cautioned, but he proved obstinate and was accordingly excommunicated.[4] This excommunication was publicly proclaimed, for it was intended to serve as a salutary lesson to turn the wavering populace from mass apostasy.[5] The former blind man had been given sight, but he had lost his spiritual home and was compelled to move on to the alien land of a new faith.

➤➤➤➤➤➤➤➤➤ 3 ◄◄◄◄◄◄◄◄◄

DISCOURSE
ON THE SHEPHERDS

ON OCTOBER 18, A.D. 31, Sejanus was arrested and executed in Rome. News from Rome could reach Jerusalem within a few days, and this news no doubt traveled by the swiftest of secret couriers. For particularly in Jerusalem there were many people who had a vital interest in changing their course and destroying certain documents they might have in their files. We can easily imagine how frantically Pilate and Caiaphas, as well as Herod Antipas—all three incriminated by their previous association with Sejanus—must have scurried to save their positions. And they succeeded brilliantly, better than most other high-placed men in the Empire.

During these weeks Jesus may well have spoken those pastoral epigrams [n] which the Fourth Evangelist stitched to-

[4] John 9, 34; Appendix II, 122. [5] John 9, 35.

gether after his own fashion into one grand pastoral discourse and very logically inserted in his narrative [6] between the end of October [7] and the end of December.[8] Jesus could count on being understood without his making everything too explicit. In this land of shepherds and shepherd kings it was an old tradition for prophets to proclaim God's judgment upon the conditions and personalities of public life in metaphorical polemics against the unfaithful shepherds.[9]

The Ethiopian Book of Enoch contains a figurative diatribe against the political masters of Palestine, who are branded the murderous shepherds of God's people.[1] In precisely the same style and spirit Jesus spoke of the thieves and robbers who had fallen upon God's flock.[2] The term "robber" (lestes, latro) that Jesus here employed was used in antiquity to designate bandits and gang-leaders. In Jesus' eyes Pilate was no better than a political gang-leader. Herod Agrippa passed virtually the same judgment upon Pontius Pilate's administrative practices: "Acts of violence, robberies, executions without pause . . ." I have discussed this in greater detail elsewhere.[n] "Where there is no justice, states are nothing but bands of robbers [latrocinia]," Augustine declared.

Again in the Old Testament we find a stern discourse on shepherds.[3] Here, however, the metaphor of the shepherds is applied not to the secular authorities, but to the high priests of the pre-Maccabaean age who made common cause with foreign rulers—Syrian in this case—at the expense of God's flock. "Woe to my worthless shepherd, who deserts the flock!"[4] In similar metaphors Jesus cried out against Caiaphas and his ilk: "[The] hireling . . . sees the wolf coming and leaves the sheep and flees; and the wolf snatches them and scatters them."[5] Is the word "wolf" a direct reference to

[6] John 10, 1–18.   [7] John 7 ff.   [8] John 10, 22.   [9] Ezekiel 34, 1 ff.
[1] Ethiopic Enoch 89, 59–90, 38.   [2] John 10, 8.   [3] Zechariah 11, 4–17.
[4] Zechariah 11, 17.   [5] John 10, 12 f.

94

the Roman she-wolf? [n] In any case, the epithet "hireling" is a perfect description of Caiaphas in the late autumn of A.D. 31.

It is plain that Jesus was no "simple artisan," no unworldly quietist. He had the keen and farsighted vision of the Old Testament prophets for the world of politics. But of course not political but metaphysical realities were decisive to him, not negations but affirmations, not invective but pronouncing who he was: "I am the good shepherd." [6] In the metaphorical language of the Ethiopian Book of Enoch 89 f. and Zechariah 11 there is also occasional mention of the Good Shepherd. Jesus, however, spoke of the Good Shepherd in the formulae of the Book of Ezekiel and the Psalms. [n] God himself, he said, is the master and shepherd of his flock. The Good Shepherd loves his flock with the love of God. At the same time he loves God's flock with all the devotion of a man who loves his people as he loves his own flesh and blood. [7] "I lay down my life for the sheep." [8] "All who came before me are are thieves and robbers. . . . I came that they may have life, and have it abundantly." [9]

It may be that Jesus never spoke of his historical role with greater nobility and simplicity than he did in those apocalyptic autumn days in the midst of his misused and once again deceived nation. It is understandable why the picture of the Good Shepherd should have become the oldest representation of Jesus in Christian art, as we see it in Dura-Europos, in the catacombs of Lucina, in the Palace of the Conservators, and in the Lateran. But these "Good Shepherds" were inspired more by the spirit of Hellenistic bucolics than by that of ancient Palestinian pastoral life and the Biblical concept of the shepherd. There is nothing lyrical about Jesus' image of the Good Shepherd. His guardian of the flock is, rather, a virile and militant figure, the incarna-

[6] John 10, 11 ff.   [7] Cf. Mark 6, 34; Luke 15, 4 ff.   [8] John 10, 15; cf. Mark 14, 27.   [9] John 10, 8 ff.

tion of a compassion not of this world, and shadowed by the
nearness of death.

➤➤➤-➤➤➤-➤➤➤ 4 ᐸᐸᐸ-ᐸᐸᐸ-ᐸᐸᐸ

AN ATTEMPTED STONING

DURING THESE WEEKS Jesus seems to have moved somewhat restlessly about Judea, turning up now here, now
there. Perhaps he occasionally spent nights on the "Mount
of Olives."[1] The visit with Mary and Martha may have
taken place at this time,[2] as well as other events that have
been fitted into Luke's "travelogue"[3] or into the concluding
chapters of the Synoptic Gospels.[4] An item of rabbinical tradition which has been much misinterpreted deals with a stay
of Jesus in the city of Lydda, which lay on the road from Jerusalem and Emmaus to Jaffa, hard by the border of Judea.
There, the tale goes, he was watched by two young scribes
whom the authorities had appointed secret witnesses.[n] We
have no particular reason to doubt this story, which is repeated in several places, and this episode, too, may be placed
somewhere during the months of November and December.

During the second half of December there was celebrated
in Jerusalem the week-long Feast of Dedication in memory
of the purification of the temple under Judas Maccabaeus.[5]
Jesus appeared at the temple,[6] and was immediately surrounded by the Sanhedrin's men and assailed with questions.
"If you are the Christ, tell us plainly." But Jesus refused to

---

[1] John 8, 1; cf. Luke 21, 37.   [2] Luke 10, 38 ff.   [3] Luke 9–18.   [4] Mark
10 ff.   [5] 1 Maccabees 4, 59.   [6] John 10, 22 ff.

say, not because he feared the consequences, but because the title "Messiah" was not sufficient for him, never was to be sufficient.[7] He replied: "The works that I do in my Father's name, they bear witness to me." This was more than a false claim of Messiahship; it was blasphemy. Earlier, in the autumn of A.D. 30, Jesus had spoken in similar terms.[8] At that time the religious authorities had not had a free hand.[9] But now they could take stronger action.[1] They were going to have him stoned.[2]

Jesus, however, as the Fourth Evangelist relates, confronted his adversaries with the words of the psalmist: "You are gods, sons of the Most High, all of you."[3] And he continued: "If he called them gods to whom the word of God came . . . do you say of him whom the Father consecrated and sent into the world, 'You are blaspheming,' because I said, 'I am the Son of God'?"[4] Nowhere else does John's Jesus express himself so indirectly, with so much circumlocution, as he does here. "To whom the word of God came . . ." The members of the Sanhedrin knew perfectly well to whom this passage from the psalm had been addressed: the religious authorities. They realized at once to whom Jesus was alluding: Caiaphas, their high priest and the president of their council. They knew, too, how the psalm continued: "Nevertheless, you shall die like men, and fall like any prince."[5] Jesus' counterattack was annihilating. In his pastoral discourse Jesus had spoken of the true and false shepherds. Now he spoke of the true and false son of God. The false one, he said, wished to sit in judgment upon the true Son, and he would do so. The true Son of God would die as the sacrifice to which his Father had consecrated him. The false son of God, however, would die the death of tyrants which the Heavenly Judge had proclaimed for him. The members of the Sanhedrin understood Jesus'

[7] Mark 8, 30; 14, 62.   [8] John 5, 18.   [9] Appendix II, 112.   [1] Appendix II, 113.   [2] John 10, 31.   [3] Psalm 82, 6.   [4] John 10, 34 ff.   [5] Psalm 82, 7.

meaning. "Again they tried to arrest him, but he escaped from their hands." [6]

There are sundry indications that stones were already flying through the air as Jesus escaped the fanatics like a bird fleeing the nets of the fowler.[n] The accounts that mention the spies in Lydda also state that Jesus had been stoned for teaching polytheistic heresies.[n] In Jewish texts the word "stoning" did not necessarily mean stoning to death.[n]

⇢⇢⇢ 5 ⇠⇠⇠

THE FLIGHT ACROSS
THE BORDER

JESUS NOW WITHDREW to the land east of the Jordan.[7] The Jordan formed the boundary between Judea and Peraea, between the territory governed by Pontius Pilate and that ruled by Herod Antipas. In other words, Jesus was putting himself under the protection of his own sovereign,[8] although he did not deceive himself into imagining that Herod Antipas offered any reliable or lasting protection. He was seeking only a breathing-spell, a last moment of peace while he prepared for the hour that was to come.

For the present he did not venture very far into Trans-Jordan. As soon as he had crossed the river boundary, he stopped and gathered his disciples about him.[9] This was the spot where John had baptized him four years earlier. Here,

[6] John 10, 39.　[7] John 10, 40; cf. Mark 10, 1; Matthew 19, 1.　[8] Cf. John 11, 7 f., and Luke 23, 7 f.　[9] John 11, 7.

in earlier days, his first disciples had joined him, those who still made up the most intimate circle around him: John, Andrew, Peter, Philip.[1] It was like a return to his beginnings —with death in sight. Once again crowds poured onto the plain of the Jordan, as they had done in the days of John the Baptist.[2] Many came to the faith, especially the inhabitants of the land east of the Jordan.[3] Others watched and spied on him; still others sought to involve him in disputes.[4] Jesus, however, went about doing good.[n]

It was in all probability during these weeks that the Pharisees were sent to Jesus, as narrated in Luke 13, 31 ff. Their purpose was to cajole him into crossing the Jordan once more, back into the sphere of their authority. They therefore came to him with a pretense of concern, and warned him against Herod. This was an attempt to lure the miscreant into a trap. Jesus replied to them: "Go and tell that fox, 'behold, I cast out demons and perform cures today and tomorrow, and the third day I finish my course. Nevertheless I must go on my way today and tomorrow and the day following, for it cannot be that a prophet should perish away from Jerusalem.'" Devastating words. Pilate was a wolf,[5] Herod a fox, cunning and full of wiles. But Jesus' words were also contemptuous. He was saying: Herod is no hero; [6] he is a mixture of wiliness and cowardice. In point of fact, no one could predict what the crafty ruler would do next.[7] We have discussed his treasonable link with Sejanus.[n] Did he intend to arrest Jesus as an "agitator," as he had arrested John the Baptist? [8] Did he wish to make a great show of having Jesus executed, on grounds that he was a messianic pretender to the imperial throne? It was by no means unlikely that Herod might be considering such a thing as a means to ingratiate himself with Tiberius, who was cur-

[1] John 1, 28 ff.   [2] John 10, 41.   [3] John 10, 42.   [4] Mark 10, 1 ff.; Luke 11, 53 f.   [5] John 10, 12.   [6] Cf. Pirkē Aboth 4, 15.   [7] Cf. Mark 9, 13.
[8] Flavius Josephus, *Antiquities* 18, 5, 2; Luke 23, 5.

rently engaged in hunting down precisely such persons.[n] But Jesus was well aware that the Pharisees had not come from Tiberias or Machaerus, but from Jerusalem. Therefore he sent them in mockery to Herod. Let the fox lay whatever plans he wished: Jesus would still die in Jerusalem. There was the seat of the Great Sanhedrin, the sole authority with the right to pass death sentences under the religious laws.[9] There was the citadel of the enemies of God, who had already slain so many men of God.[n] There, in Jerusalem, stones had already been cast at him.[1] There certain death awaited him.[2]

Among his disciples, Jesus summed up the significance of the political object lessons of the past weeks, the past decades, the past centuries.[3]

➛➛➛ 6 ⬅⬅⬅

THE DECISION
OF THE SANHEDRIN

WHILE JESUS STILL LINGERED east of the Jordan, Lazarus in Bethany fell fatally ill.[4] Jesus responded to the appeal for help from the sisters, Martha and Mary. The disciples feared the worst: "Rabbi, the Jews were but now seeking to stone you, and are you going there again?"[5] But Jesus would not be deterred. Then Thomas said: "Let us also go, that we

[9] Appendix II, 65.   [1] John 10, 39.   [2] John 11, 16.   [3] Mark 10, 42 ff.; Luke 22, 24 ff.   [4] John 11, 1 ff.   [5] John 11, 8.

may die with him."[6] Meanwhile Lazarus had already died;
and the Evangelist describes in full detail how Jesus called the
dead man back from the grave.[7] John stresses unmistakably
that Lazarus had already lain in his tomb for four days; that
the smell of decay was already noticeable; that this resurrection of a dead man took place before a great many witnesses,
among them many who were highly critical and extremely
hostile; that Lazarus did not reappear like a ghost, but
wrapped in quite tangible grave-clothes; that the people removed the cloth and bandages from him, by this very act
convincing themselves of his physical resuscitation; and that
he then actually went about[8] and resumed his previous normal life, sitting down at table before all eyes, eating and
drinking.[9]

The rabbis of the third century rejected Jesus' raisings
from the dead as necromancy and optical illusions (in the
sense of Appendix II, 52).[n] Justin Martyr tells us that this
charge was circulated even while Jesus lived.[1] In any case, it
occurred frequently in the polemics of the apostolic age; and
the resurrection of Lazarus in particular seems to have been
the subject of violent debates. A sign of this is the story of
poor Lazarus, which is told only by Luke.[2] The very name
Lazarus should warn us that something is afoot, as the rich
man remains nameless, and as the persons of Jesus' parables
were always anonymous. In the course of the tale Luke unmistakably attacks those who expressed doubts about the
other Lazarus: "Neither will they be convinced if some one
should rise from the dead."[3] The Fourth Evangelist flung
himself vigorously into this controversy.[4] Hence his emphasis on all the facts surrounding the resurrection of Lazarus;
he rules out any possibility that the feat might be interpreted
as necromancy. With the same motive Quadratus, the apolo-
gist of the days of Hadrian, emphasized that a number of

[6] John 11, 16.   [7] John 11, 38 ff.   [8] John 11, 44.   [9] John 12, 2. 9.
[1] *Dialogue* 69, 6 f.   [2] Luke 16, 19 ff.   [3] Luke 16, 31.   [4] John 11, 42.

persons whom Jesus had cured or raised from death were
still living in his time.[5]

According to John, the raising of Lazarus precipitated a
special session of the Great Sanhedrin. In his account of this
the Evangelist for the first time mentions the name of the
officiating High Priest, Caiaphas. Probably Gamaliel I, Zadok the Faster, Johanan ben Zakkai, Nicodemus, and Joseph
of Arimathea took part in this memorable session. Saul of
Tarsus may have "audited" the meeting. Discussion centered around the political situation that had arisen, after the
breathing-spell of the past weeks,[6] as the result of the new
mass following that was being attracted to Jesus.[n] The situation certainly was critical. For fourteen years the political
watchword of Caiaphas and the aim of his administration
had been the preservation of public tranquillity. Those had
been dangerous years, and Caiaphas had often had to resort
to highly questionable measures to keep things in check. But
the outward show of peace which he had imposed was the
secret of his lasting favor with Rome.[n] Since the fall of Sejanus in October 31 the imperial government was combing
the land for conspirators and pretenders to the throne. The
High Priest was in an exposed position. If at this moment
any news of political messianic movements in Palestine
should reach Rome, Caiaphas was done for. Therefore, Jesus
had to be eliminated before it was too late. Up to the present
the Great Sanhedrin had hesitated to strike at Jesus; even
now it still shrank from direct attack.[7] Caiaphas, however,
had the decisive vote.[8] This was the procedure of the council
in Jerusalem: the president of the Sanhedrin cast the last
vote.[n] Experienced councillor that he was, Caiaphas had already devised the legal theological formula which convinced
even the most reluctant members (Gamaliel, Johanan, Nicodemus, perhaps Joseph) that a radical solution was not only

[5] Eusebius: *Historia Ecclesiastica* 4, 3, 2.   [6] John 10, 40.   [7] John 7, 20.
51; 11, 47.   [8] John 11, 49.

necessary, but also just. "It is expedient for you that one man should die for the people, and that the whole nation should not perish." [9] Cast in terms of the given situation, this was, after all, one of the guiding principles of the provisions against heresy.[1] The result was that the Great Sanhedrin decided to condemn Jesus to death.[2] A proclamation of outlawry was issued, reminding all Jews faithful to the Torah of their obligation to denounce the criminal.[3] "If any one knew where he was, he should let them know, so that they might arrest him." [4]

It is no doubt this proclamation which is recorded in a rabbinical tradition preserved in Sanhedrin 43a: "The word is handed down: On the eve of the Passover Jeshu Hannosri was executed. Forty days [n] before a crier had gone forth and had cried: 'He shall be stoned because he has practiced magic and deceived and led Israel astray. Anyone who knows anything that may justify him, let him come forward and declare it.' But no justification was found for him, and so he was executed on the eve of the Passover." Ulla (c. A.D. 300) said: "Would you think he had deserved that anyone should seek to find justification for him? He was indeed a deceiver, and the All-Merciful has said: Nor shall you spare him, nor shall you conceal him (Deut. 13, 8). But it was different with Jeshu Hannosri. For he stood close to the government."

As we see, here too a cause-and-effect relationship is established between Jesus' miracle-working and the death sentence, exactly as John emphasizes.[5] The Talmud brings in this historical item as a legal precedent—the subject under discussion being dilatory or rapid execution of a sentence.[6] The duty of denunciation is taken for granted; the Talmud concerns itself only with the fact that in this special case the punishment was postponed for several weeks. As for the

[9] John 11, 50.　[1] Appendix II, 78.　[2] John 11, 53.　[3] Appendix II, 31.
[4] John 11, 57.　[5] John 11, 46 ff.　[6] Cf. Sanhedrin 11, 3, and *passim*.

"government" in whose good graces Jesus is said to have stood, the Talmud probably does not mean the house of David [7] or the wife of the Roman procurator, [8] but the ruler of Jesus' country and his legal protector, the unpredictable Herod Antipas. [9] If the round number (forty days before the Passover) may be taken as approximately correct, the passage enables us to date the proclamation mentioned in John 11, 57—sometime in February of A.D. 32.

Throughout this period Jesus did not set foot inside the city. From Bethany he retreated northward, and remained with his disciples hiding in the wilderness. [1] At the time he left the Mount of Olives and turned toward the north he may have spoken those parting words on Jerusalem which were recorded in the *Logia* and are quoted by Matthew and Luke [2]—Matthew inserting them into his account of the Passover week and Luke into the narrative of Jesus' journeys.

According to the accepted text of John, [3] Jesus fled to Samaria. There he was comparatively safe, for since his early days he had had many friends there, who were all the more ready to receive him if he were being persecuted by the Sanhedrin in Jerusalem." Meanwhile the hunt for him continued, but in vain."

For the rest, we know virtually nothing about those solitary weeks.

[7] Luke 2, 4.   [8] Matthew 27, 19.   [9] Luke 23, 7 f.   [1] John 11, 54.
[2] Matthew 23, 37 ff.; Luke 13, 34 f.   [3] John 11, 54.

$\twoheadrightarrow\!\!\twoheadrightarrow\!\!\twoheadrightarrow$ 7 $\twoheadleftarrow\!\!\twoheadleftarrow\!\!\twoheadleftarrow$

JESUS IN JERICHO
AND BETHANY

I F JESUS ALREADY KNEW in his heart that he was to die by
violence, as the oldest *Logia* traditions unanimously and
plausibly testify, we are forced to face the question: why did
he run from his pursuers and withdraw once more to the
north? Here we are touching upon one of the deepest secrets
of Jesus. Nevertheless, with all due reservations, I hazard this
reply: Jesus wished to die on the Passover.

His subsequent actions support this view. As the Passover
feast approached, Jesus and his disciples left the hiding-place
in the north in order to accompany the Galilean pilgrims to
Jerusalem by way of Jericho and Bethany.

I believe it is possible to arrive at a chronology for the last
days of Jesus' life precise to the days of the week and finally
to the hours of the last day. In this limited space, of course,
I cannot enter into all the complicated calculations that un-
derlie my reconstruction. However, I shall set down the most
important points of reference in so far as these illuminate the
course of the last days and the last journeys.[n]

Jesus and his disciples reached the pilgrims' road through
the eastern Jordan valley on a Thursday. "And they were on
the road, going up to Jerusalem, and Jesus was walking
ahead of them; and they were amazed, and those who followed were afraid." [4] They tramped on toward the south

[4] Mark 10, 32.

105

for many hours. Finally they reached the crossroads where the north-south pilgrims' road of the Galileans met the east-west pilgrims' road that led from Trans-Jordan across the Jordan and then upward to Jericho and Jerusalem. This was the region where Jesus had been baptized by John the Baptist.[5] Here, in the country east of the Jordan, he had won hordes of new adherents only a few months before.[6] Thus, he may have encountered many enthusiastic friends, who hailed him with jubilation, among the Passover pilgrims who here met and joined the Galilean pilgrims. Jesus, however, took the Twelve aside and spoke to them: "Behold, we are going up to Jerusalem; and the Son of man will be delivered to the chief priests and the scribes, and they will condemn him to death, and deliver him to the Gentiles; and they will mock him, and spit upon him, and scourge him, and kill him; and after three days he will rise." [7]

Then he had several of them go on ahead, while others remained with him. For the last two hours they climbed until Jericho rose before them, the city of festivals and horrors. South of Jericho lay the wasteland where the people of the Qumran community and the Essenes lived, the wilderness where John the Baptist had dwelt for years.

Before the gates of Jericho, Jesus was hailed with a messianic acclamation: "Jesus, Son of David." [8] In the city the crowds thronged fervidly around him.[9] Jesus spent the night at the home of the chief publican, Zacchaeus. The spacious mansion had room enough for the entire retinue of disciples and women. Early Friday morning a crowd gathered under the windows to cheer him. "He was near to Jerusalem and . . . they supposed that the kingdom of God was to appear immediately." [1] The time and place aroused the most reckless hopes. The rapid changes in the imperial government since the fall of Sejanus; the approaching Passover, which had al-

[5] John 1, 28.   [6] John 10, 41 f.   [7] Mark 10, 33 f.   [8] Luke 18, 38 f.
[9] Luke 19, 3 ff.   [1] Luke 19, 11.

7 · *Jesus in Jericho and Bethany*

ways been regarded as the time for the promised advent of
the Messiah; memories of Simon the slave-king (see page
49); the Galilean partisans' hopes for a political Messiah;[2]
the apocalyptic fanaticism of the dwellers in the desert
around the Dead Sea; the Trans-Jordan pilgrims' ardent
faith in Jesus—all these elements combined to produce an
intense excitement. According to Luke,[3] Jesus told them a
parable that was intended to check somewhat their wild
hopes of the coming of the kingdom. The overwrought
crowds in Jericho certainly only half understood his mysterious metaphorical speech. Nevertheless, Jesus and his disciples
were now able to leave the house and the city without calling
forth new messianic demonstrations.

Jesus walked ahead, alone and in silence; the disciples and
women followed at a distance.[4] On Friday afternoon they
reached the estate of Bethphage on the Mount of Olives. At
this season of the year the Sabbath rest began around six
o'clock.

Early on the Sabbath morning Jesus walked the short
distance to Bethany, the last village on the pilgrims' road to
Jerusalem.[5] Presumably he went there to attend the religious
service. In the afternoon he was a guest at the house of Simon the Leper,[6] whom he had probably healed on an earlier
occasion.

Here there took place the anointing of Jesus, which is
described very differently in the different sources, probably
because the significance of Mary's act has been obscured by
the discussion that ensued.[n] Without a word Mary (the sister
of Lazarus) poured a pound of precious spikenard over Jesus.
Judas began wrangling about social problems. But Jesus cut
him short: "You always have the poor with you."[n] Hard
words for social-minded idealists. "But you will not always
have me." Here was a defense of Mary strikingly akin to the

[2] Cf. Luke 13, 1.   [3] Luke 19, 12 ff.   [4] Luke 19, 28.   [5] Mark 11, 1;
John 12, 1.   [6] John 12, 2 ff.; Mark 14, 3 ff.

blessing of Mary in Luke 10, 42.[n] It would appear that Mary performed the anointing in the hope that Jesus would, upon his arrival in Jerusalem, ascend the throne as Messiah. ("Messiah" means "The Anointed.") Jesus had an entirely different view of his future, and gave to Mary's act a fresh meaning, interpreting it in terms of the coming Passion. "She has done what she could; she has anointed my body beforehand for burying." [7]

[7] Mark 14, 8; John 12, 7.

VII

THE
PASSOVER
OF
DEATH

❯❯❯❯❯❯❯❯ 1 ❮❮❮❮❮❮❮❮

JESUS IN JERUSALEM

Jesus spent Saturday night in Bethany. On Sunday morning he continued on from the Mount of Olives to Jerusalem. He was met everywhere with tumultuous rejoicing.
The Messiah had been upon the Mount of Olives, the mount
of the revelation! It was there the Lord God was expected to
appear to establish the kingdom of Jerusalem; there the rais-

ing up of Israel was to take place. (Indeed, later on, in the days of Nero, an Egyptian pseudo-Messiah was able to gather many thousands of adherents on the Mount of Olives for an attack on Jerusalem.) Hopes of a political Messiah revived almost inevitably at the moment that Jesus at last, in the full light of publicity, took the road from the Mount of Olives to Jerusalem.[1] The news raced along through the bands of pilgrims and preceded Jesus into the streets of the festive city.[2] The witnesses of the raising of Lazarus went about everywhere proclaiming what they had seen.[3] The resurrection of the dead upon the Mount of Olives had begun! The Messiah was coming!

Jesus was greeted with one ovation after another. Swarms of pilgrims came forward, messianic acclamations on their lips, to "lead" their king solemnly into Jerusalem. Many of them waved palms, thus making plain the political meaning of their demonstration. For the palm was the key emblem of Palestine in national heraldry and in the international emblematic language of the day. Palm trees and palm leaves are to be found on the Palestinian coins of the early Maccabees, the Hasmonaeans, the Herodians, the procurators, and the partisans; they are found also on Flavian coins celebrating victories and, above all, on the coins celebrating the advent of Hadrian. On these last coins we see Judea kneeling or sacrificing, surrounded by children bearing palms and marching in solemn procession to meet the approaching Emperor. This is how we must understand the palms of Palm Sunday: Jerusalem was celebrating the epiphany of her messianic king. Even the children crying Hosannah are included in this description of the coming of a king.[4]

The Evangelists make it perfectly plain that this political demonstration was a terrible misunderstanding, in which even the Twelve Apostles had some share.[n] Jesus responded to the ovations of his followers with a wholly unpolitical

[1] Luke 19, 37.   [2] John 12, 12.   [3] John 12, 11. 17 f.   [4] Matthew 21, 15 f.

countersign. He chose an ass on which to ride.[5] For the ass was symbolic of the king of peace who, according to the ancient rabbinical interpretation of the prophet Zechariah,[6] was to proclaim the way of humility and suffering. Yet as Jesus rode through the city gate, he spoke the lament for Jerusalem: "Would that even today you knew the things that make for peace." Jerusalem had failed to recognize the day of the advent of God.[7] Now other days would come, not days of peace, but days of the sword. Jesus foresaw the times of Nebuchadnezzar returning, the times of Pompey and Varus. He would go the way of his Passion, but he could no longer avert disaster from Jerusalem.

On the following days (Monday to Thursday) Jesus appeared daily in the temple and addressed his people. The throng of his listeners constantly swelled, if only because of the pilgrims who were entering the city each succeeding day.[8] When the people left the temple, Jesus also disappeared and remained hidden during the night on the Mount of Olives.[9] His enemies held one conference after another, and several times tried in vain to seize him.[1] The temper of the crowd was such that it was impossible to capture Jesus in the midst of his massed bodyguards.[2] His enemies therefore tried to engage him in all sorts of controversies, in order to force him to compromise himself publicly. As had once happened to John the Baptist,[3] a variety of deputations, Pharisees, Sadducees, and scribes, now came to challenge Jesus.[4] But intellectually and in argument Jesus towered so high above his opponents that all their attempts failed. A clear illustration of this is the most famous dispute of those days, the controversy over the tribute money,[5] which was started jointly by the Pharisees and the Herodians—their object be-

[5] John 12, 14.   [6] Zechariah 9, 9 ff.   [7] Luke 19, 41 ff.   [8] Luke 19, 47; 21, 37 f.; John 12, 44.   [9] Mark 11, 1. 11. 19; 13, 3; Luke 31, 37; 22, 39; John 12, 36; 18, 2.   [1] Mark 11, 18 f.; 12, 12; Luke 19, 47; John 12, 19. 36 ff.   [2] Luke 20, 19.   [3] John 1, 19 ff.   [4] Mark 12, 13 ff.   [5] Revised Standard Version says "money for the tax."

ing to force Jesus into a compromising position either theologically or politically. It ended with a double repudiation by Jesus of politics in religion—with his rejecting militant messianism and worship of the Emperor as well.[n] Worsted, his opponents withdrew.

On Wednesday there took place in the palace of the High Priest a conference of church dignitaries and councillors. The agenda called for discussion of what measures were to be taken against Jesus.[6] The situation was difficult because only two days' respite remained before the Passover festival, a time at which wild demonstrations or riots could always be expected, especially among the easily inflamed Galileans, who had been manifesting a threatening attitude ever since Jesus' entry into Jerusalem.[7] The result of these consultations was the decision to seize the person of Jesus by a strategem, and to force his execution even before the Passover feast, so that peace and public order might be preserved as far as possible.[n] It may be that Judas, the non-Galilean, had for months been a secret agent of the Jerusalem Sanhedrin assigned to work among the Galilean's disciples. At any rate, he regarded the capture of the man who had been proclaimed [8] a blasphemer and pseudo-prophet as his bounden duty.[n] For he took an oath pledging himself to commit the betrayal— an oath that may well have included a curse upon himself should he fail to carry out the task he had undertaken.[n] We may add that the need to employ a "betrayer" demonstrates how hard it had been to find and to seize Jesus. The final struggle between Jesus and Caiaphas must have been in actuality far more dramatic than the accounts of the Evangelists suggest.[n]

[6] Mark 14, 1; Matthew 26, 3 ff.   [7] Luke 22, 2.   [8] John 11, 57.

❯❯❯-❯❯❯-❯❯❯ 2 ❰❰❰-❰❰❰-❰❰❰

THE LAST SUPPER

O N Thursday Jesus celebrated the Last Supper with his
disciples. The very fact that it took place in the evening indicates that this was a Passover meal. But the Synoptic Gospels never expressly mention [9] a Passover lamb;
they say nothing about it in connection with the preparations
or the meal itself, not even at the point where the reference
to a lamb on the Passover table was virtually called for.[ⁿ]
Why not? According to John, Paul, and the rabbinical traditions concerning Jesus, the temple ritual with the slaughtering of the Passover lambs did not take place normally until
Friday—that is, until the time Jesus was being crucified.[ⁿ] Accordingly, Jesus held his Passover feast twenty-four hours before the official Passover meal of the members of the temple
community.

Jesus had a compelling reason for renouncing the Passover lamb—a reason that has hitherto been overlooked in
discussions of the Last Supper. An apostate was forbidden to
eat of the Passover lamb,[1] although he was expressly allowed
to eat unleavened bread and bitter herbs. Practically speaking, no one could prevent a heretic from preparing a feast at
home; but he would be unable to eat a Passover lamb because
he would not be permitted to bring a lamb to the temple for
ritual slaughtering. In the light of this, it is understandable
that Jesus should say not a word to his disciples about select-
ing the Passover lamb and going to the temple to have it
slaughtered there, not a word about all the ritual prepara-

[9] In spite of Mark 14, 12; Luke 22, 7.   [1] Appendix II, 123.

113

tions that played so large a part in the practice and literature of the Passover. Jesus spoke only of the domestic preparations for the meal, as these were independent of the temple slaughtering as long as the Passover lamb was omitted. This, too, explains why all the Gospels expressly mention the unleavened bread and bitter herbs and "expressly" omit mention of the Passover lamb.

Now, Jesus was not just any apostate; he was a condemned preacher of apostasy, and a warrant for his arrest had been issued. Even at a private feast he had to be alert for spies, informers, and officers of the Sanhedrin. Only in the light of these facts can we understand why the disciples, in Mark 14, 14, were told to plead: "The teacher says, Where is my guest room, where I am to eat the passover with my disciples?" Jesus needed a hidden refuge where he could celebrate the Passover undisturbed and out of danger; he needed a host who would have the courage to shelter the heretic Galilean and his outlawed company of disciples [n] for a few hours.

Celebration of a Passover meal without the lamb was, incidentally, not without precedent. The year before, Jesus had done the same with his disciples in Capernaum. All the Jews in Galilee and throughout the world who could not make the pilgrimage to Jerusalem had to celebrate the Passover without benefit of temple ritual or lamb.[2] The exiles in the desert, the Essenes, the Therapeutae were reduced to similar measures. When worship in the temple finally ceased in A.D. 70, the liturgy for the Diaspora came into general use,[3] but the Passover meal nevertheless remained one of the principal Jewish festivals. In most cases a roast kid was served instead of the Passover lamb; the kid would be slaughtered without the temple ritual, but prepared in the same manner as the Passover lamb.[4] The sacramental emphasis passed

[2] Deuteronomy 16, 5 f.   [3] Justin Martyr: *Dialogue,* 46, 2.   [4] Cf. also Eduyyoth 8, 6.

114

from the lamb to the unleavened bread and the cup of the blessing. Jesus may well have celebrated the last Passover meal with his disciples in somewhat the same manner.[n]

That Jesus should have celebrated his Passover on an evening other than the official one was also not so unprecedented as it may seem. Divergencies in the calculation of festivals among various groups and in the various provinces were quite common among the Jews of antiquity, especially in regard to the date for Passover.[n] It is therefore quite possible that certain groups of Galileans held their Passover meal in the capital a day sooner than the adherents of the temple clergy and the Sanhedrin. For that reason alone all these would have to do without the Passover lamb, as the slaughtering ritual in the temple would of course be governed by the official calculation of the Passover.

In the evening after sunset, at the customary hour of six, Jesus and his disciples assembled in the dining-room, which had been prepared according to the ritual.[n] All reclined at table.[n] Jesus took the place of the paterfamilias and spoke to his disciples: "I have earnestly desired to eat this passover with you before I suffer; for I tell you I shall never eat it again until it is fulfilled in the kingdom of God."[5] Then Jesus took up the First Cup, pronounced the prescribed blessing for the day, and, after his disciples' Amen, added: "Take this, and divide it among yourselves; for I tell you that from now on I shall not drink of the fruit of the vine until the kingdom of God comes."[n] Now all partook of the usual first course, a bit of greens and a morsel of bitter herbs, both first dipped into the common Passover bowl. After the first morsel of greens, Jesus said: "Truly, I say to you, one of you will betray me, one who is eating with me."[n] The words struck like a bolt of lightning into this group who had foregathered in this room with hopes of being safe at least for this hour.

[5] Luke 22, 15 f.

Uneasy questions were thrown about, in which Judas himself took part.[6] Then Jesus said: "It is he to whom I shall give this morsel when I have dipped it." And he dipped the bitter herbs into the passover bowl and gave the morsel to the traitor. The choice of this moment and the use of the bitter herbs had the significance of a curse.[7] Judas ate the bitter herbs and at once left the room.[8]

The Passover ritual provides for more or less general conversation on the divine revelation during the Passover night. In this connection various theophanic formulae, in the manner of Isaiah 43, are recited, such as: "I am He and no other." [n] Probably this custom already existed in the time of Jesus, and Jesus was referring to it, just as in John 8, 24 ff., he was referring to the *"Ani"* formula in the liturgy for the Feast of Tabernacles. For, according to John,[9] the words he spoke at the Passover table were altogether in the style of the divine phrases of revelation in Isaiah 43, 9 f.: "I tell you this now, before it takes place, that when it does take place you may believe that I am he."

After the traitor had been expelled from the company, Jesus lifted the platter of unleavened bread and spoke the Aramaic formula prescribed in the liturgy of the time: "This is the bread of affliction that our fathers ate in the land of Egypt. Let everyone who hungers come and eat; let everyone who is in need come and eat the passover meal." [n] Then the disciples drank the Second Cup, and the usual Passover liturgy continued until the meal proper began. Jesus took up the Passover bread, spoke the traditional words of blessing, broke the unleavened bread, and divided the pieces among the disciples. Then he spoke three sentences that went beyond the prescribed office for the Passover: "Take, eat; this is my body which is given for you. Do this in remembrance of me." [n] Then the disciples ate the roast kid that stood on

[6] Matthew 26, 25.   [7] See Deuteronomy 29, 18 f., etc.   [8] John 13, 26 ff.
[9] John 13, 19.

the table in place of the Passover lamb;[n] they also had cereals, fish, eggs, and some other dishes.

After the meal the Third Cup was poured, the so-called "Cup of Blessing."[n] Jesus raised the cup high and spoke the principal grace used at table: "May the All-merciful make us worthy of the days of the Messiah and of the life of the world to come. He brings salvation of his king. He shows loving-kindness to his anointed, to David, and to his seed in all eternity. He makes peace in his heavenly places. May he make peace for us and for all Israel. And say ye Amen."

After all the disciples had said Amen, Jesus gave the cup to them and again spoke three sentences that were not in the Passover liturgy: "Drink of it, all of you; for this is my blood of the covenant, which is poured out for many; do this, as often as you drink it in remembrance of me."[n] Then Jesus and his disciples sang antiphonally the concluding psalms.[n]

In terms of Old Testament sacramental theology, these words of Jesus could be ranked as a divine act of legislation, creating a ritual whose performance established a new relationship between God and man. The words "this is my body," which have been the subject of so much controversy, derived from the phraseology used in Old Testament Passover theology and already had a fixed place in Jewish Passover ritual. These words concern a reality of a "representative" kind. Bread and wine "represent to God" the body and blood of Jesus. Here we are dealing with a reality of a special order that is established by the divine authority of the inaugural words and cannot be grasped in terms of materialistic or spiritualistic categories. Jewish Passover theology speaks of the Passover lamb's redeeming blood of the covenant.[n] Jesus took himself to be God's Passover lamb and spoke of the expiatory effect of his bloody death as a sacrifice. The Old Testament Passover meal had already been regarded as a covenant. Jesus' Last Supper inaugurated the New Covenant. The disciples were required to repeat the new ritual of the meal at regular intervals after Jesus' death. "Do this." [1] That was no counsel; it was an unqualified commandment. The binding power of law, the obligatoriness, and efficacy of the eucharistic ritual, the sense in which it was declared a sacrament in accordance with Old Testament theology, was completely bound up with the fact that Jesus himself inaugurated this new sacrament, drawing his full authority from God. It is therefore unthinkable that the primitive Christian community, standing as it did upon the foundation of the Old Testament, could have established this sacrament of the Eucharist of its own impulse.

Among serious-minded Jews it was customary to remain together at table for several hours after the conclusion of the Passover meal and talk about the Passover miracles of the past and the future.[n] Jesus, too, remained for some time with his disciples in the room where they had supped, talking with them of things past and to come.[n] Then Jesus left the house and walked through the nocturnal streets of the city and out to the Kidron valley. The disciples followed him, again keeping a discreet distance, as they had done on the road to Jericho; probably they moved in inconspicuous small groups, possibly by different roads, in order to reach the Mount of Olives unnoticed.[2]

[1] Luke 22, 19; 1 Corinthians 11, 24 f.   [2] Luke 22, 39.

118

≫≫≫-≫≫≫-≫≫ 3 ≪≪-≪≪-≪≪

THE ARREST

EANWHILE a large and motley band of armed men marched across the Kidron valley to occupy and cordon off the Mount of Olives, and to search with lanterns and torches every hiding-place.[3] Evidently Jesus had been denounced to the Romans as a political messiah with a huge, dangerous, and unpredictable following; and those who were out to capture him were using tactics that had been developed since the early days of Herod the Great in the campaigns against Galilean guerilla chieftains.

First of all, there were the local Roman commandant of Jerusalem and his garrison troups, a whole cohort.[4] The detachment was prepared for battle.[n] Obviously, the Romans were counting on armed resistance, and in spite of all the precautions they had been taking they were rather expecting a general riot.[n] The Roman military tribune also had with him—and under his command—several officers of the temple police,[5] apparently the men with whom Judas had already negotiated when the plan for the arrest was devised.[6] These men commanded a detachment of temple police, also armed.[7] Finally, we are told of chief priests and councillors who came along probably in order to serve as witnesses or advisers should there be incidents involving the religious laws.[8] They had apparently brought their servants with them, sturdy

[3] "Have you come out as against a robber, with swords and clubs?" (Luke 22, 52).   [4] John 18, 3. 12.   [5] Luke 22, 52.   [6] Luke 22, 4.   [7] John 18, 3.   [8] Luke 22, 52.

119

fellows equipped with clubs for this nocturnal adventure.[9] Such a huge deployment of men was striking, but by no means unprecedented or incomprehensible.[1] The wooden clubs deserve our special attention; there was a good reason for their being mentioned so frequently.[n] Weapons (swords, lances, spears, bows, shields) were considered part of a man's adornment and it was therefore permissible under Jewish law for them to be carried on the Sabbath.[2] Clubs and wooden staves, on the other hand, were regarded not as decorative arms, but as pieces of wood,[3] and therefore fell in the category of things that might not be carried on the Sabbath or any other holy day.[n] Therefore this expedition cannot have taken place on the night after the official Passover meal, which belonged to the first principal holiday of the Passover week. This item of the chronology of the events of the Passion must be settled against the Synoptic Gospels, and in favor of John's Gospel.

Everything turned out differently from what the pursuers had feared or expected. Jesus did not stay in hiding; he went to his usual place.[4] Also, he made no attempt to flee, and did not hide among his disciples.[5] The troops, weapons, lanterns, signals, the traitor's signal—all had been needless and proved to be meaningless. But the prearranged operational plan was carried to its conclusion. Judas went up to Jesus, greeted him with the usual salutation, "Rabbi," and kissed him on the head; this was the customary manner of greeting a venerable rabbi.[n] Thus, the betrayal took the form of a kiss that was a sign of honor.[6] On the other hand, Judas did not speak the usual greeting, "Peace!" The disciples of Jesus had two swords among them[7]—hardly weapons enough to pit against a small army of a thousand soldiers, but enough if supplemented by "the twelve legions of angels"

[9] Mark 14, 43; John 18, 10.   [1] Cf. Acts 23, 23 f.   [2] See Shabbath 6, 4.
[3] As defined in Shabbath 9, 5.   [4] John 18, 2.   [5] John 18, 4 ff.   [6] Luke 22, 48.   [7] Luke 22, 38.

120

which the Master could call up at will.[n] Peter drew his sword
and began to use it. But Jesus would not have this. "All who
take the sword will perish by the sword."[8] This was his
forthright "no" to political messianism, and to militant
apocalypticism as well.

The military tribune rode up to the little group. Jesus was
bound, and the procession started.[9] The disciples simply
scattered and fled.[1] Nothing came of the dreaded riot. Mark
mentions a single person, a young man clad only in a linen
shirt, who tore away and took flight naked into the darkness
when the soldiers attempted to seize him.[2] Possibly this was
Mark the Evangelist himself, who is known to have been a
native of Jerusalem.[3] It may well be that Mark wished to introduce his own portrait into a "dark corner" of this nocturnal scene, as artists loved to do even in antiquity. In that case,
we have our account of the night of betrayal from at least
three eyewitnesses: Peter, Mark, and John.

⋙⋙⋙ 4 ⋘⋘⋘

THE ECCLESIASTICAL TRIAL

THE MILITARY TRIBUNE escorted the prisoner straight to
the palace of the High Priest. The traitor received his
reward and was permitted to go.[4] Jesus was interrogated at
once.[n]

According to the regular procedure of the Great Sanhe-

[8] Matthew 26, 52.   [9] John 18, 12.   [1] Mark 14, 50.   [2] Mark 14, 52.
[3] Acts 12, 12.   [4] Cf. Matthew 27, 3.

drin, a heretical teacher in Jerusalem had to be questioned by two lower courts before the highest court would hear the case.[5] Now there was no time for these formalities. Still, an attempt was made to comply with this custom to the extent of having one lower court sit on Jesus' case.

The Fourth Evangelist tells us that Jesus was "first" led before Annas, the senior pontifex—previous to the decisive hearing before Caiaphas, of which John gives a scantier account. This he justifies by obliquely informing us that he was a personal eyewitness of the hearing before Annas, as he was a personal acquaintance of the High Priest.[6] Hence he is able to give a circumstantial account of Annas' questioning.

Annas asked Jesus "about his disciples and his teaching." [7] Secret associations with secret membership lists and secret doctrines were by no means rare in Palestine in those days. This was the reason for the priest's question—which seemed all the more logical as Jesus and his disciples had lived so much in hiding during the past months. Jesus denied the charge of having organized a religious underground; he also insisted that he had nothing to do with the esoteric practices of the desert sect.[8] An episode occurred in which Jesus proved himself thoroughly grounded in legal procedure and adept at argumentation.[n] But the situation was serious. Jesus, still bound, was now brought before the Great Sanhedrin.[9]

The President of the Great Sanhedrin, who was also the son-in-law of Annas, was named Joseph. The cognomen Caiaphas may have stood for something like "inquisitor." [n] Probably he had already made a name for himself as an examining justice before he was entrusted with the office of high priest.

The trial began with the prescribed questioning of witnesses.[1] We learn nothing of the content of their testimony; presumably it had to do with Jesus' attitude toward the Sab-

[5] Sanhedrin 11, 2.   [6] John 18, 15.   [7] John 18, 19.   [8] John 18, 20.
[9] John 18, 24.   [1] Appendix II, 69.

122

bath. For this [2] had been his chronic offense, and figured also among the priests' charges against Jesus which Tertullian placed at the head of his list.[n] We know that Johanan ben Zakkai had early won a reputation for his searching and clever interrogation of witnesses.[n] It is quite possible that during this nocturnal session of the court he also conducted some of his formidable cross-examinations. In any case, it developed that the testimony of the various witnesses did not agree.[3]

Jesus' pronouncement about the temple was introduced. Apparently this aroused dangerous memories of the expulsion of the money-changers. What Jesus had then said about the temple had, evidently, been circulating ever since in many forms and been giving rise to many interpretations.[n] Caiaphas had secured several witnesses who repeated the saying in the offensive first-person version: "*I* will destroy this temple that is made with hands, and in three days *I* will build another, not made with hands." In this form the saying was plainly an assertion of divinity, and a blasphemy against the temple as well—more than enough for a death sentence.[4] But the scribes of the Sanhedrin pursued their questioning inexorably, and it developed that the witnesses had various versions of the incriminating saying—which was certainly not surprising after an interval of three years.

Up to this point Caiaphas had merely presided over the trial, in accordance with the procedural rules. Now, however, he took part in it. He stood up.[5] Mark emphasizes this, for it was not customary. The defendant stood before the court, but the President of the Sanhedrin usually sat upon the judges' bench. Nevertheless, Caiaphas rose to his feet. At this, the other members of the Seventy-one likewise rose, for so the rules required. The President stepped forward, went up to the defendant in the middle of the hall. According to the

[2] Since the events recorded in John 5, 9 ff., and Mark 2, 23 ff. [3] Mark 14, 56. [4] Appendix II, 15, 18. [5] Mark 14, 60.

prescribed legal procedure, the examining judge had the right and even the duty to intimidate the defendant.[n] This was clearly the intention of the experienced inquisitor. He wanted to startle Jesus, to make him lose his composure. "Have you no answer to make? What is it that these men testify against you?" But Jesus refused to be either surprised or frightened.[n] He knew that the President's question was no longer admissible because the testimony of the witnesses had already collapsed. By law the Sanhedrin was now obligated to pronounce the defendant innocent, and condemn the false witnesses.[n] But Caiaphas was determined to confuse the legal issue by his dramatic maneuver. He hoped to lead Jesus into a trap. Jesus saw through this, and continued to conduct himself as he had all along—he remained silent.[6] The trial had reached an impasse.

Now, however, Caiaphas played his last card. "Are you the Christ, the Son of the Blessed?" This, for Jesus, was the point at which he had to make his statement. More than that, it was the moment of revelation. His time had come.[7] And Jesus replied: "I am [*Ani hu*]; and you will see the Son of Man sitting at the right hand of Power, and coming with the clouds of heaven."[n] Whereupon the High Priest rent his garments and said: "Why do we still need witnesses? You have heard his blasphemy. What is your decision?" And they all pronounced against him a sentence of death.[8]

"*Ani hu*" was the most sacred of the theophanic formulae; it was taken from Isaiah 43 and played a great part in the liturgies of the festivals. Jesus had used it at the Feast of Tabernacles as an affirmation of who he was, and as soon as he did so, the people had taken up stones to stone him.[9] A few hours before this scene in court he had repeated the words at the Passover table.[1] Now he once again voiced this taboo formula of revelation, not any longer before the popu-

---

[6] Mark 14, 61.   [7] Cf. John 2, 4. 24.   [8] Mark 14, 61 ff.   [9] John 8, 58 f.
[1] John 13, 19.

lace or in the circle of his own disciples, but before the highest ecclesiastical tribunal of his people. Caiaphas instantly grasped the tremendous claim implicit in this *"Ani hu"* and saw the way to convict Jesus without more ado. Not saying a single word in anticipation of the court's verdict, he spoke his mind by impulsively rending his garments. For this act meant: I have this very moment heard with my own ears a blasphemy. Naturally the entire council followed his example, for no one would dare to show less piety than the High Priest.[n] Meanwhile Jesus went on, completed his *confessio* and *revelatio,* proclaimed himself the apocalyptic Son of Man.

The President now proposed that no further witnesses be heard. It was no longer necessary to examine what had happened in the past. For the defendant had just committed the greatest sacrilege of his life before this very tribunal. Nor were any witnesses needed, for the judges had heard the defendant's words with their own ears and were therefore themselves witnesses.[2]

No one raised any objections. The motion was accepted. The grand inquisitor finally spoke the fatal word: "Blasphemy."[3] Again no one objected. Caiaphas was now sure of his ground and ready to proceed with a test vote.[4] In accordance with the rules of procedure, it began with the youngest and ended with the president.[n] Caiaphas asked: "What is your decision?"[n] All without exception declared the defendant guilty of a capital crime.[5] Even such men as Gamaliel and Nicodemus condemned the blasphemer. By his virtuoso inquisitional tactics, Caiaphas had won a complete victory. In terms of ecclesiastical law, he was on perfectly solid ground. For the rules of procedure stated: "If the defendant declares: 'I have something to say in favor of my acquittal,' he must be listened to; but there must be something substantial in his

[2] Cf. Sanhedrin 7, 5.   [3] Mark 14, 64.   [4] Sanhedrin 5, 4.   [5] Appendix II, 18.

words." [n] Jesus brought forward no arguments in his own defense, and to the last he made no use of his right to protest. By this silence he acceded to the court's interpretation of his *"Ani hu."* [n]

At the conclusion of the night's business, Jesus was taken to the inner court of the High Priest's palace and kept under guard until his removal to the temple mount. There Peter had meanwhile waited—and thrice denied Jesus. All four Gospels report the denials, foremost among them being the Gospel that served as mouthpiece for the Petrine group.[6] For the denial by the first of the Apostles was an essential part of the story of that sinister night. The behavior of the Levite guards was also regarded as a characteristic feature of that night. They whiled away the time, until they were to repair to the temple, with more or less customary mistreatment of their prisoner.[n]

Shortly after dawn the official plenary session of the Great Court of Justice took place on the temple mount. Once again Jesus stood in the hall of Annas, where three years before he had driven out the money-changers with his lash. Now the master of the house, the High Priest, sat inside on the judges' bench to pronounce sentence upon him. The meeting was brief and formal; we are able to reconstruct the course of it from items in the Synoptic Gospels [n] and the rules of judicial procedure. Caiaphas opened the voting by asking the members to give their verdict. The court clerk called each member of the court by name, starting with the youngest. In each case the vote was only one word, and in each came the same word: Death. Every member of the council had the right to rescind his previous test vote and declare for acquittal. No one availed himself of this right, for Jesus himself had not opposed the verdict. Finally the President's name was called. He, too, replied: Death. Then he had the defendant brought in and pronounced the sentence.[n]

[6] Mark 14, 66 f.

126

Caiaphas' conduct of the trial was a masterpiece, from the point of view of formal legal procedure. In innumerable large and small points, which cannot be discussed in detail here, he had adhered with ostentatious pedantry to the letter of the law. Conflicts among various paragraphs of the law played an important part in the Jewish criminal code, and Caiaphas consistently played upon these to validate the fundamental decision of the council reported in John 11, 53. In other matters, to be sure, he committed infractions against the formal rules of procedure. But even the most scrupulous members of the council (Gamaliel, Johanan, Nathanael) raised no objections. Caiaphas could grant his associates spiritual dispensation at any time. He had solved the problem of schedule with particular cleverness. Jesus would have to be executed during the festival.[7] At the same time, however, public order must be guaranteed; this had been a concern of the authorities all along.[8] Both these ends were achieved by having the crucifixion take place precisely during the hours when the pious crowds were largely preoccupied with the ritual of the lambs and were also handicapped by fear of incurring defilement before the Passover meal. For this Caiaphas had to obtain from the Romans a quick confirmation and execution of the sentence.[9] His handling of this matter was his supreme coup. Because of the impending festival, Pilate was staying at the Praetorium in Jerusalem. There was no time to be lost; the High Priest and his attendants set out for the Praetorium at once, accompanied by the guards and their prisoner.

In the meantime Judas attempted to undo his crime, probably appealing to the Sanhedrin's edict: "If anyone knows anything in Jesus' favor, let him come forward and declare it." [n] But his remonstrance could in all legality be dismissed as having no substance.[1] For Jesus' blasphemy in court

[7] Appendix II, 86.   [8] Mark 14, 2.   [9] Appendix II, 112 f.   [1] Sanhedrin 5, 4; 6, 1.

weighed far more heavily than the desperate statement of a traitor: "I have sinned in betraying innocent blood." [2] In any case, Judas' objection came too late. Once the Great Sanhedrin had pronounced a death sentence upon a pseudo-prophet, the verdict was unassailable and irrevocable.[n] Judas realized that the avalanche he had started could no longer be checked, and put an end to his own life.[n]

➤➤➤-➤➤➤-➤➤➤ 5 ᛜᛜᛜ-ᛜᛜᛜ-ᛜᛜᛜ

THE POLITICAL TRIAL

IN PALESTINE it was the general practice in all official affairs to confront the Roman authorities with as noisy and large a delegation of dignitaries as could be mustered.[n] This was the strategy followed on that Friday morning. Caiaphas appeared before the Praetorium accompanied by the entire Sanhedrin.[3] We are told that the Passover meal was about to be eaten.[4] We also know that the legal authority of the Jews was limited.[n] These are valuable points for establishing the chronology of the events.

The Sanhedrin produced its charges. Not a word was spoken about the matters that had formed the subject of the religious trial. Here the indictment was altogether political: the defendant was an instigator of unrest, a partisan, a messianic king.[5] Pilate had already had more than one messianic king before his judgment seat, and he asked calmly: "Are you the King of the Jews?" Jesus affirmed that he was, but

[2] Matthew 27, 4. [3] Luke 23, 1; John 18, 28 ff. [4] John 18, 28.
[5] Luke 23, 2, and *passim*.

128

in a private hearing declared: "My kingship is not of this world." [6] Here was fresh confirmation for Pilate, who had already heard from his military tribune that Jesus on the Mount of Olives had forbidden resistance.[7] Jesus spoke of the kingdom of truth. This was enough for Pilate. Anyone who had made his career under the cynic Tiberius and the adventurer Sejanus, who had witnessed the events in the Empire during the past year, and who had managed to survive the past six months might well ask: "What is truth?" A Palestinian Jew who in the present state of world affairs could still speak of the kingdom of truth was certainly His Majesty's most harmless subject. "I find no crime in him," Pilate declared.[8]

Thereupon the accusers spoke of the torch of insurrection which Jesus had allegedly carried from Galilee to the south.[9] Seizing upon the cue of Galilee, Pilate hastened to turn Jesus over to the titular ruler of that country, who had likewise come to Jerusalem for the festival. Here was an easy gesture that enabled him to make amends for various slights by which he had offended the petty prince of Galilee.[n]

The whole parade of accusers went along to see Herod.[1] For Jesus "stood close to the government." [2] The Sanhedrin feared that the Galilean government would take the part of Jesus the Galilean, and thus foil their plans to destroy him. For in previous years the tetrarch had always "gladly heard" John the Baptist.[3] He had also long been eager to see Jesus.[4] John the Baptist unfortunately had been no miracle-worker.[5] Herod would have dearly liked to see Jesus perform a miracle, and for the sake of such a miracle was prepared to proffer his protection. But even in this hour Jesus disdained to help himself by a miracle.[n] He treated Herod with the same contempt he had earlier expressed,[6] and would not conde-

---

[6] John 18, 36.   [7] John 18, 11.   [8] John 18, 38.   [9] Luke 23, 5.   [1] Luke 23, 10.   [2] Sanhedrin 43 a.   [3] Mark 6, 20.   [4] Luke 9, 9.   [5] John 10, 41.
[6] Luke 13, 32.

scend to say a word to him. Angered, Herod listened readily to the charges against Jesus—obviously these must again have been political charges. Then he had the prisoner arrayed in the white robe of a Messiah, and in this costume of mockery sent him back to the Procurator.[n] The meaning was this: Herod thought it well to reply to the Roman's political gesture with an equally conciliatory gesture of his own; he renounced his legal authority over his own subject, and by dressing Jesus in a ridiculous costume signified that he took the defendant no more seriously than had the Procurator. "And Herod and Pilate became friends with each other that very day." Their newfound friendship was based on their common ridicule of this odd prisoner, and on a surreptitious smile at his overwrought accusers.[7]

Pilate wanted to have nothing more to do with the case, and discovered a new method of evading responsibility. "Now at the feast the governor was accustomed to release for the crowd any one prisoner whom they wanted." [8] No further details are known about this Passover amnesty,[n] but we may guess that it was a small concession granted to the Jews by way of compensating them for their loss of jurisdiction over capital crimes. At any rate, Pilate saw an opportunity to somewhat mitigate memories of the bloody rule that had prevailed while Sejanus was master in Rome, and made his offer to the people to set Jesus free. But the populace was browbeaten by the Sanhedrin's decision; the priesthood had by now won them over again completely; and they raised a great cry for the release of the scribe Barabbas, who had become a guerilla chieftain and now sat in the death cell.[9] Pilate had to be convinced that Jesus was far more dangerous to the state than the noted guerilla leader.

According to Mark and Matthew, the Procurator now condemned Jesus to death and let the customary scourging

[7] Luke 23, 12.   [8] Matthew 27, 15; Mark 15, 6.   [9] Mark 15, 11; John 18, 40.

130

take place. But according to certain hints in Luke[1] and the detailed account of John,[2] the Procurator hoped that the scourging and mocking would be sufficient and that he could yet save Jesus. By the barbarous legal practice of the Romans,[n] Jesus was first officially scourged, then unofficially left to the wanton sport of the soldiers. The crack cohort that had accompanied Pilate from Caesarea assembled rapidly. A scarlet lictor's cloak was placed on Jesus; the soldiers mocked and tormented him.[n] Pilate came forward, put an end to the business, and once again led the prisoner out to show him to his accusers: *"Ecce homo."* [3] But the priests refused to listen to Pilate's humanitarian suggestion. Amid the din of the crowd they shouted: "Crucify, crucify him!"

In Roman Palestine crucifixion was the usual means of executing a criminal who did not possess the rights of Roman citizenship.[n] In demanding this particular mode of punishment, Jesus' accusers intended to make public proclamation of three things. Slaves, rebels, and pseudo-prophets would normally be crucified. Now the false king was to be degraded by dying like a slave; Jesus was to die the death of a rebel to demonstrate the Sanhedrin's loyalty to the Emperor; and Jesus was to die the death of a blasphemer to make clear in the sight of God the piety of his accusers. Pilate said once more: "I find no crime in him."

Remembering what we have learned about Pilate from Luke 13, 1, from the testimony of Jewish and half-Jewish contemporaries, and from the evidence of his coins,[n] we are confronted with a riddle. For the Pilate we meet in the story of the Passion is not the brutal mass murderer who killed without qualm or trial the victims of his caprice and made a sport of affronting the Jews in every possible way. Instead we see a man who is making every effort to hand down a just judgment and save the life of an innocent man. A great deal

---

[1] Luke 23, 16. 20.   [2] John 19, 1 ff.   [3] John 19, 5.

has been written about the "apologetic" intent of the Gospels. It has been argued that they wished to make the Roman Procurator stand as a sterling witness to the political blamelessness of Christianity. However, it must be noted that the Pilate portrayed in the story of the Passion was not only anxious to acquit Jesus; shortly before, he had treated the case of Barabbas, the theologian's son and partisan leader, with a procastination that is really striking.[n] Pilate was not only reluctant to shed blood; he appears to have been extremely chary of any serious conflict with the Jews. Pilate's three attempts to save Jesus were all so arranged that they could not offend the leading Jews: the episode with Herod, Barabbas, *"Ecce homo."* In spite of some initial unpleasantness,[4] the tone of the negotiations was more than conciliatory; it bordered on obsequiousness. "What is your wish?" "What shall I do now?" "Shall I do this, or that?"[n] Pilate not only wanted both to spare the prisoner and to oblige the Sanhedrin; he also wanted to win the friendship of Herod.[5] These traits can scarcely have been ascribed to him by Evangelists intent on slanting the story. Rather, there emerges the picture of a man with no backbone, a portrait of an opportunist politician who has got himself into hot water and is concerned about his position. At what point had Pontius Pilate become so cautious, so complaisant, so in need of friendship? There can be only one answer to this question: since Sejanus had been put to death by Tiberius. Ever since October 19, A.D. 31, the Procurator no longer dared to pass death sentences that were in any way open to question. But he also no longer dared to provoke the leading Jews. He needed friends everywhere, in Jerusalem, in Tiberias, in Rome.[n] Pilate was in a corner. How is it, then, that in this predicament he nevertheless decided finally in favor of the execution of Jesus? Only the Fourth Gospel throws adequate light on this point.

[4] John 18, 30 ff.   [5] Luke 23, 7 ff.

132

The high priests were demanding the crucifixion of Jesus. Pilate insisted on the defendant's innocence. The political trial had reached an impasse, just as had the religious trial a few hours earlier. But again Caiaphas held his ground. At this point, finally, there began the great struggle between the politician and the high priest which was to decide the fate of Jesus.[6] And this time, too, Caiaphas had reserved a trump card for the last moment. Now he played it. "If you release this man, you are not Caesar's friend; every one who makes himself a king sets himself against Caesar."[7] And as soon as the Procurator heard this, his resistance collapsed.[8]

Pontius Pilate had always been disturbed by threats of a complaint to the Emperor.[n] This time he had a special reason for fear. For the title of Friend of Caesar, *amicus Cæsaris,* was an honor reserved for loyal senators, prominent knights, and meritorious administrators. It assured its holder a brilliant career. What loss of this title meant can be observed by the example of C. Cornelius Gallus, a Roman knight and the prefect of Egypt. On grounds of ingratitude and lese majesty Augustus stripped him of his *amicitia* and discharged him from government service. He was also forbidden admission to the imperial court, expelled from the equestrian order, and banned from the imperial provinces. Almost immediately a wave of denunciations, indictments, and annihilating decrees of the Senate descended upon C. Cornelius Gallus, making life impossible for him. In the year 26 B.C. he committed suicide.[n] The precedent that Augustus had established in this case was followed faithfully by Tiberius. It remained a warning to all administrative officials, especially in that critical winter after the fall of Sejanus. Pilate therefore knew what he might expect if Caiaphas were to go to the imperial government with his collection of incriminating evidence against the anti-Semitic Procurator of Judea, together with the latest story of Pilate's criminal leniency toward a subversive agi-

[6] John 19, 7 ff.   [7] John 19, 12.   [8] John 19, 13.

tator. Nor was Caiaphas a man given to empty threats. The situation was clear: if the Procurator released Jesus, he himself was done for; if he condemned Jesus, he could pose more convincingly than ever as the guardian of Rome and of Augustus in a restive land at a critical moment.

Hastily, Pilate mounted the judgment seat once more, hiding his fear behind a display of dignity. With the matter-of-factness of a secretary keeping minutes, the Fourth Evangelist notes the exact time and place of this memorable procedure.[9] Matthew describes how the Procurator washed his hands to demonstrate his innocence—to provide himself with a moral alibi—[1]while the crowd pronounced the terrible ancient formula of a conditional curse upon themselves.[2] Then Pontius Pilate asked the question: "Do you wish me to crucify your king?" And the priests who held the power in Palestine replied: "We have no king but Caesar."[3] Then Jesus was led away.

Pilate, however, had one more official act to perform. He dictated the *titulus,* the official description of the crime, which, according to Roman legal practice, had to be placed above the head of the crucified man. The words chosen were: JESUS NAZARENUS REX JUDEORUM. He ordered that the sign be written in three languages, so that everyone could read it. Pilate intended to cover himself politically, to be ready for all contingencies; and he desired both friend and foe to know that this was his attitude. The priests protested; they felt the subtle insult in this title. But Pilate paid no attention to them. He no longer needed to placate the Sanhedrin. He must have felt safer than he had for months. Once more he could indulge in the pleasure of baiting these people.

---

[9] John 19, 13 ff.   [1] Matthew 27, 24.   [2] Matthew 27, 25.   [3] John 19, 15.

⇶⇶⇶ 6 ⇷⇷⇷

THE CRUCIFIXION

A T NOON Pilate sent an execution squad and the three condemned men, in charge of a centurion, to the small hill of Golgotha outside the northwest wall of the city. The posts for the crosses already stood on the execution ground, left there from former crucifixions. The crossbeams had to be carried by the condemned men themselves. Following the old custom,[4] the leading women of Jerusalem met the party and gave them a jug of wine in which narcotic essences had been steeped. The mourning women accompanied the sad procession, uttering the wails and singing the songs of lamentation which were part of their trade. Jesus turned to them: "Daughters of Jerusalem, do not weep for me, but weep for yourselves and for your children."[5]

Outside the walls, on Gallows Hill, the condemned men were offered the narcotic drink.[6] Then the execution squad proceeded to its barbarous work. Jesus was crucified on the middle stake, the two criminals to his right and left. The leading men of the Sanhedrin appeared as witnesses.[7] Here Caiaphas had a priestly office to perform. He was waiting for the pseudo-prophet to confess his wrong and recant, thus "justifying" the Great Sanhedrin's death sentence. Then the grand inquisitor would have the right to—and would—absolve the apostate preacher, and the crucified man would die a blessed death.[8]

[4] Sanhedrin 43 a.   [5] Luke 23, 28.   [6] Mark 15, 23.   [7] Mark 15, 31.
[8] Appendix II, 81.

Tradition records the last words of virtually all the great personalities in history. By the very nature of the matter, these words have more or less to be taken on faith. The Gospels report seven sayings spoken by the crucified Jesus. One is found in Mark, the same one in Matthew, three more in Luke, and another three in John.[n] Are all these last words historical? Contemporary testimony indicates that crucified men at the place of execution were often surrounded by relatives, friends, and enemies, and that they spoke a good deal during the long and painful hours of waiting for death.[n] It is therefore by no means impossible that Jesus spoke all of the sayings which the four accounts of the crucifixion attribute to him. In fact, he probably said a great deal more. There was no lack of attentive witnesses to hear the words and pass them on. In this case, however, as in so many others, the Evangelists made no attempt to draw up a complete account. They set down only those sayings that appeared to them especially significant; in some instances they preserved only abbreviated key words of these sayings.

This last point must be remembered whenever we are dealing with quotations from Old Testament or liturgical texts. For ancient Jewish writers were accustomed to cite such texts only by the initial words, leaving the knowledgeable reader to fill in the entire text for himself. They did so even when the actual emphasis fell not upon the initial words, but upon later words that would not be cited. Consequently, we can neither accept nor reject the Gospel tradition of Jesus' last words out of hand. Every saying must be individually examined for its credibility. The prerequisite to any such objective examination is an adequate understanding of the background, in liturgy and in the particular circumstances, of each reported saying.

The first saying of Jesus on the cross was [9] an intercessory prayer: "Father, forgive them; for they know not what they

[9] Luke 23, 34.

136

do."[n] Attempts have been made to derive this saying from Isaiah 53, 12. But the text of Isaiah with which Jesus and the apostles were familiar spoke not of intercession, but of a voluntary death by way of sacrifice and atonement. This we now know because of the great scroll of Isaiah from Qumran.[n] Therefore the words of intercession cannot have been fabricated by the early church in the interests of its dogma and its desire to comply with Scripture. It must have been a genuine saying of Jesus, fully in the spirit expressed in the "love your enemies" passage in Matthew 5, 44. What is more, both Stephen and James the Just died martyrs' deaths with words of forgiveness on their lips, thus following the example set by Jesus on the cross.[n] But Jesus' saying differs from these others by the invocation at the beginning: "Father." Jesus directed a wholly personal appeal to "his" father, and prayed that the guilt might be lifted from the people for whom, shortly before, he had pronounced his apocalyptic lament;[1] he prayed for Caiaphas, who had brought him to the cross and who now stood by waiting to receive his recantation and to commend him at the last to the grace of God.

The bystanders, led by the priests, responded with shouts of mockery.[2] Only the thief sensed the hidden nobility of the man who was sharing the criminal's lot with him, and said to him: "Jesus, remember me when you come to your kingly power."[3] If these words were a fabrication of the primitive church and its special dogmas regarding the Christ, we would expect here that Jesus would be addressed as "Messiah" or "Lord." But in the oldest manuscripts, the form of address is the plain name "Jesus." Nevertheless, the malefactor invoked Jesus, as God himself was invoked in the formal language of liturgy: "Remember me." And Jesus replied in a similar manner, promising the criminal a place in Paradise unconditionally, as only God can promise: "To-day."

[1] Luke 23, 29.   [2] Luke 23, 35.   [3] Luke 23, 42.

Those standing beneath the cross were not only scoffers. Among the group were also the Apostle John and several of the faithful women from Galilee. Among these was Jesus' mother.[4] Mary's appearance at Golgotha was a declaration of adherence. By coming she was announcing that she belonged to the community of her outlawed son.[n] This meant cutting herself off from James and his brothers, who still held aloof from Jesus; and for a woman in ancient Palestine it meant that she was depriving herself of a home and protection at the very moment that she was losing her son in addition to the husband whom she had already lost. Jesus knew this. And a crucified man had the right to make testamentary dispositions even from the cross. Now Jesus took advantage of this right, and, using the formal language of Jewish family law, he placed his mother under the protection of John: "Woman, behold your son!" And to the disciple: "Behold your mother!" [5]

In all the Gospels there is a kind of break at this point.[n] Jesus hung silent on the cross, perhaps unconscious for a time. The high priests vanished, and henceforth are mentioned no more in any of the accounts. The other members of the Sanhedrin also withdrew. Where to? They were going to attend services. At half past one o'clock in the afternoon the daily liturgy began in the temple. On this day it would be taking place earlier than usual because this year the eve of the Passover coincided with the eve of the Sabbath [6] and an extensive program of ritual had to be completed before the Sabbath rest began at six o'clock. First of all, the lamb for the daily sacrifice at the temple had to be slaughtered.[n] Then the twenty-four elders of the priestly orders, who were present in the Holy City only on the three great pilgrimage feasts, assembled for the sacred ritual of atonement which marked the eve of the Passover. The innumerable Passover lambs

[4] Mark 15, 40; John 19, 25.   [5] John 19, 26 f.   [6] Mark 15, 42; John 19, 14.

138

were slaughtered, and the priests sprinkled the expiatory
Passover blood upon the altar. Meanwhile the temple trumpets announced the hours of prayer and summoned the
whole city to evening worship. The Passover slaughtering
continued. The Levites struck their harps and sang the
psalm: "I shall not die, but I shall live, and recount the deeds
of the Lord. . . . The stone which the builders rejected
has become the chief cornerstone."[7] Trumpets and bugles
proclaimed far and wide the solemn event—God at the blood-
sprinkled altar was making a covenant of reconciliation and
peace with his people. Then the festive crowd, bearing their
lambs, left the temple mount; the Passover lambs were
brought home to be roasted, and before six o'clock the fathers
of the families commenced the Passover meal, on this day
beginning with the Sabbath blessing that renewed the memory of the Seventh Day of Creation:

"Thus the heaven and the earth were finished and all
the host of them. And on the seventh day God finished his
work which he had done, and he rested on the seventh day
from all his work . . . which he had created through his
logos." [n]

At the place of execution outside the city wall all had
grown quieter by one o'clock. Only the indispensable witnesses of the execution were still standing beneath the
crosses, and a number of curiosity-seekers, a few women, and
some friends.[n] The soldiers of the guard played dice. The
centurion was prepared for a long afternoon and evening.
Crucified men usually took many hours to die.[n]

"At the ninth hour Jesus cried out with a loud voice,
'Eloi, Eloi, lama sabachthani?' which means, 'My God, my
God, why hast thou forsaken me?'"[8]

In the Qumran psalms the "teacher of righteousness" declares again and again: "Thou hast not forsaken me [*lo
asabthani*]."[n] Jesus said otherwise. He had put his trust in a

[7] Psalm 118, 17. 22.   [8] Mark 15, 34.

God whom he alone knew, no one else.[9] He had proclaimed this God as a man of the ancient world had to do, in a world in which there were many gods: [n] this is my God, the God in whom I believe, the God who cries to you through the instrument of my voice. He had testified to this belief in his God and this claim on God in that moment of confession before the highest ecclesiastical tribunal of his people, testified in the boldest imaginable manner.[1] For that act he had been condemned to death.[2] Would the God whom Jesus had proclaimed now reveal himself before the eyes and ears of Jesus' judges, return faith for faith, and acknowledge Jesus as his? Nothing of the sort happened. The God whom he had faithfully professed had abandoned him. He had publicly forsaken him. So Jesus himself declared. There can be no doubt that the passage in Mark 15, 34, is genuine. No one in the primitive church would have dared to invent such a saying. And no analyst of the Gospels has any right to minimize the importance of this saying. None of the Qumran heretics had ever been so forsaken by God as the crucified heretic on Golgotha.

But even in the inferno of his abandonment by God, Jesus did not surrender his faith in God. Eli, Eli . . . He did not die renouncing God.[n] He clung fast to "his" God, called to him: "My God, my God." The God of Jesus had forsaken his prophet, but Jesus would not let him go. His faith cried out, but did not waver; not for a moment did he waver. In that exclamation he attained his ultimate freedom and independence, his ultimate boldness and maturity, his ultimate humanity. At that moment he realized his most mysterious potentiality.

The prayer Jesus uttered on the cross was Psalm 22. In accordance with the Jewish practice in citation discussed above, Mark sets down the initial verse of the psalm. Presumably, however, Jesus spoke the entire psalm, at least as far as

[9] Matthew 11, 27.   [1] Mark 14, 62.   [2] Mark 14, 64.

the cry of thirst,[n] and probably right on to the serene concluding verse.[3] Certainly this was not the recantation that the high priest had been waiting for, nor the despairing cry of a shattered spirit. What the bystanders heard was a psalm that played a conspicuous role in Jewish messianic theology in the time of Jesus.[n] To the scribes and priests this was the most frightful of blasphemies, to hear a condemned man on the accursed rood praying this eschatological psalm of suffering. Yet at this point no one was inclined to rend his garments as a demonstrative act against the blasphemer.[n] Instead, they refused to admit the meaning of the words, pretended they were other than they were, deliberately misheard, and, jeering, said: "Behold, he is calling Elijah." [4] They mocked at his thirst and offered him vinegar to drink.[5]

Jesus prayed the twenty-second psalm "at the ninth hour" —that is to say, between two and three o'clock in the afternoon. From then on the only prayers Jesus used were the prayers of his forefathers, the prayers for the Sabbath, for night, and for death. But in the mouth of the crucified Jesus they acquired a new and unique meaning. He prayed, by way of anticipation of the Sabbath that he would not see, the blessing for the Sabbath, prayed in a murmur as would a man weary unto death: "And thus was finished . . . and God finished . . . and rested from all his work." Out of this prayer the Evangelist John retained only a single word— perhaps he heard only that one word clearly—the decisive word that occurred twice: "Finished." He took this as the essence, the central meaning of all the work of Christ. What God had begun by the Word in the days of the Creation, God finished by the Word in the days of the Redemption.[6] Jesus, looking back upon the work of his life, could declare: "It is finished." [n]

At three o'clock the trumpets of the temple resounded

[3] Psalm 22, 31.   [4] Mark 15, 35.   [5] Mark 15, 36; John 19, 29.   [6] John 1, 3; 19, 28.

throughout the city. The hour of evening prayer had come. Jesus on the cross heard it, and spoke the prayer that all Israel was praying at this hour: "In thy hand are the souls of the living and the dead. . . . Into thy hands I commend my spirit, thou hast redeemed me, O Lord, thou God of truth. . . . In the name of the Lord, the God of Israel: may Michael be at my right hand, Gabriel at my left hand, before me Uriel, behind me Raphael, and above my head the presence of God." [n] Jesus, however, spoke the prayer in the form in which he had learned it in childhood: "Abba, into thy hands I commit my spirit." He pronounced the words in a loud voice, as custom required.[n] His mother, who long before had taught him this very prayer, was standing at a distance, and listened. "And having said this, he breathed his last." [n]

When the soldiers came to break the limbs of the crucified men, in order to cut short their ordeal and hasten their removal, Jesus was already dead. This, says the Fourth Evangelist, was in fulfillment of the prophecy that "not a bone of him shall be broken." [7] By the beginning of the Sabbath, Jesus already lay in his grave—and rested on the Seventh Day.[8]

Jesus was not buried casually in potter's field,[9] but was interred in an honorable tomb.[n] From this we may conclude that Pilate and some of Jesus' Jewish judges were no longer easy in their consciences.[n] According to Matthew and the Judao-Christian tradition of Jesus, the tomb was guarded for several days.[1] These accounts have been partly embellished by legend and apologetics, but they include many ancient elements and possibly a nucleus of history.[n]

The Synoptic chronology of the Passion is self-contradictory.[n] If on the night of the arrest the police forces of the Sanhedrin went out to the Mount of Olives armed with wooden clubs,[2] that night could not have been the holiday

[7] John 19, 36.   [8] John 19, 31. 42.   [9] Appendix II, 95.   [1] Matthew 27, 62 ff.   [2] Mark 14, 43.

night after the official Passover meal.[3] The Fourth Gospel is perfectly plain: it fixes the time of Jesus' death as that of the ritual of the Passover lamb.[n] The Book of Revelation gives the same timetable.[n] Likewise Paul,[n] likewise Peter,[n] likewise Tatian,[n] likewise the ancient rabbinical tradition already quoted: "On the eve of the passover Jeshu of Nazareth was executed." [n] A similar time was later given by the *Toledoth Jeshu.*[n]

⋙⋙⋙ 7 ⋘⋘⋘

THE EMPTY TOMB

ON THE MORNING after the Sabbath rest the women and disciples found the tomb of Jesus empty. Thus the Four Gospels unanimously relate, and also the fragments of Judao-Christian gospels. But the Gospels contain neither the first nor the only accounts of the empty tomb. There has never been a Christian tradition concerning Jesus or the tidings of resurrection which did not stress the empty tomb. This is revealed in the phraseology used in regard to Easter, which did not vary from the beginning to the end of the apostolic age. The crucial underlying ideas were always those of "awaking" and "arising." They are older than Christianity itself, already to be found fully formulated in Daniel 12, 2. 13. The saints of God are to "sleep" until God "awakens" them on the Last Day. Then they will "arise" and leave their graves as a man leaves his bed in the morning.[n] Such were the tidings the apostles unremittingly proclaimed from

[3] In spite of Mark 14, 12.

Easter on: the resurrection of the dead, which God has promised for the Last Days, had already begun. The Lord had "risen." Everywhere that this term is encountered in connection with the Easter tidings, the fact of Jesus' empty tomb is presupposed. And it begins to occur regularly and indisputably in the oldest formulation of the Christian tidings with which we are acquainted: the Petrine formulae in the Acts of the Apostles.[n] We find the same point in the pre-Pauline profession of Christ in 1 Corinthians 15, 4; in the Epistles of Paul;[4] in all the Gospels; in the late apostolic age. The entire primitive church unanimously testified to this fact: that on Easter morning the tomb of Jesus was empty. And even Jesus' opponents reluctantly—and therefore all the more credibly—bear witness to the fact of the empty tomb. This includes both Jewish opponents and, as new evidence indicates, Roman opponents also.

According to Acts 2 ff., the tidings of the first Apostles in Jerusalem frequently encountered extreme resistance—but no one ever took issue with their tale of the empty tomb, although the tomb of Jesus was only a few hundred yards from the walls of Jerusalem. According to Matthew,[5] not even the Sanhedrin dared to contest the fact of the empty tomb; instead it endeavored to find a rational explanation which would also serve its own interests, and put forward the theory that the disciples had stolen the body of Jesus. Matthew, who was writing his account in Palestine or Syria between A.D. 65 and 70, expressly adds: "And this story has been spread among the Jews to this day."[6] For Justin Martyr, writing in the second century, the controversy was still a live one. In the course of his argument he mentions an official circular letter of the Sanhedrin, and apparently quotes verbatim the key sentences: "A certain Jesus of Galilee, an apostate preacher whom we crucified; but his disciples stole him by

[4] Romans 6, 4, and elsewhere.　[5] Matthew 28, 1 ff.　[6] Matthew 28, 15.

night from the tomb in which he had been placed after his removal from the cross; they did this in order to persuade men to apostasy by saying that he has awakened from the dead and ascended into heaven." [n] Eusebius, in his commentary on Isaiah 18, 1, also mentions a circular letter of this sort issued by the Great Sanhedrin, apparently in keeping with the regulation that it keep the people informed of its acts.[7][n] John [8] assumes and refutes another such discreditable rumor: that the gardener had for some reason secretly removed Jesus' body. Tertullian is familiar with both theories, theft by the disciples and removal by the gardener, and heaps scorn upon the gardener's alleged motive: that in haste and secrecy he had removed the body of Jesus so that his lettuce seedlings should not be trampled by the crowd of visitors to the tomb which might be expected.[n] We find both these theories set down, in a number of variations and connections, in the *Toledoth Jeshu*. There it is expressly stated that the Jewish authorities themselves examined the grave and found it empty.[n]

Matthew already suggests that the story of the disciples' stealing of the corpse was fabricated principally in order to offset the effect the report of the empty tomb would have upon the Romans.[9] Eusebius tells us that within a short time all of Palestine buzzed with the tale.[1] Roman administrative chiefs in the provinces were required to report to the imperial government on all important events, measures, and problems within their jurisdiction.[n] Pilate would have had to make a report on the execution of Jesus, and he must have been particularly conscientious about all such official duties during those critical months. Had any rumors been circulating concerning the tomb of Jesus, he would not have dared to ignore them or fail to report them. According to Tertullian, the Procurator had sent an account of the situation to Rome by

[7] Sanhedrin 11, 3.   [8] John 20, 15.   [9] Matthew 28, 12 ff.   [1] *Historia Ecclesiastica*, 2, 2, 1.

the speediest couriers, and had asked for instructions: "This whole story of Christ was reported to the emperor by Pilate. . . . Nothing was found in the tomb but the cloths in which he was buried. The chief men of the Jews . . . spread the story about that the disciples had stolen him." [2]

Eusebius, too, speaks of the report made by Pilate.[n] Tertullian was a lawyer, and Eusebius had excellent connections at the imperial court. Their accounts therefore at least deserve consideration. But Tertullian and Eusebius were Christians. Do we have any non-Christian references to the existence of such a report by Pilate? There must once have been such. For in Eusebius we also find mention of pagan records, actual documents of Pilate's on the subject of Jesus.[n] Unfortunately, these have been lost. They must surely have been forged—presumably by pagans wishing to parry the so-called documents of Pilate which Christian and pro-Christian apologists were always forging. But their value as evidence consists precisely in this: that the pagan forgers never attempted to deny the Procurator's duty to file a report. Rather, they shared with the Christian forgers whose work they were combating the assumption that Pilate had had to report to the Emperor on the case of Jesus of Nazareth.

One original document dating back to the oldest controversy over the empty tomb is, probably, the Inscription of Nazareth, which has been preserved in Paris since 1878 and which was published in 1930. It is a summary of an imperial edict directed against the robbery of corpses and the desecration of graves. Perhaps it is based upon a rescript of Emperor Tiberius, and may possibly be the Emperor's reply to Pontius Pilate's report on Jesus, the empty tomb, and the rumors that the body had been stolen.[n]

Paul expounds the significance of the empty tomb in terms of historical theology by drawing upon the chronology

---

[2] *Apologeticus*, 21. Translation by T. R. Glover, Loeb Classical Library. Cf. ibid. 5.

of the days of the Passion. Jesus had been executed on the eve of the Passover, as God's Passover lamb.[3] He rose again on the second day of the Passover week. This second holiday was called, in the Passover calendar, the Day of the First Fruits. For it was on this day that gifts of the first fruits of the new harvest were brought to the temple.[n] In this timing Paul saw a divine pledge: the Risen One was "the first fruits of those who have fallen asleep." [4] He was the first fruits who promised the coming harvest, the beginning and archetype, the guarantee and forecast of the coming awakening of the dead.[5] At any moment, Paul felt, the next events in the divine program for the end of the world might unfold. Then the dead would arise from their sleep and leave their graves, just as Christ awakened on Easter morning and left behind him the empty tomb.[n]

∗∗∗∗∗∗∗∗∗ 8 ∗∗∗∗∗∗∗∗∗

THE APPEARANCES OF CHRIST

T HE EMPTY TOMB was a "sign" susceptible to many interpretations.[6] The Christian interpretation of it was determined by the epiphanies, the successive appearances of the risen Christ.[n] The pre-Pauline creed,[7] which probably originated in Antioch, gives the earliest list of these appearances.

Peter leads off the list—chronologically speaking. That is to say, Peter was the first of the Twelve Apostles to whom

---

[3] 1 Corinthians 5, 7.   [4] 1 Corinthians 15, 20.   [5] 1 Corinthians 15, 23 ff.
[6] Cf. Mark 16, 8; John 20, 2.   [7] 1 Corinthians 15, 3 ff.

Christ appeared. The evidence for this is to be found not only in the New Testament, not only among the adherents and friends of Peter; his adversaries testify to it also.[n] In the days of the primitive church, Peter's primacy was always regarded as a doubly significant token in view of Peter's preceding denial of Jesus. Christ's appearance to Peter, like all the other appearances, was in the nature of a call.[8] The crucial words to Peter are given in the Gospels in differing versions, and dated at different times.[n] But their historical meaning is everywhere the same, everywhere unambiguous: that Jesus was now confirming the promise he had made years before when he conferred the name of Peter upon Simon [9] and appointed him the responsible leader of the future church. Without that first appearance before Peter, without an express call on the part of the risen Christ, the special position of Peter in the primitive church would be historically incomprehensible. For Peter was not the man to forge such a special position for himself by virtue of his personality.[n]

Only one other individual besides Peter is mentioned by name among the witnesses. This was James the Just.[1] There is only the merest mention in the New Testament of this special appearance before James, but the incident is cited also in a semi-legendary fragment of the Judao-Christian gospel tradition which is preserved by Jerome.[2] There the appearance to James is given as Christ's first appearance. This suggests that the verse 1 Corinthians 15, 7, existed originally in some separate source, and that we have here an old list rivaling that of 1 Corinthians 15, 5.[n] In the latter, Peter comes first, in the former, James; in both instances the other disciples take second place.[n] Here we catch a glimpse of an ancient contest over priority between Peter and James the Just. Both lay claim to having been the first to see the Risen Lord; both base their claim to primacy in the church upon

[8] Cf. 1 Corinthians 15, 8.   [9] John 1, 42; Mark 3, 16; cf. p. 80.
[1] 1 Corinthians 15, 7.   [2] *De viris illustribus,* 2.

this matter. For in both cases the epiphanies signify a special
call.

In the West, Peter was the victor. In Antioch there existed
a special and highly important local tradition concerning
Peter; this was why the Antioch list of the witnesses of
Christ's appearances placed Peter's name at the head. Paul
was closely connected with the tradition of the Antiochian
church; consequently, he took over this Antiochian list
headed by Peter's name. The Western gospel tradition mentioned only the appearance before Peter [n] and said nothing at
all of the epiphany before James.

The Judao-Christian gospel tradition of Jerusalem and the
Semitic East took issue with this, and emphatically insisted
that James, pontifex maximus of the East, had been vouch-
safed the first appearance of Christ.[n] These asseverations
carried no weight in the West. The Judao-Christian gospels
were rejected out of hand. In Antioch the Jamesian version
of things was simply incorporated into the story; the Anti-
ochians seem to have been sublimely unconcerned that this
resulted in a doubling of the appearances of Christ before the
Twelve Apostles.[n] Nevertheless, the epiphany before James
could not be entirely suppressed even in the victorious list of
the Western church. Paul could not ignore the special epiphany granted his great antagonist. He contented himself with
weakening its effect by placing himself at the end of the list.
The Acts of the Apostles favored the traditional policies of
the Western church, while at the same time attempting to
reconcile differences. Consequently, in Acts nothing is said
of the special appearance before James, but at the same time
it is indicated that James was a Christian by the day of the
Ascension, if not sooner, and his brothers likewise.[3] James
was the oldest of the sons of Joseph, and we may conclude
from Acts 1, 14, that he had immediately brought his
younger brothers Joseph, Judas, and Simon into the group

[3] Acts 1, 14.

of disciples. James succeeded in doing what Jesus had failed to do all his life—to win over the sons of Joseph. Subsequently, James accomplished a great deal more. It is impressive to see what this man made of his call, his birth, his church.[n]

The name of the Apostle John is not to be found at all in the Antiochian list of witnesses. None of the Gospels speaks of a special appearance of Christ to John, not even the Gospel of this favorite disciple. It is true that the Johannine school later made a timid and halfhearted attempt to claim a special place for the favorite disciple in the history of Christ's appearances. In John 21, 7, John appears as the first to recognize the risen Jesus. But this is, as it were, an afterthought, born of the general overemphasis upon Christ's appearances. John the Apostle attaches no importance to having seen the risen Christ himself, nor to the testimony of others to his appearances. "Blessed are those who have not seen and yet believe." [4] His concern is with the historical Jesus of Nazareth.[5] For him personally the empty tomb is enough.[6] He lays the greatest stress upon the circumstance that he and not Peter was the first witness to the empty tomb, that he and he alone regards the empty tomb not only as the starting-point of faith in the Easter miracle, but also as a sufficient foundation for it. The favorite disciple sees the empty tomb and believes.[7] He needs no additional epiphanies. It is this that gives to the Johannine annunciation of the Christ and to the Easter message their unique and unassailable positions in the controversy centering around the appearances of Christ —a controversy initiated principally by Paul.[n]

According to the Gospel of John,[8] the first person to see and recognize the risen Christ was neither Peter nor James the Just nor John the Apostle, but a woman, Mary Magdalene. Mark,[9] too, forcefully stresses the priority of Mary Mag-

[4] John 20, 29.   [5] John 1, 14, 39.   [6] John 20, 2 ff.   [7] John 20, 8.
[8] John 20, 11 ff.   [9] Mark 16, 9.

150

dalene. But in the list of witnesses in 1 Corinthians 15, 5 ff., Mary Magdalene is not mentioned at all. Why is this? Because she was a woman. Under Jewish law, women were not qualified to bear witness.[1] Therefore the primitive church refrained from including female witnesses in this list. And, indeed, in the Gospel accounts of Easter we can sense distinctly how inconvenient, troublesome, and embarrassing all female testimonies to the resurrection seemed to the men of the early church.[n] Hence we can be certain that the early church did not invent these accounts. On the contrary, it did its best to suppress them, led by Paul, who was pre-eminently a student of the Torah.[2]

Only the Fourth Evangelist had the historical and theological courage to proclaim the unrivaled priority of Mary Magdalene as being the first to have seen Jesus after his resurrection; John alone included her in his story of the apostolic Easter tidings.[3] In so doing he was certainly acting in the spirit of Jesus. For no account of the appearances so plainly points up the synonymity of the risen Christ with the historical Jesus as does this first appearance before Mary Magdalene. Christ's appearance before the faithless first apostle reveals the loyalty and mercy of the Lord.[4] That first appearance before the despised and frightened girl from Magdala was a manifestation of the unqualified kindness of Jesus Christ, a kindness without precedent.

There are a number of divergent accounts concerning Christ's appearance before the Twelve.[n] In addition, there were the appearances to Thomas, to the disciples at Emmaus, to the hundreds of brethren, and others.[n]

In these various accounts the Gospels aimed at conveying three facts. In the first place, the risen Christ was a vital personality who acted according to a definite plan, bearing witness to himself by appearing whenever, wherever, however,

[1] Appendix II, 72.   [2] Cf. 1 Corinthians 14, 34 f.   [3] John 20, 17 f.
[4] Luke 22, 31 f.; John 21, 17.

and before whomever he pleased. In the second place, the risen Christ existed in a new form of existence whose character was neither spiritualistic nor materialistic. He was not a man, like the reawakened Lazarus; yet he had flesh and blood and partook of food in the presence of his disciples. He was not a ghost, no "materialization" of a dead man who still lay in the grave; and nevertheless he could pass through closed doors. The Evangelists and their authorities could not explain this; they could only state it as a fact, only "testify" to it. The appearances of the risen Christ are genuine signs, simultaneously overwhelming and debatable. Here is a miracle whose validity some will always doubt. Even the disciples could not bring themselves to believe the testimony of the first eyewitnesses.[5]

The opponents of Jesus had their own explanation of the appearance of Christ, just as they had of the empty tomb. They contended[n] that Jesus had always practiced magical raisings of the dead, and that his own "resurrection" was nothing but a necromantic trick.[n] By way of rejoinder the Gospels all emphasize the inseparable relation between the appearances and the empty tomb, and insist that Jesus was not a bodiless *pneuma*.[6] John is making a similar point when he develops the numerous analogies between the resurrection of Lazarus and the resurrection of Jesus.[7] The Judao-Christian tradition of Jesus also states emphatically that the Risen One was no "bodiless demon."[n] Jesus himself hands the high priest's servant his shroud, as a sign that he has risen in the body.[n] Among the Jewish Christians there is evident a tendency, even more radical and anti-Pauline than in the Fourth Gospel, to refrain from all "proofs of sight." In so doing they hoped to outflank those of the opposite camp who might attack the story of the resurrection as wholly subjective and unverifiable. Pagan authors took up the arguments of the Jewish opponents and scoffed at the hysterical hallucinations

[5] Mark 16, 14; John 20, 29.　　[6] Luke 24, 37 ff.　　[7] John 11, 42 ff.

of Mary Magdalene and the magical practices of the disciples.[n] These controversies seem to have been raging early in the apostolic age. For we find Matthew [8] bringing forward the Roman guards as witnesses to the resurrection. The pagans nevertheless continued to argue that Jesus had appeared only to his followers,[n] and this thesis has often been repeated by Christian dogmatists. But it is overturned by 1 Corinthians 15, 7 f. For before the resurrected Christ showed himself, James was neutral or skeptical, and Paul a fanatical opponent of Jesus.

The epiphany of Jesus was not an occult manifestation, but a historical summons. This is true of the special appearances before individuals,[9] but also of the appearance before the Twelve. Thus, Matthew [1] speaks of the command that the risen Christ gave to the Twelve to go out among the nations to baptize.[2] In fact, the period between Easter and Pentecost ushered in a new development in the evolution of Christian baptism. During the first weeks of A.D. 28, John had come forward proclaiming the necessity for baptism. Soon Jesus entered the new baptist movement as an active member, and his disciples proclaimed and performed the Baptist's baptism until about the end of the year 29.[3] Then Jesus withdrew from sight of the public for many months. In the autumn of 30 he gathered his disciples about him again and began a new ministry of his own, in which no mention is ever made of any practice of baptism. This ministry ended with the crucifixion in the spring of 32. A few weeks later the disciples of Jesus came forward with an entirely new message of baptism, and baptized thousands, in the name of Jesus, the Risen Christ. How had this new rite of baptism arisen? According to Matthew, it rested on a command given by the Risen Christ.

[8] Matthew 28, 11.   [9] Galatians 1, 15 f.   [1] Matthew 28, 19 f.   [2] Cf. Mark 16, 15 f.   [3] John 4, 1 f.

VIII

JESUS' WITNESS TO HIMSELF

⟫⟫⟫ 1 ⟪⟪⟪

THE WORLD'S END?

IT USED TO BE THOUGHT that the message of Jesus had been, above all, the proclamation of the approaching end of the world, and that all his words and acts were more or less bound up with this imminent expectation. Taking this idea as their starting-point, some persons therefore wondered whether a psychiatric investigation of the personality of Jesus

154

would not be in order,[n] and even adduced Mark 3, 21: "He is beside himself." But, as we have already seen, this phrase was a mere stratagem on the part of Jesus' friends, spoken at a critical moment in which the question of imminent expectation of the end was not at all under discussion (see page 85).

Jesus was convinced that the history of God and his creation had a goal.[1] But he did not consider it his task to enlighten mankind regarding the end of all things and the wonders of the world to come. Nor did he ever belong among those who proclaimed tidings of the coming end of the world. That Jesus' message did not have this eschatological character can be proved on three counts. One of these derives from examination of the sources, the second from theological controversy, and the third from the history of ideas.

Source criticism reveals that among the *Logia* there was not a single saying about the approaching end of the world. Apparently this fact has hitherto gone unnoticed, but it deserves reflection. For the *Logia* in all probability represent the oldest of Christendom's books on Jesus. To be sure, not all of the sayings are authentic and unfalsified; many are colored by the theology of John the Baptist's adherents, or by that of the primitive church, and have little or nothing to do with Jesus. In the light of these influences it is all the more astonishing and remarkable that no saying concerning the imminent end of all things found its way into the *Logia*.

On the history of controversies: the silence of the *Logia* has its counterpart in the silence of Jesus' opponents. It has likewise gone unnoticed hitherto that polemical writings say not a word about fanatical eschatological statements on the part of Jesus; neither the Jewish contemporaries of Jesus whom we meet in the New Testament, nor those in the

[1] Luke 11, 2.

ancient rabbinical texts mention the matter. If Jesus had been a prophet of the imminent end of the world, the polemical writers of the post-apostolic age would surely have made a point of it, and would not have missed the opportunity to scoff at the failure of such prophecies.

From the history of ideas we learn that apocalyptics and oracles prophesying the imminent end of the world were extremely common among the Palestinian Jews in the age of the New Testament.[n] We need only recall the Baptist's movement, to which Jesus, too, belonged for a while. But even in those early days, and, above all, during the time of his principal ministry in Galilee, Jesus went far beyond the Baptist; this is true both for the content of his message and its effect on history. What distinguished his message from that of the Baptist's community, and what was the secret of his unique historical impact?

In the oldest of the gospels the first words spoken by Jesus are "The time [*kairos*] is fulfilled." [2] Not the future but the present was the decisive element in Jesus' message; he was concerned with his own time. In this his message differed fundamentally from the apocalyptic tidings of the day, including those of John the Baptist. The kingdom of God is in the midst of you.[n] Satan is cast down.[3] He is strong, his might is far beyond human powers, but one stronger than he has bound him.[4] "But if it is by the finger of God that I cast out demons, then the Kingdom of God has come upon you." [5] This "today," Jesus says, has been the goal of all history since the very beginning.[n] Today is being made the decision as to the nature of tomorrow, the decision on the historical function and destiny of Peter, on the salvation or destruction of Jerusalem, on the future of mankind.

The disciples and followers of Jesus did not understand this message of the importance of the present moment. They

[2] Mark 1, 15.   [3] Luke 10, 18.   [4] Mark 3, 27.   [5] Luke 11, 20; cf. Mark 1, 24.

were wholly children of their times, furiously tossed upon
the waves of Jewish political and apocalyptic messianism,
inflamed by hopes that the coming of the Messiah was imminent. Jesus was not at all fond of the messianic idea (see
pages 160 ff.). His disciples and contemporaries, however,
continued to regard Jesus as the secret Messiah and went on
hoping from week to week that he would seize power, reveal himself to the full in triumph and glory.

After the apocalyptic feast during the agitated Passover of
the year 31 the Galileans were all ready to proclaim their
fellow countryman Jesus as the Messiah.[6] According to
Mark,[7] Peter said to Jesus: "You are the Christ"—imagining
that Jesus would promptly respond to this acclamation by
proclaiming himself the Messiah, setting himself at the head
of his disciples and friends, and marching on Jerusalem.
James and John, their minds dominated by the spirit of political messianism, proposed that the Samaritans be wooed by
an apocalyptic miracle, the bringing down of fire from
heaven.[8] The two sons of Zebedee asked, in view of the impending seizure of power, for the two places of honor beside
the throne of the Messiah.[9] Jesus, however, was not pleased
by the messianic salutation, "Son of David."[1] At Jericho he
had great difficulty curbing the enthusiasts who were convinced that the apocalyptic kingdom of the Messiah would
dawn immediately after Jesus' entry into Jerusalem.[2] In Bethany he interpreted the anointment, which was intended in a
messianic sense, in terms of his coming Passion.[3] In Jerusalem the excited disciples and pilgrims celebrated the arrival
of Jesus as a messianic advent.[4] At Gethsemane Peter drew
his sword, intending to evoke the assistance of the heavenly
legions in the messianic war.[5] But all these messianic hopes
on the part of the disciples were dashed. Jesus died with-

[6] John 6, 14 f.   [7] Mark 8, 29.   [8] Luke 9, 54.   [9] Mark 10, 37.   [1] Luke
18, 38 ff.   [2] Luke 19, 11.   [3] Mark 14, 8.   [4] Mark 11, 8 ff., etc.   [5] Mark
14, 47; Matthew 26, 51 ff.; John 18, 10 ff. 36.

out defending himself; no miracle saved him from the cross, and the disciples could only confess resignedly: "We had hoped [again and again] that he was the one to redeem Israel." ⁿ

A great deal of light is thrown upon the whole problem of eschatological expectations in that brief dialogue on the cross recorded in Luke 23, 42 f. The thief pleaded: "Jesus, remember me when you come in your kingly power." ⁿ Here we have, focused upon Jesus, the popular, apocalyptic expectations of the times. The thief was aware of the inscription on the cross and took the INRI in earnest, believing that it meant the kingdom would be coming soon. Jesus, was to be the messianic ruler of the kingdom of God.[6] Jesus, however, promised that the thief's prayer would be fulfilled in a manner beyond the man's belief. "Truly, I say to you, today you will be with me in Paradise." Jesus tacitly but unmistakably corrects the eschatological hopes of the petitioner. His reply says nothing whatsoever about the coming kingdom of the Messiah; it speaks only of the "now," only (in the figurative language of parables which Jesus loved) of "Paradise." There can be no doubt that this reply was not invented by the early church.

For amid the portentous events of Easter the buried hopes of a Messiah stirred once more, and with renewed force: "Lord, will you at this time restore the kingdom to Israel?" [7] The resurrection of the dead had begun. According to Jewish belief, however, the resurrection was only the first act of the eschatological drama. Therefore the end of all things was at hand. As long as Jesus lived he did his best to check the messianic expectations of his disciples. He always flatly refused to make any prediction concerning the time that the world would come to an end.[8] But now the eschatological fever reached its height, and spread in widening circles.[9] The

[6] Cf. Mark 10. 37.   [7] Acts 1, 6.   [8] Mark 13, 32; Acts 1, 7.   [9] Acts 2, 39 ff.

first Apostles, Paul, James the Just, and the kinsfolk of Jesus were all seized by it.[n] Anyone who would not believe in the approaching end of the world was considered a poor Christian.

In such an atmosphere a good many spurious oracular sayings may have penetrated into the traditions concerning Jesus. A few sayings about a second coming may have been construed from genuine phrases of Jesus.[n] Others were probably devised by the primitive church in order to bolster those whose faith in the approaching end of the world was beginning to waver.[n] In addition, Jewish prophecies, either recent or of older date, were soon being passed along as the Lord's sayings.[n] The Gospel of Matthew, written in the apocalyptic years shortly before the destruction of Jerusalem, displays most clearly the church's tendency to multiply the number of oracular sayings having to do with the end of the world.[n] Genuine sayings of Jesus were reinterpreted or rephrased to accord with this expectation of the imminent end.[n] Jesus' message in regard to the present time was thrust into the background, and John the Baptist's proclamation of the approaching Kingdom of Heaven was henceforth regarded as a complete general formulation that covered the message of Jesus and of the Apostles also.[n] The end of the world was considered to be so close that the Apostles would have to accelerate their missionary work, and could not, for that reason alone, take time to go among the Samaritans or the pagans.[1] "You will not have gone through all the towns of Israel, before the Son of Man comes."[n]

Inevitably, reactions set in. The siege and destruction of Jerusalem (A.D. 70) took its course without the hoped-for appearance of the messianic kingdom. There was real danger that belief in Jesus would be shaken by the failure of his pseudo-messianic oracular sayings to come true. In this critical situation, certain of the alleged sayings of the Lord

[1] Matthew 10, 5 ff.

159

concerning the imminent end of the world were qualified, as for example in Mark 13, 32.[n] But the hope persisted for a long time[n] among Christians, and caused a good many ironic smiles among Jews and pagans.[n]

⤜⤜⤜ 2 ⤛⤛⤛

THE MESSIAH

THE WORD "Messiah" was not used by Jesus. A sober statistical study of the concept of the Messiah in the New Testament, and in critical analysis of the incidence of the title in the Gospels, clearly demonstrates this.

The term *"Christos"* (Messiah) occurs only about fifty times in the Four Gospels, and never in a clear and incontestable statement of Jesus' about himself.[n] On the other hand, we find it about two hundred and eighty times in the rest of the New Testament, excluding the Gospels. From the very beginning the affirmation of Jesus as the Messiah seems to have been a fundamental article of faith among the disciples, and accordingly recurs in almost all credos of the primitive church.

Let us examine the use of the concept in each of our sources of information on Jesus.

Our first and fundamental observation must be to note an omission. The concept of the Messiah does not occur at all in the *Logia*. This is also true of kindred titles such as Son of David, King of Israel, King of the Jews. In short, this source does not record any affirmation by Jesus himself that he was the Messiah. Now, the *Logia* represent not only the oldest

Christian book on Jesus, but also the only book of the primitive church which attempted to include only sayings by Jesus himself, nothing said to him or about him. Therefore, the testimony of the *Logia* is of fundamental importance to our problem, and forces us to conclude that Jesus did not refer to himself as the Messiah.

Can the Four Gospels prove the opposite?

In Mark there is no certain evidence that Jesus called himself the Messiah; on the contrary, we find many tokens that he rejected the title, or else stripped it of its political meaning and interpreted it in terms of the theology of suffering.

The Gospel of Matthew, however, presents a completely different picture. Matthew had a theological interest in the concept of the Messiah. This was an outgrowth of the tendency of his circle to re-Judaicize the message of Jesus. Consequently he inserted references to the messianic idea throughout his Gospel, and at crucial places put the statement into Jesus' mouth. All this was part of a campaign to rewrite history for dogmatic ends, and must therefore be set aside as we attempt to extract from the documents the real historical material concerning Jesus.

Luke was almost as interested in the church's messianic dogma as Matthew. But he abided by his resolution to write the story as it actually happened,[2] and did not join in the attempts of the group around Matthew to inject the messianic dogma into Jesus' witness to himself.

John also was keenly interested in the church's messianic dogmas. He expressed this interest by according a great deal of space in his Gospel to messianic professions and messianic controversies. In this context it is all the more conspicuous that Jesus always avoided naming himself as the Messiah, that he either passed over or sharply rejected any such attributions—in complete concordance with the *Logia,* with the

[2] Luke 1, 3.

earliest material recorded in Mark and Luke, and in marked contrast to the presentation in the Gospel of Matthew.

The ancient rabbinical tradition of Jesus, which has independent value as a source, nowhere records that Jesus affirmed himself to be the Messiah. On the other hand, the medieval polemical work *Toledoth Jeshu* does cite large numbers of such assertions. But it has no value as an independent source.[n] Thus, a critical study of the Jewish texts concerning Jesus confirms the results of an analysis of the Gospels: that Jesus did not refer to himself as the Messiah.

→»→»→» 3 «←«←«←

THE SON OF MAN

THE TERM "Son of Man" stands at the opposite extreme. The title occurs in the Gospels about eighty times. Confirmation of it is found in all of the five New Testament traditions of Jesus as designated by scholarly criticism: the *Logia*,[3] the tradition of Mark,[4] the material found only in Matthew,[5] the material found only in Luke,[6] and the tradition of John.[7] In the Gospels the epithet "Son of Man" is used only by Jesus himself, never by his disciples, followers, petitioners, or enemies.[n] It appears to have been a favorite concept of Jesus; we find evidence for it from the beginning to the end of his public ministry. He used it more frequently than any other title of authority, and often employed it as a direct counter to "Messiah" and similar terms.[8]

---

[3] Matthew 8, 20; Luke 9, 58. [4] Mark 2, 10. [5] Matthew 25, 31.
[6] Luke 17, 22. [7] John 5, 27. [8] Mark 8, 31 ff.

Its absence from the rest of the New Testament is as significant as its frequent presence in the Gospels. For outside the Gospels "Son of Man" is found only four times in the New Testament. And in the creeds of the primitive church, multifarious as they are, the epithet "Son of Man" is not encountered a single time.[n] In other words, the primitive church never constructed a dogma around the idea of the Son of Man. It cannot therefore be asserted that the primitive church introduced the concept of the Son of Man into any of the traditions in the interests of any particular community's theological idea. The exact contrary is the case. The primitive church found the idea of the Son of Man imbedded in the oldest traditions, but did not incorporate it into its doctrines, did not even use the term or attribute its use to the first disciples of Jesus, those who had been his followers during his lifetime. Rather, it treated it as a taboo designation that Jesus Christ had reserved for himself, much as the synagogue treated God's designation of himself (Yahweh).

The history of the term "Son of Man" in later Jewish literature substantiates our conclusions. The daring author of the fourth Book of Ezra (c. A.D. 80) was the only apocalyptic of the Christian era who still spoke of the heavenly son of man who was to come henceforth,[n] and he was the last to do so. The Syrian Apocalypse of Baruch (c. A.D. 100), which had been revised to insure orthodoxy, no longer mentioned the term. "Son of Man" vanished also from the Slavonic and Hebrew texts concerning Enoch. The Ethiopian Book of Enoch was still read only in Christian circles; it was banned in the synagogue. In the Talmud the term "Son of Man" was cited only in connection with Daniel 7, being at the same time time given a collective sense as referring to God's chosen people. There can be no doubt that the rabbinate had begun to avoid the apocalyptic epithet "Son of Man," in all probability on the initiative of Gamaliel II of the Great Sanhedrin at Jamnia (A.D. 80–100). Why? The answer is given in the Jerusalem Talmud by a writer from Caesarea, Rabbi Abbahu: "If a man says, I am the Son of Man, he will come to an end that he will rue." [9] This is an unmistakable allusion to Jesus. Obviously, as early as the apostolic age Jewish writers were already fighting Jesus' affirmation of himself as the Son of Man, and from the time of Gamaliel the Younger on they fought this apocalyptic term precisely because it was Jesus' most characteristic designation of himself. Thus the Jewish literature supplied negative testimony to the use and importance of the term "Son of Man" as employed by Jesus.

There remains the problem of which "Son of Man" sayings were actually spoken by Jesus and which were embellished or even added to the texts. I cannot here go into the necessary full-scale analysis of the sources, but shall briefly present the results of my researches.

The Galilean Enoch tradition spoke of the *filius hominis absconditus;* the Son of Man for a time dwells in concealment in the heavens, to step into the light in all his power and glory on the day of his epiphany, when he will sit in judgment upon the unrighteous and take vengeance upon the enemies of God. Jesus was the *filius hominis incognitus.* Thus his self-witness accorded in every sense with the oldest and best-verified "Son of Man" sayings. He lived incognito in the midst of men, among his people, among the disciples of John the Baptist, among his own disciples—lived inconspicuously, misunderstood, a source of offense, the butt of attacks and scoffing.[1] But he, the *filius hominis incognitus,* was also master of the law; he had the authority to sit in judgment and to forgive sins.[2] He was cursed and condemned.[3] Yet the ultimate fate of men would depend upon the position they took in regard to him.[4] He was powerless and defenseless, homeless, persecuted and betrayed.[5] But he

[9] Jerusalem Ta'anith 2, 1.   [1] Luke 7, 34; 11, 31; Mark 9, 9.   [2] Mark 2, 10. 28; John 5, 27.   [3] Luke 6, 22 f.; 12, 10.   [4] Mark 8, 38; Luke 12, 8.
[5] Luke 9, 58; 22, 48.

had come to seek and to save the lost sheep—come not to enslave, but to serve and to give his life for the redemption of many.[6]

Jesus had said all this not as though it were apocalyptic speculation that could be greeted with belief or disbelief, but with the transcendent authority of a great stranger from another world, so that individuals believed or disbelieved in him. He spoke of belief in the Son of Man and accepted worship. To one who spoke thus it is only possible to reply yes or no.

➤➤➤-➤➤➤-➤➤➤ 4 ᐸᐸᐸ-ᐸᐸᐸ-ᐸᐸᐸ

THE SON OF GOD

I THANK THEE, Father, Lord of heaven and earth, that thou hast hidden these things from the wise and understanding and revealed them to babes; yea, Father, for such was thy gracious will. All things have been delivered to me by my Father; and no one knows the Son except the Father, and no one knows the Father except the Son and any one to whom the Son chooses to reveal him." [7]

This saying was long considered to be inauthentic on the grounds that such words could not conceivably have been spoken by a Jew of ancient Palestine; that they betray the influence of the Gnostic spirit; and that therefore they must have been the product of the Hellenistic Christian community and a sample of early Hellenistic dogma. This argument is faulty. For we find Ikhnaton, Pharaoh Amenophis IV, who proclaimed a new God and a new form of worship

[6] Luke 19, 10; Mark 10, 45.   [7] Matthew 11, 25-27.

in 1370 B.C., saying in the hymn to the Sun (discovered at Tell el-Amarna in 1887):

> *"Thou art in my heart.*
> *No other knows thee but thy son Ikhnaton,*
> *Thou hast initiated him into thy plans and thy power."* [n]

Many similar passages can be found in the Gathas [n] of Zarathustra (c. 600 B.C.). Accordingly, it cannot be said that such phrases are conceivable only in the age and the environment of the early Christian Gnostics. Meanwhile, however, documents have been found which prove that such language was not unheard of even among the Jews of ancient Palestine. In times before Jesus, the "Teacher of Righteousness" says in the Qumran Psalms:

> *"I give thanks unto Thee, O Lord*
> *for Thou hast illumined my face . . .*
> *But the prophets of deceit . . .*
> *have said of the vision of knowledge,*
> *'It is not sure,'*
> *and of the way Thou desirest,*
> *'There is no such thing.' . . .*
> *Through me hast Thou illumined*
> *the faces of full many. . . .*
> *For Thou hast made known to me*
> *Thy deep mysterious things . . .*
> *That Thy glory may be shown forth. . . .*
> *Only with God on High*
> *are all the works of righteousness; . . .*
> *that all His works may know*
> *how mighty is His power,*
> *how plenteous His love*
> *to all who do His will."* [8] [n]

[8] From *The Dead Sea Scriptures* by Theodor H. Gaster (Copyright © 1956 by Theodor H. Gaster. Reprinted by permission of Doubleday & Co., Inc.), pp. 142–6.

These phrases, which initially had a wholly personal and virtually autobiographical meaning, soon became established as ritual formulas, and in this sense, lacking their original force, became the general property of the desert sect and were used liturgically. Thus, for example, we find in the great community prayer at the end of the "Manual of Discipline":

"I will sing with knowledge. . . .
I will shelter knowledge with sound counsel. . . .
For He from the Wellspring of Knowledge
has made His light to burst forth,
and mine eye has gazed on His wonders. . . .
Through His mysterious wonder
light is come into my heart;
mine eye has set its gaze
on everlasting things.
A virtue hidden from man. . . .
Blessed art Thou, O my God,
Who hast opened the heart of Thy servant unto
*   knowledge.*
Direct all his works in righteousness
and vouchsafe unto the son of Thine handmaid
the favor which Thou hast assured to all the mortal
*   elect. . . .*
And there is none beside Thee
to controvert Thy plan;
none to understand all Thy holy thought,
none to gaze into the depths of Thy secrets,
none to perceive all Thy wonders. . . .
Who can compass the sum of Thy glory?
And what is mere mortal man
amid Thy wondrous works? . . .
What thought can it comprehend? [9] [n]

[9] From *The Dead Sea Scriptures* by Theodor H. Gaster (Copyright © 1956 by Theodor H. Gaster. Reprinted by permission of Doubleday & Co., Inc.), pp. 119–22.

It is evident that we here have considerable precedent for the terminology used in Matthew 11, 25–27. In the light of these scrolls, it can no longer be asserted that the language of this saying of Jesus would have been inconceivable among the Palestinian Jews of the early imperial age, and that therefore the saying cannot be attributed to Jesus, but must have sprung from the Hellenistic primitive church. As far as linguistic precedent goes, the saying could certainly have been spoken by Jesus.[11] But, in speaking so, was Jesus perhaps merely taking up and varying the motifs and formulae of the desert sect? Perhaps Matthew 11, 25 ff., attests that on crucial matters Jesus was a pupil of the Qumran, no more. If this were true it would surely be a surprising turn of affairs, doubly surprising after all that I have said above concerning the interrelationships among the Qumran sect, John the Baptist, and Jesus (see pages 75 ff.).

But Matthew 11, 25 ff., echoes the Qumran texts only in a formal, linguistic sense. Actually, in using this linguistic formula Jesus was making a claim that was not only a repudiation of the Qumran sect, but also a challenge to the whole Qumran tradition and to the whole of Palestinian Judaism in his time. "No one knows the Father except the Son." No Jew before or contemporary with Jesus had ever dared to make such a claim. The Jews had always proclaimed the God of their forefathers, the God of Moses, the God of the Torah; they had always anchored their ideas about God firmly in their tradition by citing proofs from the Scriptures; they had deduced their criticism of the times and their predictions of the future from the Scriptures, their ideals and precepts from the Torah. Jesus did none of these things. He offered no scriptural proofs; he did not go in for exegesis of the Torah. Instead, breaking with this practice, he declared: No one knows the Father except the Son.

Is there a possibility that the saying may have sprung

from the pre-Hellenistic, Aramaic-speaking early Christian community? My answer is: No. For no one in the early Jerusalem Christian community, or in any other, would ever have dared to invent such a saying for Jesus. Jesus himself and Jesus alone could have been so bold and so solitary, so free and independent, so absolutistic. Indeed, it is amazing that the members of the early church transmitted this disturbing saying at all, and it is perhaps not accidental that it was received into the oldest and in many respects most original of the books on Jesus, the collection of *Logia*.[n] But the apostolic church did everything in its power to neutralize this "scandalous" saying and the revolutionary aspect of Jesus which it expressed. The Jesus of the Synoptic Gospels does bring forth scriptural proofs and does practice exegesis of the Torah, again and again. But the words quoted in Matthew 11, 25 ff., tower above the layers of the Synoptic tradition like a lonely and primordial peak—the solid rock of the authentic Jesus.

Matthew 11, 25 f., was a prayer, and not one that occurred by chance, for the special relationship between Father and Son came forth in a unique manner in the prayers of Jesus. The *Logion* opens with a benediction: "I thank [or "praise"] Thee, Father." The next clause concerns the paradoxical nature of the divine revelation. Then comes Jesus' "yea," the most personal word in this highly personal *Logion;* it is without analogy and no one could have invented it. "Yea, Father, for such was Thy gracious will." "Gracious" is the technical term for the sovereign and conditional, the inscrutable and yet ultimately paternal will of God.[n] Praying and adoring, the Son submitted to this will a priori. Now he had understood this will, and he gave his assent to it, said his "yea," as Luke makes plain by the context and the introductory formula of blessing.[n] This *Logion,* with sudden and breath-taking clarity, affords insight into the wholly personal relationship between Father and Son,[n] shows us the

assent to the Father's will existing side by side with understanding of the Father—a reciprocal relationship, constantly
re-expressed in prayer, in which the will of the Father wres-
tles with the will of the Son, in which the mind of the Son
struggles to fathom the Father and his decisions. From this
one sample, we can form some conception of the nature of
Jesus' solitary hours of prayer which the Gospels mention
several times.[1]

→»→»→» 5 «‹«‹«‹«‹«

THE BACKGROUND TO
THE PASSION

THE JUST MAN will be scourged, tortured, bound, blinded
with fire, and when he has endured every kind of suffering will at last be impaled on the cross." So Plato declares
in his *Republic*.[2]

There can be no doubt that Jesus never read the works
of Plato. But he knew human beings at least as well as Soc-
rates or Plato. And he knew that his era was the setting for
a conflict of quite another sort from the conflict between
the righteous and the unrighteous—namely, the struggle between God and the world. In view of this, if for no other
reason, Jesus must have foreseen his violent death from the
very beginning.

Jesus was familiar with the Old Testament and its predictions of a Passion. He knew the apocalyptic texts concern-

[1] Mark 1, 35, etc.   [2] II, 5, 361 e.

ing the sufferings of the Son of Man, and knew also contemporary tracts on martyrs.[n] He was aware of and spoke of
the cruel death of John the Baptist.[3]

Jesus also knew the Torah and the current legal provisions against heretics. Therefore, he could not help knowing
what he might expect as soon as he deliberately violated the
law and incited others to do the same. He was aware of this
as any partisan leader must be aware of what is in store for
him when the hour strikes. Knowing the balance of power
among the various authorities in Palestine, Jesus could calculate pricisely what would happen, could easily foresee the
various stages of the proceedings. Whether he spoke of it beforehand, and if so when, where, and to what extent, is an
entirely different question. For information about that we
can look only to the Gospels.

Jesus' pronouncements concerning his Passion fall into
five categories, as we find them in the Gospels.

The first category includes those sayings in which Jesus
spoke of the necessity of his suffering in the form of a *mashal* (parable, figurative phrase, riddle), without any allusion to when, where, how, whence, or through whom it
would come. "I came to cast fire upon the earth; and would
that it were already kindled. I have a baptism to be baptized
with; and how I am constrained until it is accomplished." [n]
"Truly, truly, I say to you, unless a grain of wheat falls into
the earth and dies, it remains alone; but if it dies, it bears
much fruit." [n] In these sayings no specific details are given.
But with what dark power Jesus spoke here of the inevitabil-
ity of his Passion, and of its meaning.

The second category comprises those sayings concerning
the Son of Man which speak in a wholly general way, and
in terms of the fundamental principle, of the path of suffering to be followed by the Son of Man—but without making
any specific predictions.[4] Sometimes these sayings are linked

[3] Mark 9, 13.   [4] Matthew 8, 20; Mark 14, 41, etc.

with a brief scriptural reference that we cannot always ver-ify.[5] Once, without an express allusion to Scripture, there is an explication of the meaning of the Son of Man's suffering: he gives "his life as a ransom for many."[n]

The third category contains the numerous pronounce-ments upon the Passion in which Jesus, in full knowledge of the specific judicial situation, spoke of the peril of death which threatened him particularly in Jerusalem. The city of God had time and again killed the prophets of God.[6] It would also reject and kill him.[7] "For it cannot be that a prophet should perish away from Jerusalem."[n] It was with this in mind that Jesus said in Caesarea Philippi: "If any man would come after me, let him . . . take up his cross and follow me."[8] The messianic march upon Jerusalem, of which the chief apostle dreamed, would become a march to death. For Jerusalem had been the city of mass crucifixions since the days of Antiochus, of Demetrius, of Alexander Jannaeus, and, above all, since Varus.[n] This was in the mind of Thomas when he declared, just before they set out for the Mount of Olives: "Let us also go, that we may die with him."[9]

The fourth category consists of the three so-called pre-dictions of the Passion.[1] All three are linked with the idea of the Son of Man, and at the same time with the legal author-ities of Jerusalem; but they are distinguished from the fore-going group of sayings by the abundance of details. Delivery to the high priests, scribes, and councillors, rejection and condemnation, delivery to the Gentiles, mockery and abuse, execution, resurrection after three days—such are the items enumerated in these predictions. They agree, with startling exactitude, with the later course of events. Consequently, these three predictions of the Passion are nowadays generally considered to have been prophecies after the fact. Yet they

[5] Mark 9, 12; 14, 21.   [6] Luke 11, 47 ff.; 13, 34.   [7] Mark 12, 1–8.
[8] Mark 8, 34.   [9] John 11, 16.   [1] Mark 8, 31; 9, 31; 10, 33 f.

do not contain a single event—from the delivery to the Great Sanhedrin to the execution—which Jesus could not have known in advance and therefore foretold simply on the basis of the legal provisions against heretics, of his legal status at the time, and of the judicial prosecution he had already experienced. The only real enigma is his announcement of a resurrection after three days. Jesus certainly never thought that when he died "everything would be over."[2] The idea of resurrection was familiar to him.[3] And even the specific mention of "three days" was natural enough. "For the Holy One, blessed be He, does not leave His own in distress for more than three days."[n] But if Jesus had made a precise prediction of his resurrection after three days, everything that the Gospels say about the despair of the women and disciples and their surprise on Easter morning would be completely incomprehensible. We are therefore left with the conclusion that the primitive church took liberties with the final phrases of the three "predictions of the Passion" (which were probably highly obscure in their original form).

To the fifth category belong those sayings about the Passion which contain elements more reminiscent of the theology of the church than of Jesus himself. A typical example of this type is Luke 24, 26; in any case, it occupies a special position because it alleges to be a saying of the risen Christ. And we hear not of the Son of Man, but of the Messiah. Moreover, he is alleged to have added a detailed scriptural proof.[4] This is all characteristic of the church's theology at the time of Luke, and not at all characteristic of Jesus.

But the sayings in regard to the Passion in categories 1–4 fit without difficulty into the oldest tradition, and in their original form do not exceed what any man of common sense and open eyes, who found himself in Jesus' situation, could reasonably have predicted. And certainly Jesus had a notable share of common sense and clear-sightedness.

[2] Cf. Luke 12, 49 f.; John 12, 24.   [3] See Daniel 12, 2 ff.   [4] Luke 24, 27.

6

I AM HE!

IN THE SAYINGS of Jesus as found in the Gospels we encounter again and again that phrase of revelation: "I am He." Perhaps this mysterious phrase harbors within itself the most authentic, the most audacious, and the most profound affirmation by Jesus of who he was. The question is important enough to justify a separate discussion of the phrase, its early history, its roots, and its significance.[n]

The temple in Jerusalem was the site of the presence of God. Hence, the great temple festivals were in essence theophanic celebrations in which the assembled hordes of pilgrims from all over the world experienced that presence. This was particularly true of the great pilgrim festival in the autumn, the Feast of Tabernacles. According to Jewish belief, the manifestation of God during worship took place by means of the Word. Consequently, God's proclamations of Himself, as set forth in the liturgy, played a decisive part at the Feast of Tabernacles.

The scriptural passages read for the holiday were those concerning the revelation of the Torah on Mount Sinai. To these were appended the introductory words: "I am the Lord your God, who brought you out of the land of Egypt, out of the house of bondage. You shall have no other gods before me." [n]

At this same feast the "Hallel" psalms[5] were sung.[n] Psalm 115, 9–11, reads:

[5] Psalms 113–118.

174

> *"O Israel, trust in the Lord!*
> *He is their help and their shield.*
> *O house of Aaron, put your trust in the Lord!*
> *He is their help and their shield.*
> *You who fear the Lord, trust in the Lord!*
> *He is their help and shield."*

Here the name of God alternates in a triple refrain with the emphatic He (Hebrew *hu*).

Psalms 46, 50, and 81 were also sung.[n] Psalm 46 is an antiphonal song for a choir. In Psalm 46, 2 ff., the choir of Levites sings:

> *"Therefore we will not fear . . .*
> *Though its [the sea's] waters roar and foam. . . .*
> *The holy habitation [tent, tabernacle] of the Most*
>   *High.*
> *God is in the midst of her. . . ."*

In 46, 10, the voice of God replies:

> *"Be still, and know that I am God."*

And the choir sings in conclusion (46, 11):

> *"The Lord of hosts is with us."* [n]

In Psalm 50, 7, God says:

> *"Hear, O my people, and I will speak,*
> *O Israel, I will testify against you.*
> *I am God, your God."* [n]

In Psalm 81, 8 ff., we find:

> *"Hear, O my people, while I admonish you!*
> *O Israel, if you would but listen to me!*
> *There shall be no strange god among you;*
> *you shall not bow down to a foreign god.*
> *I am the Lord your God,*
> *who brought you up out of the land of Egypt."* ▪

Possibly many of these texts date back to the temple worship of the days before the Exile.[n] But even during the Exile
some kind of Feast of Tabernacles was undoubtedly celebrated, a temple festival without the temple. In any case,
much evidence suggests that the divine formulae of self-
proclamation as we have them in the Tabernacles psalms
influenced the great prophet of the Exile, the so-called
Deutero-Isaiah (that is to say, the author of Isaiah 40–55).
We can recognize such influence in, for example, the great
divine oration of Isaiah 43, 1 ff. The crucial sentences of this
theophanic address read in the Qumran Isaiah scroll, which
is the oldest text of Isaiah that we now have:

> *"Fear not, for I have redeemed you.*
> *I have called you by your name, you are mine.*
> *When you pass through the waters I will be with you*
> *For I am the Lord, your God. . . .*
> *Fear not, for I am with you. . . .*
> *You are my witnesses, whom I have chosen.*
> *That you may know and believe me, and understand*
> *   that I am he.[n]*
> *Before me was no God formed,*
> *Neither shall there be any after me.[n]*
> *I, I am the Lord,[n]*
> *And besides me there is no savior.*
> *I have declared it [to Abraham]. . . .[n]*
> *And you are my witnesses.*
> *I am God.[n]*
> *Yea, since the day was I am he. . . .[n]*
> *I am the Lord your Holy One*
> *who made a way in the sea,*
> *a path in the mighty waters. . . .*
> *I, I am he*
> *who blots out your transgressions for my own sake:*
> *and I will not remember your sins."[n]*

It is plain that the leitmotif of this revelation is the theophanic word "I." Sometimes we encounter the simple "I"

176

exerting unusual weight because the personal pronoun is grammatically unnecessary; sometimes we find the "I" repeated, sometimes the formula with a predicate, "I am God," "I am Yahweh," and sometimes the formula of annunciation without any predicate, "I am." This is all preceded by the introductory formulae, "Fear not," or "Ye shall know, believe, understand that I am He." Then there are enlargements of these formulae: "I am since the day was," "I am from eternity to eternity," "I am God and there is no other."

All these formal elements are found in other speeches of God in Deutero-Isaiah.ⁿ But again and again special emphasis is placed upon the theophanic formula "I am He," Hebrew *"Ani huah"* and *"Ani hu,"* Aramaic *"Ana hu,"* Greek *"Ego eimi."* ⁿ

The first word of this formula in Hebrew, *"Ani"* (= *Anochi* = I), is the dominant proclamation of God in Deuteronomy 5, 6; Psalm 46, 11; 50, 7; and 81, 11. The second word is the personal pronoun (= *huah* = He) which we meet in Psalm 115, 9 ff. Thus, the theophanic formula *"Ani hu"* in Deutero-Isaiah can be understood as a combination of the liturgical *"Ani"* with the liturgical *"hu."* So combined it means "I am He." Now, in the Semitic languages the personal pronoun of the third person is also frequently used as a copulative verb, equivalent to am, are, is. If we wish to understand *"Ani hu"* in this sense, it then means "I am." Both of these possible translations are used in the Greek Bible (*"Ego eimi autos"* and *"Ego eimi"*), but the second is preponderant. In any case, the Deutero-Isaianic theophanic formula *"Ani hu"* may be regarded as an all-inclusive summary of God's self-revelatory declarations in the ritual of the Feast of Tabernacles.

In Deuteronomy 32, 39 f., we encounter a whole flock of such self-revelatory formulas:

> *"See now that I, even I, am He*
> *and there is no god beside me;*

I kill and I make alive;
I wound and I heal
and there is none that can deliver out of my hand.
For I lift up my hand to heaven
and swear, as I live for ever . . ." [n]

Elsewhere, too, in the later strata of the Old Testament canon, the formula *"Ani hu"* is found in a variety of modified forms.[n] In the Greek and Aramaic translations of the Old Testament we clearly recognize the tendency to amplify or multiply these self-revelatory formulae of the original text.[n] And in the ritual language of Palestinian Judaism *"Ani hu"* played a significant part.

In the texts of the desert sect, the use of the name "Yahweh" was strictly taboo. Instead the letter *aleph* or four dots were used.[n] Often, however, the emphatic "He" (*huah*) or else the circumlocution "The Eternal" was employed instead of "Yahweh." There can be no doubt that both these substitutes were chosen in connection with the self-revelatory formulae of Isaiah 40 ff.[n]

From the number of scrolls of Isaiah which have been found, we may judge that this book was a special favorite of the members of the desert sect. In Isaiah we read: "In the wilderness prepare the way of the Lord." [6] The Manual of Discipline states in 8, 13 f.: "They are to be kept apart and to go into the wilderness to prepare the way of the *huaha* there, as it is written: 'In the wilderness prepare the way of. . . .'" Here the name of Yahweh in the quotation is replaced by the four dots (= Yahweh), but in the text of the desert sect by the secret name *"huaha,"* which is presumably a compound of *"huah"* (He) and *"A"* (= *Elohim* = God).[n] In Nahum 1, 2, we find: "Yahweh takes vengeance on his adversaries and Yahweh keeps wrath for his enemies." (The Revised Standard Version uses "LORD" instead of "Yahweh." See Preface to that translation.) The Damascus

[6] Isaiah 40, 3.

text[7] has in place of this: "He [*hu*] takes vengeance on His adversaries, and He keeps wrath for his enemies."

God says to Abraham: "Seekest thou the God of Gods? I am He."[8] And in the next chapter: "I am He, fear not, for I am before the days were."[n] In the book of Elijah, at the end of his final manifestation, God says: "Know now that I am He."[n]

A whole liturgical history underlies the self-revelatory formulae in Deutero-Isaiah. It is only natural, therefore, that in their turn these formulae affected liturgy. In the great scroll of Isaiah from Qumran the divine self-revelatory sayings are often given special prominence by the way the texts are arranged for reading on the various holidays.[n] It appears that these self-revelatory passages, with their emphasis upon the "I," were especially chosen to be read at some of the theophanic feasts—at, say, the Feast of Tabernacles, which in the desert had to be held away from the temple. On the Sabbath of the week of Tabernacles the Levites in Jerusalem sang the Song of Moses,[9] which contains a wealth of such Deutero-Isanianic self-revelatory formulae.[n] Thus the theophanic formula *"Ani hu"* from Isaiah 40 ff. won for itself a firm place in the liturgy of the Feast of Tabernacles, alongside the older formulae from the psalms. This must already have happened before the birth of Christ. Proof of this is to be found in an often misinterpreted saying of Hillel the Elder, who taught in Jerusalem under Herod the Great. "When Hillel the Elder was in good spirits at the distribution of waters [a rite at the Feast of Tabernacles] he was in the habit of saying: 'When *Ani* is here, all is here. When *Ani* is not here, who then is here?' "[n]

This saying is a riddle,[n] a *mashal*, intended for the amusement of the pilgrims to the temple, for such entertainments were the duty of every scribe at the Feast of Tabernacles.

---

[7] 9, 5.   [8] Revelation of Abraham 8.   [9] Deuteronomy 32, 1 ff. and, in particular, 39 ff.

This saying of Hillel can be translated as we have just done.[n] If so, it refers to the miracle of God's manifestation at the Feast of Tabernacles, to the presence of the divine *Ani* in the temple. To be sure, the saying can be taken differently and translated as follows: "When I am here, all are here. When I am not here, who then is here?" [n] But Hillel never suffered from megalomania, least of all in the temple, where, naturally, not the scribe but the priest was the important person. Hillel's intention, in using this provoking and mystifying phrase, was to propound a riddle that cast light on the Great Mystery of the Feast of Tabernacles. At the altar the choir of priests sang: "God is in the temple." And the voice of God replied: "Be still and know that I am God." [1] The Levites sang: *"Ani, ani hu."* [2] Hillel summed up the whole theology of the Feast of Tabernacles in the one sentence: when the divine *Ani* is here, all is here.

Our interpretation of this saying of Hillel's accords with an ancient rabbinical account of the liturgy of Tabernacles in the second temple. On each day of the festival week the priests arranged a ceremonial procession around the altar, during which they sang repeatedly: *"Ani we hu"* and *"Hosanna."* [n] The refrains of litanies have, historically, undergone many interpretations, for such refrains are always mysterious and equivocal.[n] Perhaps the phrase may be understood in this way: the procession consisted of two groups of priests, who sang the litany responsively in the manner of Psalm 46. One choir sang the theophanic formula *"Ani hu,"* the meaning being that of Psalm 46, 10, and the wording that of Isaiah 43, 10. Thereupon the other choir answered, in the spirit of Psalm 46, 11, and Psalm 118, 25, with the cry *"Hosanna!"* ("Then help us!") The temple priests were allowed to pronounce the most holy name of Yahweh. Therefore, they also were allowed (in contrast to the Levites in Psalm 46, 1. 10) to proclaim the theophanic formula *"Ani hu."*

[1] Psalm 46, 5. 10.   [2] Deuteronomy 32, 39.

But they avoided pronouncing the name of Yahweh distinctly. It is therefore understandable that they also began to conceal the holy *"Ani hu"* under a disguise, using the dualistic formula *"Ani we hu*. This means "I and he." This substitute also was susceptible to theophanic interpretation, for both elements, *"Ani"* and *"hu,"* were common references to Yahweh.[n]

The formulae *"hu," "Ani,"* and *"Ani hu"* were used not only in the ritual for the Feast of Tabernacles, but also in the Passover liturgy. The Hallel psalms were sung several times during the Passover, both in the temple and in the home.[n] In the domestic Passover liturgy the father at the family table narrated the miracles of God on the night of the Egyptian Passover.[3] Then he quoted Deuteronomy 26, 8: "And the Lord brought us out of Egypt . . . with signs and wonders." Whereupon he spoke the following words of interpretation: "The Lord brought us out of Egypt—not by an angel, nor by a seraph, nor even by an envoy, but the Holy One, praised be He in his glory, he himself, as it is written: I will pass over the land. I will . . . I will, I the Lord." A further passage, possibly a later addition, inserts five more emphatic "I's": I and not an angel; I and not a seraph; I and not the envoy; I, the Lord, I am he and no other.[n] The concluding formula once again comes from Deutero-Isaiah,[n] whose reiterated "I's" seem to have influenced many other passages in the ancient Hebrew literature. In a late litany of prayer for the reconstruction of the temple the word *"hu"* appears no less than twenty-two times as a substitute for "God," altogether in the style of the familiar Hallel psalm.[n]

As these Deutero-Isaianic formulae of self-revelation became established in Jewish liturgy, the rabbinical theologians applied them and interpreted them. We often encounter the emphatic *"hu"* as a substitute for the divine name "Yahweh." [n] But far more stress was laid upon the self-revelatory

[3] See Exodus 12, 27; Deuteronomy 6, 21 ff.

"*Ani*." In an ancient rabbinical commentary on the book of
Exodus we find: "The Eternal is the same in the past and
the same in the future, as is written: 'Behold now that I, I
am, and there is no God beside me. . . . I will lift my hand
to heaven and will say: I live eternally. . . . I am the first,
and at the last I am the same.' " [n] In the late rabbinical commentary on Exodus, Joshua ben Levi (Lydda, c. A.D. 230)
says of the decalogue: "Moses spoke all the words except for
the two which God himself out of His own mouth spoke to
the Israelites, namely: 'I am the Eternal, your God.' And:
'Thou shalt have no strange gods before me.' " [n] It is plain
that the exclusive "*Ani*" appears here as the key theophanic
term, and is therefore reserved for God's affirmation of Himself. Consequently, theologians were fond of mediating upon
this "*Ani*" (= *Anochi*). Adducing the emphatic "*Anochi,
Anochi*" of Isaiah 51, 12, they declared "*Anochi*" to be the
surrogate word for Yahweh, a secret name for the Re-
deemer,[n] or a symbol of the redemption in itself. "The word
Anochi is the sign of the First Redemption. For it is said: I
[*Anochi*] will go down with you to Egypt and I [*Anochi*]
will also bring you up again.[4] The word *Anochi,* however,
also serves as the sign of the Last Redemption. For by this
word they will be restored, as it is said: Behold, I [*Anochi*]
will send you Elijah the prophet." [5] In short, the self-revelatory word "*Anochi*" was considered the token and pledge of
God's determination to save man in the first days and the last
days.[n]

So much for the dominance of Deutero-Isaianic self-
revelatory formulae in Jewish liturgy and theology. How this
development came about can here be sketched only tenta-
tively. But it is possible to describe with fair certainty the
stage in the evolution of these formulae which had been
reached in the early period of Jesus' life—that is, by around
A.D. 20.

[4] Genesis 46, 4.   [5] Malachi 4, 5.

In A.D. 20, Isaiah 40–45 was being widely read and quoted. The emphatic *"hu"* was a favorite term for referring to God. Theology was much concerned with the divine self-affirmations contained in *"Ani"* and *"Ani hu."* The Hallel psalms, in which *"hu"* equaled "God," were firmly established in the rituals of the two principal pilgrimage feasts, Tabernacles and the Passover. Psalms 46, 50, and 81 formed part of the special liturgy of the Feast of Tabernacles. In the theology of the Feast of Tabernacles the theophanic word *"Ani"* had assumed importance, as the above-mentioned story of Hillel indicates. It is therefore virtually certain that even then the priests paraded around the altar repeating the secret formula *"Ani we hu"* (= *Ani hu*). Such was the significance, in theology and liturgy, of the theophanic formula *"Ani hu"* in the days of Jesus. We must view the Gospel accounts of Jesus' self-revelatory sayings in the light of this situation.

In Mark 6, 45 ff., Jesus appears to the troubled disciples before dawn in the middle of the stormy lake of Gennesaret. They cry out, for at first they take him for a ghost (*phantasma*). But he says to them: "Take heart, it is I, have no fear." Then he enters the boat, and immediately the wind subsides. This story must derive from a very old, much discussed, and widely disseminated tradition. For in Mark 6, 49, we find the Evangelist plainly combating a polemic account which evidently tried to dismiss the whole affair as a ghost story.[n] And in Mark 6, 50, the reader is informed that all the persons in the boat saw the miracle and can testify to it. All this is reminiscent of the Easter controversy with its problem of ghostly appearances and its lists of witnesses.[n] This cannot, however, be a remnant of the Easter story which inadvertently found its way into the wrong place in the narrative. For in both Mark and John [6] the story is inseparably linked with the feeding of the multitude in the spring of A.D. 31.

[6] John 6, 16 ff.

183

The "It is I" in **Mark 6, 50,** is ambiguous. It can be understood as a normal statement ("It is I, Jesus"); but it can also
be intended as a divine self-revelation (*"Ani hu"*). Three
elements favor the theophanic interpretation. The first is the
time. According to Mark,[7] the incident took place in the
spring; according to John,[8] at the time of the Passover. Now,
as we have seen, the divine self-revelatory formulae had a
fixed place in the Passover ritual. The second element is the
storm. The appearance of Jesus walking on the sea can be regarded here as an epiphany of the God who rules the waters,
who is glorified in the Passover liturgy.[n] The third element
is the framework in which the words are placed. For the
"Take heart" and "Have no fear" which introduce and conclude the "It is I" in Mark 6, 50, are a part of the divine formula of self-revelation.[n]

In the Gospel of Mark, Jesus alone uses this *"Ani hu."* No
mortal man other than he is permitted to use such language.
The exclusiveness of the phrase is most strongly emphasized
in Jesus' prediction of the self-proclaimed "Christs" of the
future. "Many will come in my name, saying, 'I am He!' and
they will lead many astray." [9] Here Matthew naïvely interpo-
lated the further statement ("I am the Messiah"), thereby
weakening the self-affirmation of divinity to a messianic
claim.[1] Luke, however, retained the mysterious "I am He!"
and transmitted the tradition without making any additions.[2]

In Mark 14, 62, it is also the Passover season. Once more
Jesus says *"Ani hu."* This time, however, the ambiguous self-
affirmation takes place before the judges who are trying him
by religious law, and Caiaphas immediately seizes upon this
dangerous phrase and cries: Blasphemy! Matthew, in telling
the story, once again rephrased the theophanic formula in
terms of his messianic dogma, and thereby stripped it of its
true significance.[3]

[7] Mark 6, 39.   [8] John 6, 4.   [9] Mark 13, 6.   [1] Matthew 24, 5.   [2] Luke
21, 8.   [3] Matthew 26, 64.

In A.D. 68 a contemporary of Mark and Matthew composed an apocalyptic pamphlet which is contained within the Ethiopian *Ascension of Isaiah* and which may well be of the highest importance for the history of the tradition and interpretation of Jesus' self-revelatory statements.[n] I quote the crucial sentences:

"After it is consummated, Beliar the great ruler, king of this world, will descend . . . in the likeness of a man, a lawless king, the slayer of his mother. . . . This king will persecute the plant which the Twelve Apostles of the Beloved have planted. Of the Twelve one will be delivered into his hands. . . .[n] And all that he hath desired he will do in the world; he will do and speak like the Beloved and he will say: 'I AM God and before me no god was formed.'[n] . . . And all the people in the world will believe him. And they will sacrifice to him and they will serve him, saying: 'This is God and beside him there is none other.' And the greater number of those who shall have been associated together in order to receive the Beloved will turn aside after him. And he will set up his image before him in every city. And (after the execution of one of the Twelve) he shall bear sway three years and seven months and twenty-one days.[n] And many believers and saints having seen Him for whom they were hoping, who was crucified, Jesus, the Lord Christ, and those also who were believers in Him—of these few in those days will be left as His servants, while they flee from desert to desert, awaiting the coming of the Beloved. And after one thousand three hundred and thirty-two days the Lord will come with His angels and with the armies of the holy ones from the seventh heaven with the glory of the seventh heaven, and He will drag Beliar into Gehenna and also his armies . . . and his fire will consume all the godless, and they will be as though they had never been created." [4]

Plainly, the ruler referred to is the matricide Nero; it is

[4] Translation by R. H. Charles.

well known that the imaginations of the apocalyptics of those days dwelt in fascination upon Nero.[n] The apocalyptic writer is here taking up arms against Nero's metaphysical claims. He quotes the Emperor as declaring in the style of Isaiah 43, 10: "I am God, and before me no god was formed." This phraseology, as the author emphasizes, corresponds to the language of Jesus. This is the most important aspect of the entire text. For from it we learn that the apocalyptic writer and his readers were familiar with some *Logia* in which Jesus spoke of himself in the same style as Isaiah 43, 10: "I am God and before me no god was formed." The pamphlet in all probability dates from the spring of A.D. 68, and is therefore somewhat later than the Gospel of Mark (probably A.D. 60–2) and considerably earlier than that of John (probably A.D. 96–100). The self-revelatory formula of Jesus alluded to in this pamphlet cannot be traced to the annals of Mark, for there is nothing comparable in the Gospel of Mark.[5] Rather, the author must have been drawing upon an independent tradition about Jesus which only partially parallels the *Logia* underlying the Gospel of John.[6]

John has the Samaritan woman say: "I know that the Messiah is coming (he who is called Christ); when he comes, he will show us all things."[7] But Jesus replies to this tentative question: "I who speak to you am He." This *Logion* has always hitherto been regarded as an indirect assent to the title of Messiah. But such an interpretation is hardly correct. Rather it would seem that John intends the reply of Jesus to be understood in terms of the theophanic formula *"Ani hu."* We can list six observations in support of this view.

1) Nowhere else does the Fourth Evangelist report any claim by Jesus to be the Messiah.[n]

2) The verb "to show" is a favorite expression in Deutero-Isaiah, often linked with the theophanic formula *"Ani hu."* It is used fourteen times altogether in passages speak-

[5] See Mark 6, 50; 13, 6; 14, 62. [6] John 8, 58. [7] John 4, 25.

ing of the mysteries of the past, present, and future, which God alone knows and will make known.[n] The same verb in John 4, 25, seems intended to prepare the reader for a divine self-revelation in the manner of Deutero-Isaiah.

3) In the Qumran text of Isaiah 52, 6, God says: "Therefore shall my people know my name on that day, for I am He that doth speak: behold, here am I."[n] The crucial phrase of revelation ("I who speak to you am He") appears once more almost without change in John 4, 26.

4) According to the testimony of several of the Fathers of the Church, Jesus said: "I am He that doth speak: behold, here am I."[n] Either this is based upon an independent *Logia* tradition, or else it is a paraphrase of the passage of John already quoted. In any case, it is a confirmation of our interpretation of John 4, 26, as carrying the same meaning as Isaiah 52, 6.

5) In John 1, 49 ff., Nathanael speaks of the "King of Israel" (= Messiah), but Jesus of the "Son of Man."[8] Jesus uses the established titles as a point of departure, but he amends then and goes beyond them.[9]

6) The Samaritan woman stubbornly sticks to her messianic notion.[1] She fails to grasp the hidden meaning of *"Ani hu."* This, apparently, was Jesus' intention. He appears to have deliberately chosen the obscure revelatory formula from Isaiah 52, 6, without either accepting or rejecting the Samaritan woman's messianic terminology. His self-revelation was thus couched as a *mashal*.

We may wonder whether Jesus actually pronounced the theophanic formula for the first time on this occasion. For in all the other accounts in the Gospels the use of *"Ani hu"* by Jesus is linked with one of the two great festival seasons, Passover or Tabernacles. In John 4, 26, however, the season is the middle of winter,[2] far from the time of either feast. We

[8] Cf. Mark 8, 29 ff.   [9] Cf. John 3, 2 ff., etc.   [1] See John 4, 29. 39.
[2] Cf. John 4, 35.

must therefore ask why the Evangelist chose this particular place to include a theophanic saying. My answer is as follows:

John emphasizes[3] that in Judea Jesus confided his secret to no one. Later[4] John declares that Jesus had met with no understanding in Judea. In between is the story of the Samaritan woman, which culminates in the enigmatic theophanic pronouncement[5] and the Samaritans' profession of faith in him.[6] There is no doubt that the Evangelist intends to say that Jesus spoke his first significant but still half-obscure words concerning his secret not in Judea or in Galilee, but in Samaria, and that by so doing he evoked a considerable response, although by no means complete understanding. Jesus' remarks about the great harvest[7] and the later reproach, "You are a Samaritan,"[8] accord fully with this interpretation.

So also does an item out of the religious history of the times. Jesus had a contemporary who occasionally gave voice to such mysterious theophanic formulae: the Samaritan and Gnostic Simon Magus,[n] who lived fairly near Sychar[9] and who later tried to establish relationships with the Apostles.[1] How did a Samaritan come to use these theophanic words? The Fourth Evangelist attempts to answer this question, or at least to hint at an answer to it.[2] He appears to imply that the Samaritan Gnostic heard the theophanic formula from Jesus, and stole it.

In those chapters in John which deal with the major period of Jesus' ministry, and which parallel Mark 1 ff., the theophanic formula appears more frequently, and step by step is made plainer.

The Evangelist speaks of Jesus' walking on the water during the Passover season.[3] Here, too, the *"Ani hu"* forms the

---

[3] John 2, 24. [4] John 4, 44. [5] John 4, 26. [6] John 4, 42. [7] John 4, 35 ff. [8] John 8, 48. [9] John 4, 5. [1] Acts 8, 9 ff. [2] John 4, 26 ff. [3] John 6, 16 ff.; cf. John 6, 4. 10.

climax, just as it does in Mark.[4] Here too the self-affirmation is linked with the formula of revelation: "Fear not." It is rare that the Fourth Evangelist repeats or corroborates a Synoptic account so precisely. Here the agreement is particularly significant, for we are dealing with the scattered and obscured accounts of the Gospels concerning the apocalyptic Passover season of A.D. 31.

Following this, the Gospel of John contains an account, with material found in this Gospel alone, of the Feast of Tabernacles and the thrice-repeated *"Ani hu."* [5] This section is rich in allusions to the ritual of Tabernacles. The self-revelatory formulae are accompanied by other key phrases from the Deutero-Isaianic theophanic speeches. The mention of Abraham, which crops up apparently without transition [6] and seems closely united with the crowning theophanic formula,[7] is reminiscent of the interpolation in the Targum [8] of the figure of Abraham in the words spoken by God in Isaiah 40–55. Certainly this was not accidental.[n] As John reports it, it was only now that Jesus' opponents grasped the tremendous meaning, the claim implicit in his *"Ani hu"*—and were moved to take up stones against this blasphemer.[9]

We encounter the theophanic formula *"Ani hu"* once again in John 13, 19. Here, too, resemblance to the Deutero-Isaianic text is unmistakable. There God speaks: "Behold, the former things have come to pass, and new things I now declare; before they spring forth I tell you of them." [1] "You are my witnesses . . . whom I have chosen, that you may . . . believe . . . that I am He." [2] Here Jesus speaks: "I tell you this now, before it takes place, that when it does take place, you may believe that I am He." [3] We must note that this same assertion is again made in the Pass-

---

[4] Mark 6, 50. [5] John 8, 24. 28. 58. [6] John 8, 33 ff. [7] John 8, 56 ff.
[8] A translation, or paraphrase, of some portion, or portions, of the Old Testament in the Aramaic of Judea or Galilee. [9] John 8, 59. [1] Isaiah 42, 9; cf. 41, 23. [2] Isaiah 43, 10; cf. 43, 12. [3] John 13, 19.

over season, and again it is spoken only among the disciples.

In religious life in ancient Palestine the liturgical *"Ani hu"* was used in two specific situations: in the temple ritual of the Feast of Tabernacles, and in the private liturgy for the eve of Passover. Analogously, Jesus used this formula at the time of Tabernacles as a public self-revelation, and at the Passover only within the circle of his intimates.[n]

John omits the trial before Caiaphas and therefore says nothing of Jesus' *"Ani hu"* before the Great Sanhedrin.[4] John also fails to record the Synoptic prediction of the coming of the false Christs and their deceptive theophanic declarations.[5][n]

It is clear that our chief evidence for Jesus' use of the theophanic formulae comes from Mark and John, who in other ways also provide the most important testimony on the story of Jesus and are in agreement on decisive matters. John's account of the early revelation in Samaria[6] stands by itself; but then there could be no complement to it in Mark because the Synoptic Gospels report nothing at all about Jesus' early ministry. On the other hand, Mark 6, 50, and John 6, 20, can easily be synchronized. The further accounts in Mark and John form an interlocking pattern,[n] one taking up where the other leaves off, in accord with John's evident intention to fill in gaps.

In an explication of the oracles of Balaam[7] provided by the rabbinical school of the Torah at Caesarea, Rabbi Eleazar Hakkapar (c. A.D. 170) says: "God saw that a man, son of a woman, would come forth in the future who would endeavor to make himself God and to lead the whole world astray. Therefore he spoke: 'Beware that you do not err by following that man.' For it is said: 'A man is not God. . . . And if he says he is God, he is a liar. And he will lead men astray and say that he is going and will come back again at the end of days.' Is it not so that he spoke thus, but he will

---

[4] Cf. Mark 14, 62.   [5] Mark 13, 6.   [6] John 4, 26.   [7] Numbers 23, 19.

190

not be able to do it." [n] Here we recognize a polemic against Jesus in the guise of a scriptural exegesis. The idea is that even as far back as the time of Balaam God warned against the future preacher of apostasy, Jesus.

Some hundred years later we find Rabbi Abbahu of Caesarea citing another item derived from the same tradition. Here Balaam himself is made to repeat the blasphemous words used by Jesus: "If a man says, 'I am God,' he is a liar; if he says, 'I am the Son of Man,' his end will be such that he will rue it; if he says, 'I shall ascend to heaven,' will it not be that he will have spoken and will not be able to perform?" [n]

There can be no doubt that such passages were aimed specifically against the theophanic phrases of Jesus. The actual wording of those phrases does not coincide with the wording in the Gospels. The Balaam story in Numbers 23, 19, was subjected to an intensive rereading—a procedure possible with early consonantal rabbinical texts of the Bible—in order to "find" these passages. There is, therefore, no need to comb the Gospels for sayings that exactly correspond to the ones quoted. In general, the rabbis were not trying to co-ordinate or correct the accounts of the Gospels. They simply took no notice of them. Polemics against Jesus were based upon their own traditions concerning him and were still independent of the Gospels.

Nevertheless, we have still to decide what episode in the history of Jesus was involved here. We can arrive at this by determining which of the sayings in the Gospels most nearly coincide with the Jewish version. The more or less private self-revelations must logically be ruled out. [n] Only the public theophanic sayings can be in question, especially the self-revelations Jesus made in the presence of his opponents. [8] The closest parallels to the quotations of Jesus which Rabbi Abbahu paraphrases are to be found in John 8: "I am He," [9]

[8] John 8, 24 ff. 58; Mark 14, 62.   [9] Cf. John 8, 24. 28. 58.

and "when you have lifted up the Son of Man."[1] Rabbi Eleazar's quotations, on the other hand, largely correspond with Mark 14: "He says he is God,"[2] "He says he is going and will come back again at the end of days."[3] The argument corresponds precisely with the charge after Caiaphas had passed his verdict: Jesus wished to lead everybody astray.[n] All this suggests that Rabbi Eleazar's data and arguments were based directly or indirectly upon the circular letter which Caiaphas had to send out after the execution of Jesus,[4] and which, according to the assertions of the primitive church and the Fathers, was actually sent.[n] If this is so, then the saying of Jesus quoted by Eleazar may be adduced in order to cast new light on Mark 14, 62. It would appear that Jesus, in this interrogation by Caiaphas, did not speak of the imminence of the last days, but rather spoke of his coming again "at the end of days." For then it makes sense that Eleazar should confine himself to stating that Jesus will not be able to fulfill his prediction of returning at the "end of days"; and we at last understand why the rabbis made no allusion to an unfulfilled second coming.

With this we have fairly well completed our list of witnesses to Jesus' theophanic sayings. It is ample and unanimous enough. Mark and John, canonical and extra-canonical sources, Christian and anti-Christian testimony, all agree. There can, therefore, be no doubt that these theophanic formulae had their source in Jesus himself. We cannot say that Jesus actually spoke all the theophanic sayings attributed to him by our various witnesses, that he spoke only these, or that he spoke them in exactly the situations and using exactly the words reported. But we can with confidence maintain that the theophanic formula *"Ani hu"* was of crucial importance in Jesus' revelation of himself.[n]

Judging by the linguistic form,[n] the earlier history, and

[1] Cf. John 8, 28.   [2] Cf. Mark 14, 62.   [3] Cf. Mark 14, 62.   [4] Appendix II, 87.

the content of the *"Ani hu"* formula, there can no longer be any doubt of what Jesus meant when he used it. He was in all deliberation using the Old Testament and liturgical formula of God's self-revelation. He wished to convey that in his life the historical epiphany of God was taking place.

This self-affirmation is in no way consonant with the dream of the Messiah which dominated the Christology of the primitive church. Hence it was that primitive Christianity did not know quite what to make of Jesus' *"Ani hu"* and often pushed it aside, reinterpreted it, or changed it. This was done principally by Matthew, the foremost exponent of messianic dogma in the early church.

Jesus' theophanic formula was equally incompatible with the intense apocalyptic expectation of the coming of the Last Days which dominated both Jewish and Christian thought in the early Christian era. Jesus told his opponents that only future revelation would bring his secret fully to light.[n] There was logic behind this statement, but this logic had nothing to do with the eschatological fever that expected the end of the world to come from one day to the next. The great event in the history of revelation had already taken place; God was present. Anyone who spoke in such terms was not interested in apocalyptic oracles and the appointing of a date for the end of the world. But the group around Matthew was increasingly interested in just those questions. Matthew therefore gave short shrift to Jesus' theophanic sayings. The rendition of Jesus' words in Matthew 26, 64, is a vivid example of the apostle's distortion of Jesus' original message.[n]

Consequently, the theophanic formula employed by Jesus is still another negative factor in our examination of the Gospels for messianic dogma and eschatological hopes. At the same time, this formula agrees perfectly with all that we have discovered concerning Jesus' essential doctrines. The kingdom of God is in the midst of you. Why? Because God is in the midst of you. Jesus called himself the Son of Man.

But in assuming this title he likewise claimed for himself the majesty and power of God.[n] He referred to himself as the Son of God, thereby averting the possible misunderstanding that "heaven," so to speak, would be "empty" during the historical epiphany of God. But at the same time he emphasized that the Father had "delivered all things" to the son.[5] With a clarity that often made him enemies, Jesus stated that this creative and redeeming plenitude of power had nothing to do with human virtuousness and perfection, certainly not with Pharisaic blamelessness.[6] With even greater frequency and clarity, however, Jesus stated that the divine dignity and power could not save him from suffering and dying. On the contrary, it is only against the background of his theophanic words that Jesus' predictions of his Passion reveal their gravest meaning: that the epiphany of God on this earth was to be consummated in the *passio humana* upon the cross.

The theophanic formula used by Jesus was the purest, the boldest, and the profoundest declaration by Jesus of who and what he was.

It was the purest declaration because in this one case Jesus abstained from using the figurative language of the ancient Orient, which is so often an obstacle to modern Western man's understanding of the sayings of Jesus. In this one case no elements of mythology, Gnosticism, mysticism, speculation, metaphysics, or theory entered in, no proof by scriptural texts, no dogmatic doctrines about pre-existence, incarnation, virgin birth. Here theology ceased, for this was, this is, theophany.

It was the boldest declaration. "I am He"—this meant: where I am, there God is, there God lives and speaks,[n] calls, asks, acts, decides, loves, chooses, forgives, rejects, suffers, and dies. Nothing bolder can be said, or imagined.

It was the profoundest declaration. The historical epiphany of God was fulfilled in the form of a man, not only of a

[5] Luke 10, 22.   [6] Mark 1, 9; 10, 18.

194

fallible, suffering, mortal man, but of a human man; in the form of a new humanity and brotherhood, in the forward-looking form of a wholly new *humanitas*. God himself had become man, more human than any other man in the wide expanse of history.

APPENDIXES

and

NOTES

S. establishes the historical Jesus — but nothing as to what he was or claimed to be.

S. believes these events; B. can't find them

Much of the story is based on gospel narratives substantiated by historical occurances which declare their possibility.

KEY TO ABBREVIATIONS

in

APPENDIX II *and* NOTES

Aboda — Aboda zara
Aboth — Pirkē Aboth
Aboth de R. Nathan — Aboth
of Rabbi Nathan
Apoc. Abrah. — Apocalypse of
Abraham
Apoc. Mos. — Apocalypse of
Moses
Asc. Isa. — Ascension of Isaiah
Ass. Mos. — Assumption of
Moses
B (before Talmud tractates) —
Babylonian Talmud
3 Bar. — Greek Apocalypse of
Baruch
S. Baruch — Syrian Apoca-
lypse of Baruch
B. Bath. — Baba Bathra
Ber. — Berakoth
Bikk. — Bikkurim

Billerbeck — (H. L. Strack
and) P. Billerbeck: *Kom-
mentar zum Neuen Testa-
ment aus Talmud und
Midrasch*, 4 vols. Munich,
1922–8, 1951.
B.M. — Baba Mezia
Cant. r. — Canticum rabba
C.G.C. — *Catalogue of Greek
Coins in the British Mu-
seum.*
C.I.L. — *Corpus Inscriptionum
Latinarum.* Berlin, 1862–
1909.
Dmd. — The Damascus Docu-
ment
D.S.M. — "Manual of Disci-
pline," *The Dead Sea
Scrolls,* Vol. II, Millar Bur-

rows, ed. New Haven, 1951.
Eduy. — Eduyyoth
En. — Enoch
E. Enoch — Ethiopian Enoch
Ep. Ar. — Letter of Aristeas
Euseb. *H.E.* — Eusebius: *Historia Ecclesiastica*
Ex. r. — Exodus rabba
4 Ezr. — Fourth Book of Ezra
Gen. r. — Genesis rabba
Ginza — Mark Lidzbarski: *Ginza.* Göttingen, 1925.
Git. — Gittin
Herm. — Hermas: *Pastor*
   m. — *mandatae*
   sim. — *similitudines*
Hor. — Horayoth
Hul. — Hullin
Ign. — Ignatius
   Eph. — To the Ephesians
   Smyrn. — To the Smyrnaeans
J (before Talmud tractates) — Palestine Talmud
Jos. — Flavius Josephus
   Ant. — *Antiquities*
   Apion — *Against Apion*
   Jew. W. — *Jewish War*
   Life — *Life*
Jub. — Book of Jubilees
Keth. — Kethubboth
Kid. — Kiddushim
Koh. r. — Koheleth rabba
Lev. r. — Leviticus rabba
Mak. — Makkoth
Mart. Isa. — Martyrdom of Isaiah
Meg. — Megilla
Megillath Taanith — "Scroll of Fasts"

Mek. Ex. — Mekilta Exodus
Men. — Menahoth
Mid. — Middoth
Midr. Sam. — Midrash on the Book of Samuel
Midr. Tann. — Midrash Tanna debe Eliyyahu
Mishle r. — Midrash on the Book of Proverbs
M. K. — Mo'ed Katan
M.P.L. — *Patrologia, Series Latina,* J. P. Migne, ed.
Nu. r. — Numeri rabba (Midrash on Numbers)
Otsar — E. L. Sukenik: *Otsar Ha-megilot Ha-genuzot.* Jerusalem, 1954.
Pe'a — Pe'a
Pes. — Pesahim
Pesikta — Pesikta de Rab Kahana
Pesikta rabb. — Pesikta Rabbathi
Ps. Clem. *Hom.* — Pseudo-Clementine Homilies
Ps. Clem. *Rec.* — Pseudo-Clementine Recognitions
Ps. Phil. — Pseudo-Philo's Liber Antiquitatum, *Biblicarum,* Guido Kisch, ed. South Bend, Indiana, 1949.
Ps. Sol. — Psalms of Solomon
Rev. Abr. — Revelation of Abraham
R.H. — Rosh Ha-shana
Sanh. — Sanhedrin
S. Deut. — Siphre Deuteronomium
Semah. — Semahoth
Shabb. — Shabbath
Shebu. — Shebu'oth

Sib. — Sibylline Oracles
S. Num. — Siphre Numeri
Soph. — Sopherim
Sukk. — Sukka
Taan. — Ta'anith
Talmud W. — *Wörterbuch über die Talmudim und Midraschim,* Jacob Levy, Vols. I–IV. Berlin and Vienna, 1924.
Targ. Jer. — Jerusalem Targum I
Tehillim — Midrash Tehillim
Terum. — Terumoth
Test. — Testament
    Benj. — Benjamin

Jos. — Joseph
Lev. — Levi
Naphthali — Naphthali
Test. Abr. — Testament of Abraham
Thr. r. — Threni rabba
Tos. (before Mishnah tractates) — Tosephta
T.W.z.N.T. — *Theologisches Wörterbuch zum Neuen Testament,* Gerhard Kittel, ed., Vols. Iff. Stuttgart, 1933–.
Yeb. — Yebamoth
Yom. — Yoma

JOURNALS AND PERIODICALS

H.T.R. — *Harvard Theological Review*
H.U.C.A. — *Hebrew Union College Annual*
J.B.L. — *Journal of Biblical Literature*
J.Q.R. — *Jewish Quarterly Review*
Nov. Test. — *Novum Testamentum*
S.B.T. — Studies in Biblical Theology
Th.L.Z. — *Theologische Literaturzeitung*
Th.Z. — Theologische Zeitschrift

V.T. — *Vetus Testamentum*
Z.A.W. — *Zeitschrift für die alttestamentliche Wissenschaft*
Z.D.M.G. — *Zeitschrift der deutschen morgenländischen Gesellschaft*
Z.N.W. — *Zeitschrift für die neutestamentliche Wissenschaft*
Z.R.G.G. — *Zeitschrift für Religions- und Geistesgeschichte*
Z.Th.K. — *Zeitschrift zur Theologie und Kirche*

APPENDIX I

POLITICAL RULERS IN THE TIME OF JESUS

ROME	PALESTINE
B.C.	B.C.
44 Assassination of Julius Caesar	37 Herod I (the Great) King of Judea, etc.
30 Suicide of Antony and Cleopatra; Augustus emperor	
12 Quirinius viceroy of the East (with intervals to A.D. 17)	8 Herod I degraded
	7 Jesus born
	4 Death of Herod I, leaving Archelaus ethnarch of Judea (to A.D. 6), Herod Antipas tetrarch of Galilee (to A.D. 39), Philip tetrarch of Iturea, etc. (to A.D. 34)

A.D.

14 Death of Augustus; Tiberius emperor

15 Sejanus prefect of Rome

31 Sejanus executed

37 Death of Tiberius; Caligula emperor

A.D.

6 Judea under Roman procurators

18 Joseph Caiaphas high priest

26 Pontius Pilate procurator of Judea

28 Jesus baptized

32 Jesus crucified

36 Pontius Pilate recalled

37 Joseph Caiaphas deposed

APPENDIX II

THE PROVISIONS AGAINST HERETICS

THE JEWS OF ANCIENT PALESTINE were familiar with the concept of the heretic. The Old Testament itself threatened dire penalties against any who opposed the Law. The early rabbinate translated these threats into practice by applying them to specific cases. They did not, however, ever draw up a systematic penal code. Yet we must be familiar with the legal practices in the age of the New Testament if we are to understand the conflicts and actions of the Great Sanhedrin. I have therefore compiled a summary of the most important provisions against heresy, numbering them for easy reference.

It must be emphasized again that the ancient Jewish lawbooks did not have any such systematic arrangement.[1]

1. Whoever wittingly and deliberately violates the Sabbath prohibitions or any other prescript of the Torah is a blasphemer.

[1] The above lines and the numbered sections that follow have been translated, for the convenience of readers of this American edition, from *Jerusalem und Rom,* by Ethelbert Stauffer (Bern: Francke Verlag; 1957), pp. 113 ff. Only those sections are cited here to which reference has been made in this book.—Translators' note.

(Ex. 20, 8; Nu. 15, 30 ff.; S. Num. 15, 30 f.; Lev. r. on 1, 2. On the other hand, an unintentional violation of the Sabbath can be atoned for by a simple sin-offering; see Shabb. 7, 1.) [2]

2.　He must be warned. (Nu. 15, 32; Deut. 9, 3 ff.; 17 ff.; Sanh. 5, 1; 7, 8.)

6.　The Great Sanhedrin in the temple at Jerusalem pronounces justice on the authority of God. (Deut. 17, 8–12; Simon ben Shetach in Sanh. 19 a; J Sanh. 1, 18 b; Jos. *Ant.* 4, 8, 14; S. Deut. 17, 12; Hor. 1, 1; Tanchuma Nasa 202 a.)

7.　Opposition to the Great Sanhedrin's right to pronounce justice is punishable by death. (Deut. 17, 12; Sanh. 11, 1 ff.; cf. Ex. 22, 27, Targumim and Mek. Ex. 22, 27.)

15.　Whoever vilifies or profanes the temple is to be punished by death. (Jer. 7, 11 ff.; 26, 11; Tos. Sanh. 13, 5; R.H. 17 a; J Ber. 9, 13 b; Ps. Phil. 25, 9; Acts 6, 13; 21, 28.)

18.　Whoever arrogates to himself divine honors or privileges is a blasphemer. (Ezek. 28, 2 ff.; Ps. Sol. 2, 28 f.; Mek. Ex. 15, 7. 11; S. Deut. 21, 22; Sanh. 10, 1.)

30.　A "misleader" is a Jew who has enticed, or attempted to entice, another Jew to practice idolatry or to become an apostate. (Deut. 13, 7 f.; Sanh. 7, 10; Cant. r. 2, 13; Pesikta 51 a.)

31.　Every Jew is obligated to denounce a "misleader." (Deut. 13, 8; Sanh. 7, 10; Lev. 5, 1; Sanh. 4, 5.)

33.　To expose a "misleader," the use of "secret witnesses," though not permitted in any other cases at law, is approved. Two loyal men who are fit to bear witness are set to keep watch over the suspected person until he betrays himself. Then the witnesses are to seize him at once and bring him before the Great Sanhedrin in Jerusalem. (Deut. 13, 7–10; Sanh. 7, 10; Sanh. 67 a; contrary example, J Sanh. 3, 21 c.)

34.　In difficult cases the Great Sanhedrin in Jerusalem sends out two agents who are to watch the suspect, catch him in the act, arrest him, and bring him to Jerusalem. (Tos. Sanh. 10, 11; J Sanh. 7, 25 c-d; J Yeb. 16, 15 d.)

[2] For Key to Abbreviations, see page 199.

42. A "misled town" is a town or village wherein a large-scale defection has arisen as the result of the agitation of a preacher of apostasy. (Deut. 13, 13 f.; 1 Mac. 9, 23. 58; Jub. 1, 20; Ps. Phil. 25, 5. 9 ff.; 26, 2; Sanh. 1, 5; 10, 4. 6; Tos. Sanh. 14, 1; Sanh. 111 B Baraitha.)

43. The Great Sanhedrin in Jerusalem must have a thorough investigation made on the spot by official envoys, in order to determine the extent of the defection; the instigators, the apostates, and the innocent must be sharply distinguished. (Deut. 13, 15; Ps. Phil. 25, 3 ff. 6. 8; Sanh. 10, 4; Acts 8, 3; 9, 1 f.; 22, 4 f. 19; 26, 10–12.)

52. A pseudo-prophet is a preacher of apostasy who seeks to lead Israel astray by dreams, visions, lying oracles, magic, necromancy, deception of the senses, or genuine miracles. (Deut. 13, 2 f.; 18, 20 ff.; Lev. 19, 31; Jer. 28, 1 ff.; Mart. Isa. 3, 1; Sib. 3, 63 ff.; Sanh. 8, 7. 11; 11, 4 f.; Tos. Sanh. 14, 13; Sanh. 90 a; S. Deut. 13, 2; J Hor. 3, 48; cf. Cant. r. 17 a.)

54. The pseudo-prophet is usually regarded as an instrument of hell, filled with the spirit of Belial, by whose power he performs the misleading miracles. (Lev. 20, 6; Deut. 18, 10 f.; Mart. Isa. 2, 12 ff.; Dmd. 12, 2 f.)

55. A pseudo-prophet must be sentenced by the Great Sanhedrin and executed in Jerusalem. (Deut. 13, 6; 18, 20; Dmd. 12, 2 f.; Sanh. 1, 5; cf. Luke 13, 33.)

59. If a man is suspected of apostasy, the circumstances of his birth are to be investigated. For the *mamser* (bastard) is inclined toward rebellion and blasphemy. (Lev. 24, 10 ff.; Targum same place; S. Lev. 24, 10 ff.; Kalla 41 d. The *mamser* must be distinguished from the *beduki* and the *shethuki*. The *beduki* is a child whose birth still requires investigation [Kid. 4, 2; B Kid. 74 a; J Kid. 4, 65 d]. The *shethuki* is a child whose father can no longer be determined [Kid. 4, 1; B Kid. 69 a; 73 a; Yeb. 100 b].)

60. As long as a *mamser* leads a life pleasing to God, nothing insulting shall be said about his birth. (Tos. Eduy. 3, 4 [459]; Kid. 70 b; 71 a Baraitha; Tos. Kid. 5, 2 [341]; Lev. r. 24, 10; Rashi on Ex. 12, 38, and Lev. 24, 10. Also Aboth 5, 20 ff. in Codex M [in Karl Marti–Georg Beer: *Aboth* (Giessen; 1927), p. 157]: "Every-

one who casts aspersions [upon another because the circumstances of his birth] is himself tainted.")

61.   If the *mamser* becomes an apostate, his illegitimate birth shall be spoken of publicly and unsparingly. (Lev. 24, 10 f.; Tos. Eduy. 3, 4 [459], Lev. r. 24, 10; Meg. 25 b; Soph. 9, 11.)

62.   A person is characterized as an illegitimate child when he is named with the name of his mother. For he "has no father." (Lev. 24, 11; Mek. Ex. 12, 6; Lev. r. 24, 10; Nu. r. 6, 2; 25, 1; Mishle r. 7, 23, end.)

64.   The Great Sanhedrin in Jerusalem is the ultimate court of appeal for all difficult cases and questions at law. (Deut. 1, 17; 17, 8 ff.; Jos. *Ant.* 4, 8, 14; Sanh. 11, 2; S. Deut. 17, 8; Sanh. 14 b; J Sanh. 1, 19 c.)

65.   The Great Sanhedrin in Jerusalem is the sole court empowered to impose death sentences in all cases and types of apostasy. (Deut. 18, 8 ff.; Jos. *Ant.* 4, 8, 14; Sanh. 11, 3; Sanh. 41 a Baraitha; Aboda 8 b.)

69.   Every case of apostasy must be corroborated by at least two witnesses. (Deut. 19, 15; cf. Susanna 36 ff.)

70.   The testimony of the witnesses for the prosecution must agree completely in all material matters, down to the most trifling details and incidentals. (Aboth 1, 9; Susanna 54 ff.; Sanh. 4, 1; 5, 1 ff.; Mak. 1, 3–8; Tos. Sanh. 5, 5; 6, 3.)

71.   Once sentence has been pronounced, it cannot be reversed even though one of the witnesses for the prosecution should recant. (Simon ben Shetach in Sanh. 6, 23 b. But cf. Sanh. 4, 1; 6, 1; b Sanh. 33 b Baraitha.)

72.   Women are not qualified to bear witness. (Jos. *Ant.* 4, 8, 15; Shebu. 4, 1; Nu. r. 10 [159] b; J Yom. 6, 2.)

78.   The corruptor of the people must die so that the corruption will not spread. (Deut. 17, 7; 22, 21 ff.; 24, 7; S. Deut. on these passages; Jos. *Ant.* 18, 5, 2, 118; 1 Cor. 5, 6. 13; Ps. Phil. 25, 5; Sanh. 43 a; Gen. r. 94.)

79.   The wicked man must be destroyed so that God's wrath will be lifted from the people. (Nu. 25, 13; Deut. 13, 6. 18; Targumim on Deut. 13, 6; S. Deut. 13, 6; Ps. Phil. 25, 3; Sanh. 10,

6; cf. 2 Sam. 20, 21 f.; 21, 14; J Terum. 8, 46 b [below] in Talmud W. III, p. 177 a.)

80. The punishment of the godless man is meted out for his own salvation and that of the people. (Ps. Phil. 25, 3. 5; 26, 1; Sanh. 8, 5; Sanh. 71 B Baraitha; Sanh. 113 b; Rashi on Deut. 21, 17.)

81. Should the condemned acknowledge and repent their guilt before execution, they are assured of God's forgiveness and a share in the future world. (Jos. *Ant.* 7, 19 ff.; Deut. 13, 18; Ps. Phil. 25, 7; Sanh. 6, 2; Sanh. 43 b; Semah. 2, 9.)

83. The prime aim of punishment is deterrence. (Deut. 17, 12 f.; 19, 19 f.; 21, 21; S. Deut. on these passages; cf. 1 Tim. 5, 20.)

86. Such executions are therefore to be performed at the time of the great pilgrimage festivals (Tabernacles, Passover, Whitsun), and their purpose will best be achieved by having them done on the eve of the first principal holiday when the swarms of pilgrims from all over the world are already assembled in Jerusalem, but the holiday peace has not yet begun. (Sanh. 11, 3; Tos. Sanh. 11, 7; S. Deut. 13, 12; Rashi on Deut. 17, 13.)

87. In special cases the Great Sanhedrin in Jerusalem is to announce the execution by official envoys and circular letters to all communities. (Sanh. 11, 3; Sanh. 89 a Baraitha.)

88. These circular letters must list the forename and family name of the executed person, the names of the witnesses, the verdict, justification of the verdict, and a brief account of the execution. (Tos. Sanh. 11, 7; Midr. Tann. on Deut. 17, 13.)

95. Criminals who have met death by stoning or hanging are to be buried in potter's field. (Ps. 26, 9; Tos. Sanh. 9, 8 f.; Sanh. 6, 7; Sanh. 45 b Baraitha.)

107. In the year 4 B.C. the right of Herod I to pass death sentences in Galilee and Trans-Jordan was transferred to his son Herod Antipas. (Jos. *Jew.* W. 2, 6, 3; Mark 6, 16; Luke 13, 31; 23, 7.)

112. Around A.D. 30 the imperial government (under Sejanus) deprived the Great Sanhedrin in Jerusalem of its right to pass death sentences. The Great Sanhedrin was permitted to issue

warrants for pursuit and arrest, and could make arrests. But the
court sessions that might lead to a capital trial had to be approved
beforehand by the procurator. The Great Sanhedrin continued to
have the right to pass death sentences in matters of religious law,
but was required to turn the condemned man over to the procurator for confirmation and execution of the sentence. (J Sanh. 1,
18 a Baraitha; 7, 24 b; B Sanh. 41 a Baraitha; Aboda 8 b Baraitha;
Shabb. 15 a; Philo, *Legatio* 302; Jos. *Ant.* 20, 9, 1, 202; Acts 22, 30;
25, 9.)

113. After the fall of Sejanus (October 18, A.D. 31), Pilate in
practice occasionally gave the Great Sanhedrin a freer hand. But
the fundamental judicial situation remained unchanged. (Acts 7,
54 ff.; 26, 10; Megillath Taanith 6; cf. Ernst Bammel: *"Der 28.
Adar,"* H.U.C.A. 28, 1956.)

122. A ban was pronounced upon the apostate, the conse-
quence of which was his excommunication. (John 8, 49; 9, 22.
34 f. R.H. 24 b-25 a; cf. Tos Sanh. 12, 9; 13, 4; Ps. Phil. 26, 5.)

123. On Passover eve the apostate was not allowed to eat of
the Passover lamb. On the other hand, he was permitted to eat
unleavened bread and bitter herbs. (Ex. 12, 43. 48; Ezek. 44, 9 ff.;
Mek. Ex. 12, 43; Pes. 96 a; Yeb. 71 a.)

NOTES

These notes are intended for scholars. Well-known source authorities or monographs are quoted only seldom. On the other hand, there is a large collection of references wherever I advance observations or theses of my own, or deal with new problems and subjects that have been treated too briefly in research. There is no space here for thorough demonstration and discussion. For this reason I have had to refer more frequently than I like to my own papers in specialist journals; in these I have given a full account, with all the pros and cons, of particular hypotheses.

CHAPTER I

P. 3, l. 6 FOR PETRINE FORMULAE, see Acts 2, 22 ff.; 2, 36; 3, 13 ff.; 4, 10; 4, 27 f.; 5, 30 f.; 10, 37 f.; 13, 23 ff. For pre-Petrine evidence concerning Jesus in the Pauline epistles, see 1 Cor. 11, 23 ff.; 15, 3 ff.; etc. For the source value of the Gospels, see T. W. Manson, "The Life of Jesus: A Study of the Available Material," *Bulletin of the John Rylands Library*, Vols. 27–30 (Manchester, 1943–7); "John the Baptist," ibid., Vol. 36 (1954), p. 395 ff.

p. 4, l. 3 There can be no doubt that the collection of *Logia* existed in written form even before Mark. For the Jews of ancient Palestine were far readier with the pen (see Koh. r. 12, 12) and far more literate (consider the Qumran scrolls) than is generally assumed. They were particularly fond of collections of sayings (Ahikar; Proverbs; Ecclesiastes; Wisdom; Sirach; Pirkē Aboth, etc.). Apparently the sayings of Johanan ben Zakkai were also collected in writing; see W. Bacher, *Agada der Tannaiten* (2nd ed., Strassburg, 1903), p. 41. The collection of *Logia* was the oldest Christian book on Jesus. Even so, it obviously contained, along with authentic and revised sayings of Jesus, many Jesus-like sayings from before and after his time, including some sayings of John the Baptist. Naturally, the collection of sayings circulated in several versions (cf. Dan., Tob., Mark, Acts, Mekilta, *Toledoth Jeshu,* and similar writings). None of those versions has been preserved, but we now know several later forms of the same type of work (Oxyrynchus, Nag Hammadi, etc.).

p. 4, l. 17 Pliny the Younger, *Ep.* 10; Tacitus, *Ann.* 15, 44; Suetonius, *Claudius* 25, etc.; see J. B. Aufhauser, *Antike Jesuszeugnisse* (2nd ed., Bonn, 1925).

p. 5, l. 20 For material from the Mandaean writings and the Koran, see Ethelbert Stauffer, *"Antike Jesustradition und Jesuspolemik im mittelalterlichen Orient,"* Z.N.W., Vol. 46 (1955), pp. 1 ff., 264 ff. Michael Asin et Palacios, *Logia et Agrapha Domini Jesu, Patrologia Orientalis,* Vol. 13 (Paris, 1916), p. 327 ff., and Vol. 19 (Paris, 1926), p. 529 ff., contain 233 Islamic sayings of Jesus.

p. 5, l. 30 For the Chinese Lives of Jesus of the seventh century, see P. Y. Saeki, *The Nestorian Documents and Relics in China* (2nd ed., Tokyo, 1951), p. 206 ff. and *passim.* For their connections with the *Toledoth Jeshu,* see Stauffer in *Nov. Test.,* Vol. 1 (Leiden, 1956), p. 96 ff. For the Taoist Life of Jesus, see *The Chinese Recorder,* Vol. 55 (Shanghai, 1924), p. 109 ff.

p. 6, n. 6 In John 5, 1, the feast is that of Tabernacles. See below, note to page 73, line 11. Hence there is no need to transpose chapters 5, 6, and 7—a transposition often suggested on grounds of the synchronization of John 5, 1, with the Passover of John 6, 4.

p. 7, l. 13 See John 2, 12; 2, 13 ff.; 3, 24; 18, 12; 18, 28 ff.

p. 9, l. 20 Presumably there was originally hidden in Mark 6, 14. 16, and 8, 28, the imputation of necromancy in the sense of Ps. Clem. *Rec.* 2, 13, 1 f., where the Samaritan Simon Magus explains his miraculous powers. Thus C. H. Kraeling, "Was Jesus Accused of Necromancy?" *J.B.L.,* Vol. 59 (1940), p. 146 ff. This accords with the imputation in John 8, 48, and the rabbinical polemics against Jesus as a practitioner of magic and necromancy. See, e.g., Sanh.

Notes

43 a; Pionius, *Acta Sanctorum* for February 1: *"Dicunt [Judaei]
Christum necromantiam exercuisse."* (See below, note to page 101,
line 17.)

CHAPTER 2

P. 13, l. 1 Rom. 1, 3; Mark 10, 47 f.; Matt. 12, 23; 21, 9; Rev. 5, 5;
22, 16.

p. 13, l. 3 See Num. 1, 2; Jos. *Ant.* 6, 4, 1 and *passim.*

p. 14, l. 5 See Ethelbert Stauffer, *Jerusalem und Rom* (Bern, 1957),
chaps. 3, 5, and 7.

p. 14, l. 24 Neh. 10, 35; Taan. 4, 5; J Taan. 4, 2; Euseb. *H.E.* 3, 32, 4.

p. 14, l. 27 Cf. Euseb. *H.E.* 1, 7.

p. 15, l. 2 Euseb. *H.E.* 3, 20; 3, 32, 3.

p. 15, l. 12 Rom. 9, 4 f.; Acts 5, 5; cf. 1 Thess. 2, 15; Jos. *Apion.
passim;* Tacitus, *Hist.* 5, 3 ff.

p. 16, l. 17 See Deut. 20, 18 ff.; Targ. Jer. Vol. 1, *ad loc.* For the after-
effects of the controversy about Jesus, see Kalla 18 b; 41 d; Sanh.
107 b; Sota 47 a.

p. 16, l. 27 See Matt. 3, 13; John 2, 12. It is also possible that the
Christology of the early Church, based on priestly theology, presupposes Jesus being born by parthenogenesis of Mary of the House
of Aaron.

p. 16, l. 32 A list of ditch-diggers on a Vatican papyrus enumerates
several hundred persons. In about 65 cases there appears, instead of
the usual patronymic, the note *"apatōr."* See Friedrich Preisigke,
Sammelbuch (Berlin and Leipzig, 1913), No. 5124.

p. 17, l. 14 Hence the striking mention of Tamar, Rahab, Ruth, and
Bathsheba in Matt. 1, 3 ff.—four women in the genealogical table
of the Israelite kings who became mothers under more or less
dubious circumstances. An Arabic parallel to this is the courtesan
Zarca in the family tree of the Omayad Caliph Merwan I, which
provided his enemies with many occasions for attack. See W. R.
Smith, *Kinship and Marriage in Early Arabia* (London, 1907), p.
171.

p. 17, l. 15 Shabb. 104 b; Sanh. 67 a; Pesikta rabb. 100 b. Such phrases
were typical of polemical writings. Thus, for example, Rabbi
Nehemia (*c.* A.D. 150) calls the hated Emperor Titus, in S. Deut.
328, p. 139 b, the "son of Vespasian's wife"—*"ben ishtho shel
Ispasianos."*

p. 17, l. 19 Tos. Hul. 2, 24 and *passim;* Origen, *Cels.* 1, 32 and frequently. But the Greek Celsus is the first to offer an explanation of

Luke 1, 26 ff., from the point of view of the "history of religion"; see Origen, *Cels.* 1, 37.

p. 17, l. 22 See Nathan Adler and M. Seligsohn, *Une Nouvelle Chronique samaritaine* (Paris, 1903), p. 41 ff.; *Ginza,* Right-hand part, 382 (Lidzbarski, p. 410, 32). But the Mandaeans gave a perverted account of the virgin birth from the demonological, not pornographic, aspect; see, e.g, *Ginza,* Right-hand part, 56 (Lidzbarski, p. 50, 15 ff.). The counterpart to this, in a positive sense, is the mythological story of the birth of John the Baptist in the *John Book,* p. 116 ff. (Mark Lidzbarski, *Das Johannesbuch der Mandäer* [Giessen, 1915], p. 115 f.) For the connections among the disciples of the Baptist, the Samaritans, and the Mandaeans in traditional history, see Stauffer, *Z.N.W.,* Vol. 46 (1955), p. 13 f.

p. 18, l. 24 Matt. 1, 19; cf. Deut. 22, 23 f.; S. Deut. § 239 f.; 242; Sanh. 7, 9; Git. 6, 2; John 8, 5.

p. 18, l. 26 Matt. 1, 20. 24; Luke 2, 5; cf. 3 Macc. 4, 6 ff.; Gen. r. 26; Tos. Keth. 1, 4.

p. 18, l. 29 Matt. 1, 25; Luke 2, 22 ff.; cf. Isa. 43, 1; Ps. 2, 7. An Arabian example is given in W. R. Smith, op. cit., p. 169 f.: the Omayad Abu Sofyan had a son by a courtesan. His name was Ziyad, "Son of his father"—i.e., an unknown father. Abu Sofyan later adopted the child, thus legally admitting him to the dynasty of the caliphs of Damascus. An example of the opposite in familial law is the disowning of a child; see Gen. 21, 9 ff.; Luke 15, 19; Ex. r. 46, 4 ("They are not my sons; I know them not; their mother committed adultery and bore them"). See P. M. Meyer, *Juristische Papyri* (Berlin, 1920), p. 25 ff., for the disinheriting of a daughter by the formula of disowning.

p. 20, l. 19 J Sota 9, 10; Euseb. *H.E.* 1, 7, 17.

p. 20, l. 25 Origen, *Cels.* 1, 51.

p. 21, l. 7 Justin, *Dial.* 78, 5, etc.

p. 21, l. 31 D. F. Strauss, *Das Leben Jesu* (Tübingen, 1835), Vol. 1, p. 199 ff. Repeated with some additions in *Leben Jesu für das deutsche Volk* (1864).

p. 21, l. 34 Thus, e.g., Emil Schürer, *Geschichte des jüdischen Volkes im Zeitalter Jesu Christi* (Leipzig), Vol. 1, and E. Klostermann, *Lukasevangelium,* both in all editions.

p. 23, l. 11 Theodor Mommsen, *Staatsrecht* (Leipzig, 1887), Vol. 2, p. 1094.

p. 24, l. 11 The classic book by L. Mitteis, *Reichsrecht und Volksrecht in den östlichen Provinzen des Römischen Kaiserreichs* (Leipzig, 1891), is still of fundamental importance for understanding the history of Syrian law. However, it deals more with the law of inheritance than with that of taxation.

p. 25, l. 15 Lactantius, *De mortibus persecutorum* 23, 1 ff. Cf. 26, 2 ff.; 36, 1 f. That Roman census officials were already handling the survey and assessment in this manner in the early imperial age in Palestine is proved indirectly by the hitherto entirely neglected account of Flavius Josephus in *Ant.* 5, 1, 21. In this passage Josephus was evidently illustrating the brief note about the survey in Josh. 18, 9, out of his knowledge of the Roman methods of surveying and assessment in his own time.

p. 25, l. 21 S. L. Wallace, *Taxation in Egypt from Augustus to Diocletian* (Princeton, 1938), gives a brief survey of the period of the principate. E. Seidl reports regularly on recent research into juristic papyrology in *Studia et Documenta Historiae et Juris.*

p. 25, l. 33 Luke 2, 2: *"apographēi";* cf. the same term in Acts 5, 37.

p. 26, l. 2 Jos. *Ant.* 18, 1, 1; 18, 2, 1 and *passim.*

p. 27, l. 5 The Nabataean coins may be found in *C.G.C.,* "Arabia, etc." (1922), p. 3 ff. The report on the tax collector under Vespasian was noted by Mommsen in *Römische Geschichte* (Berlin, 1885), Vol. 5, p. 479. Mommsen himself comments: "It was not unprecedented for a vassal state to be brought into the sphere of the imperial taxation. This occurred in, for example, the Alpine regions."

p. 27, l. 10 See *C.G.C.,* "Galatia, etc." (1899), p. 233 ff.; B. V. Head, *Historia Nummorum* (2nd ed., Oxford, 1911), p. 780; A. R. Bellinger, "The Coins," in *Excavations at Dura-Europos,* Final Report, Vol. 6 (New Haven, 1949), p. 86.

p. 27, l. 30 One of the first to recognize the authenticity of the inscriptions without reservation was the great Mommsen (*Ephemeris Epigraphica* [1881], p. 537 ff.), who as late as 1872 had still declared: "Up till now not a single expert has defended the genuineness of this monstrosity" (*C.I.L.,* Vol. 5, 1, p. 15 * No. 136 *).

p. 28, l. 30 The coins of Herod the Great in *C.G.C.,* "Palestine" (1914), p. 220 ff.; A. Reifenberg, *Ancient Jewish Coins* (2nd ed., Jerusalem, 1947), p. 42 f. Two facts indicate how much the ban on silver coinage rankled in the hearts of the Jews: (1) Josephus pretends that Herod I also struck silver coins—indeed, silver ones especially (see Jos. *Jew. W.* 1, 18; 4, 358); (2) the Jewish rebel chieftains of A.D. 66 ff. and A.D. 132 ff. immediately coined their own silver money.

On the titles *Amicus Caesaris* and *Socius Populi Romani* see Jos. *Ant.* 16, 9, 3 f.; 16, 10, 8 f.; also E. Bammel in *Th.L.Z.,* Vol. 77

(1952), column 205 ff. Josephus' principal source in this matter is Nicholas Damascenus, who went personally to Rome with Herod to bring about a reconciliation with the Emperor and naturally made much ado about the success of his labors on behalf of reconciliation.

p. 30, l. 14 The tradition embodied in Josephus apparently also preserves memories of Quirinius' *imperium maius.* See *Ant.* 18, 1, 1.

p. 30, l. 23 Ulpian, *Digests* L, 15, 4 § 2. On the question of the *idia* in the papyri, see H. Braunert, *"Studien zur Bevölkerungsgeschichte des ptolemäischen und römischen Ägypten,"* in *The Journal of Juristic Papyrology,* Vol. 9–10 (Warsaw, 1956), p. 305 ff. Braunert rightly emphasizes that papyri relating to the place of registration for the Egyptian census are still scanty, and that we must be careful on that account alone when drawing conclusions in respect to Palestine by analogy with Egyptian conditions. To my mind, the key word to elucidate the specific technique of taxation used in Roman Palestine is the ancient Jewish term *patria* in Luke 2, 4. It is here the equivalent of the Egyptian *idia* and reveals how Quirinius adapted Roman tax techniques to the land of Israel by drawing upon familial law.

p. 30, l. 30 As late as 1872 the Turkish government encountered great difficulties in registering property in Palestine for fiscal purposes, because most of the land there was held collectively. See H. Schaeffer, *Hebrew Tribal Economy* (Leipzig, 1922), p. 129 f.

p. 31, l. 4 This is proved by the declaration which the two Davidites, Zechariah and Jacob, presented to the predatory Emperor Domitian in the hope of averting confiscation of their property. This declaration was drawn up in the correct legal terms used for property and taxation, and was handed down with equal accuracy. See Euseb. *H.E.* 3, 20, 2.

p. 31, l. 28 Tertullian says (*Adv. Marc.,* 4, 19): *"Sed et census constat actos sub Augusto nunc in Judaea per Sentium Saturninum."* C. Sentius Saturninus was legate to Syria from 9 to 6 B.C. The note in Josephus (*Ant.* 17, 2, 4) favors the year 7 for the mass protests of the Pharisees (see below, note to page 38, line 15).

p. 32, l. 11 Ign. *Eph.* 19, 2 f. For the astral-historical phrase *"tŏ plēiroma tou chronou"* in Gal. 4, 4, see the astral-technical term *"stoichea"* in the context (4, 3. 9) and the mysterious words in Pseudo-Philo's *Antiquitates Biblica,* 19, 15: *"Istic mei, apex magnus, momenti plenitudo et ciati gutta, et omnia complevit tempus."* Cf. also Heb. 9, 16; Eph. 1, 10; Rev. 1, 16; Herm. *sim.* 9, 12, 3, and others. In the Mandaean *John Book* 66 ff. (Lidzbarski, p. 75 ff.), the theme of the star is transferred to Elizabeth and her son John.

p. 32, l. 14 Johannes Kepler, *De stella nova* (Prague, 1606), pp. 129 f., 134 f. That same year Kepler published a bulky supplement in which he linked his new hypothesis as to this dating with Luke's synchronization of the birth of Jesus and the reign of Herod the Great. See *De Jesu Christi . . . vero anno natalito* (*Sylva Chronologica*), p. 7; 9; 25 and elsewhere. From 1607 to 1614 Kepler expanded and partially modified his theory in numerous letters and other writings.

p. 33, l. 7 W. Spiegelberg, *Demotische Papyrus aus den Kgl. Museen zu Berlin* (1902), p. 29 ff.; P. Schnabel, *"Der jüngste datierbare Keilschrifttext,"* *Zeitschrift für Assyriologie,* Vol. 36 (1925), p. 66 ff. Cf. also F. X. Kugler, *Sternkunde und Sterndienst in Babel* (Münster, 1907 ff.), Vol. 1 ff.

p. 33, l. 33 Rabbinical writings on the constellation of the Last Days (the Fishes) in Billerbeck, Vol. 4, pp. 1046, 1049. Mandaean material on Jupiter, Saturn, the Fishes, and the time of the Messiah in *Ginza,* Right-hand part, 18 (Lidzbarski, p. 408 ff.) and *The Book of the Zodiac* (ed. E. S. Drower, London, 1949), pp. 60 ff., 70, 119 and *passim.* Cf. also Test. Lev. 18, 3; Dmd. 7, 18 ff. A special study of this subject is in preparation.

p. 34, l. 6 Matt. 2, 3. Perhaps we may also synchronize this with the oracle of the approaching downfall of Herod in Jos. *Ant.* 17, 2, 4, 43. (See below, note to page 38, line 19.)

p. 34, l. 23 We mention only the Gemma Augustea, the triumphal reliefs on the Bowl of Boscoreale, and the coins of the year 7 B.C.

p. 34, l. 24 Stauffer, *Jerusalem und Rom,* chap. 2. The inscription of Philae is apparently the oldest monument on which Augustus is glorified as *Zeus Eleutherios.* This title makes its appearance in the official forms for oaths only from 5 B.C. on. Cf. J. Vogt, *Die alexandrinischen Münzen* (Stuttgart, 1924), Vol. 1, p. 18; Seidl, *Der Eid im römisch-ägyptischen Provinzialrecht* (Munich, 1933), Vol. 1, p. 19.

p. 36, l. 9 Our text speaks expressly of the sons of Herod I, but not until 6, 7 ff.

p. 36, l. 27 L. Ginzberg, *Legends of the Jews* (Philadelphia, 1946), Vol. 2, p. 254 ff.; Vol. 5, pp. 393 f., 401 ff. Undoubtedly themes from the Church's tradition and apocryphal childhood stories are mixed in with this. There is even mention of a census. In short, Moses was set up as a rival figure who was to eclipse the image of Jesus. Contrariwise, Clement of Alexandria endeavored to strip some of the glory from the beginnings of Moses as they were related in Jewish tradition. See Leopold Cohn's edition of Philo, *ed. maior* (Breslau, 1923), Vol. 4, p. 121 ff.

p. 37, l. 2 The expression *juvenes* leaps into the author's mind at this point because he is employing an established phrase from Deut. 28, 50. The motif of the king's "fierceness" comes from the same source. (Cf. also Jos. *Ant.* 6, 12, 6 f.) Besides, we must never forget that we depend on an extremely poor Latin translation at second or third hand. But the *Ass. Mos.* is preserved for us only in this one translation and manuscript.

p. 38, l. 15 Jos. *Ant.* 17, 2, 4, 42. Here we apparently have a protest against the census oath and the superhuman imperial titles included in the oath, to which at this very time there had been added the honorific title *Zeus Eleutherios*.

p. 38, l. 19 Jos. *Ant.* 17, 2, 4, 43 ff. For the interpretation of this highly allusive text, see Schürer, op. cit., Vol. 2, p. 512 f.; H. Willrich, *Das Haus des Herodes* (Heidelberg, 1929), pp. 104, 182 f. Niese's punctuation in 17, 43, is dubious. What does *"epiphoitēisis"* mean here? For this passage Liddell and Scott propose the translation "manifestation."

p. 42, l. 21 In critical times even the Roman emperors persecuted and attempted to exterminate the Davidites. See Euseb. *H.E.* 3, 12; 3, 20; 3, 32. *"Ben [Bne] David"* = "son [sons] of David." Cf. the *"Bne Baba"* (not *Sabba*) in Jos. *Ant.* 15, 7, 10; B. Bath. 4 a. We must not minimize, as ancient and modern scholars have tended to do, the potential political force of these dispossessed royal clans in the Semitic Orient.

p. 42, l. 31 See Stauffer, *Jerusalem und Rom,* chap. 7.

CHAPTER 3

P. 44, l. 21 Sabb. 104 b; Origen, *Cels.* 1, 28.

p. 44, l. 32 See Ethelbert Stauffer, *Jerusalem und Rom* (Bern, 1957), chaps. 3, 7, 9.

p. 45, l. 2 Cf. Luke 2, 21 ff. 41 ff.; John 7, 37 ff.; Mark 14, 12 ff.; 15, 34; Luke 23, 46; John 19, 30, etc.

p. 45, l. 4 According to Luke 1, 36, Mary was a kinswoman of Elizabeth, who, according to Luke 1, 5, was of the House of Aaron.

p. 45, l. 5 The offering of the turtledoves in Luke 2, 24, is, according to Lev. 12, 8, the sacrifice fitting for the poor.

p. 46, l. 2 Cf. John 19, 25, with Mark 15, 40, and Matt. 27, 56. Also Mark 1, 19 f.; Matt. 20, 20 ff., etc. John never mentions his father,

Notes

Zebedee, by name, nor does he name his mother, his brother, Jesus' mother, or himself.

p. 46, l. 17 Regular opportunities for this were provided by the pilgrimage festivals from A.D. 7 on. See Luke 2, 42. 44.

p. 48, l. 10 B. Bath. 74 b and *passim*. See Franz Delitzsch, *Ein Tag in Capernaum* (Leipzig, 1873), p. 144, note 12.

p. 50, l. 34 See Jos. *Life*. 17; J Keth. 4, 29 b; J Shabb. 16, 15 d.

p. 51, l. 10 1 Macc. 1, 56 f.; Ps. 1, 2.

p. 52, l. 5 Luke 2, 24; 4, 17 f.; John 7, 15.

p. 55, l. 8 Almost all the coins mentioned in this section will be found in the coin catalogues of the British Museum. Some are in A. Reifenberg, *Ancient Jewish Coins* (2nd ed., Jerusalem, 1947). For radius of distribution and period of circulation, A. R. Bellinger, "The Coins," in *Excavations at Dura-Europos* (New Haven, 1949), is of importance.

p. 56, l. 31 Illustration in Stauffer, *Christ and the Caesars* (4th ed., London, 1954), facing p. 81.

p. 59, l. 13 S. Krauss, *Talmudische Archäologie* (Leipzig, 1910), Vol. 1, p. 248.

p. 59, l. 16 The polemic against Bileam the Lame is late and shows no sign of historical memory, but merely the postulate that a contemptible opponent should not lack physical infirmities.

p. 59, l. 20 Luke 2, 52 ("*hēilīḳia*," as in Luke 19, 3); John 2, 1; 4, 6 and *passim*. In Luke 19, 3, of course, Zacchaeus, not Jesus, is "small of stature." Otherwise many would have climbed up into trees, and Zacchaeus would not have attracted attention (cf. Luke 19, 4 f.).

p. 59, l. 25 According to the "Letter of Lentulus" (see below), Jesus had blue eyes. See E. von Dobschütz, *Christusbilder* (Leipzig, 1899), p. 308 ff.

p. 60, l. 13 See Akiba's polemic against a beardless man, Koh. r. on 10, 7.

p. 60, l. 27 John 19, 23. We have no serious grounds for rejecting this statement. Cf. note to page 160, line 11. We must also remember the priest's *sindones* and the high priest's *petalon* of James the Just; see Euseb. *H.E.* 2, 23, 6; Epiphanius, *Haer.* 29, 4, and 78, 14.

p. 60, l. 29 Thus Delitzsch, op. cit., p. 134. Further information in S. Schemel, *Die Kleidung der Juden im Zeitalter der Mischna* (Rostock, 1912); Billerbeck, Vol. 3, p. 423 and *passim*.

p. 61, l. 7 The most famous is the so-called "Letter of Lentulus"; see J. B. Aufhauser, *Antike Jesuszeugnisse* (Bonn, 1925), p. 43. The description of Jesus by the Islamic Jew Kab el-Akbar in Thalabi is likewise valueless because governed by ascetic postulates; see

S. M. Zwemer, *Die Christologie des Islam* (Stuttgart, 1921), p. 42.

p. 62, l. 9 See Stauffer, *"Agnostos Christos,"* in *The Background of the New Testament and Its Eschatology,* ed. by W. D. Davies and D. Daube in honor of S. H. Dodd (Cambridge, 1956), p. 281 ff.

CHAPTER 4

P. 64, l. 16 See Mark 14, 3; Luke 4, 44; 13, 7 f. 34; Acts 18, 25 and *passim.*

p. 64, l. 20 See Sanh. 90 a; 106 a; 107 b; Agobard in *M.P.L.* 104, col. 87; *Ginza,* Right-hand part, 147 (Lidzbarski, p. 50), and elsewhere. In all these cases the decisive characteristic of this early period is Jesus' unclouded relationship to the Torah.

p. 66, l. 6 John 2, 24: *"ouk episteuen"*—*"non credebat semetipsum eis."*

p. 66, l. 9 Cf. John 1, 26; Luke 10, 22; also Ethelbert Stauffer, *"Agnostos Christos,"* in *The Background of the New Testament and Its Eschatology* (Cambridge, 1956). John links the dignity of Sonship with Jesus' superiority over the Torah—a dignity which, according to John, did not reveal itself so completely in that early period, and was not intended thus to reveal itself as it did later in the main period (John 5 ff.).

p. 67, l. 2 John 1, 16 ff.; 3, 29 ff.; Mark 2, 19; Luke 4, 19.

p. 67, l. 4 For response, see John 2, 23; 3, 26; 4, 1. 41. For rebuffs, see John 1, 11. 46; 4, 44; Matt. 8, 10; Luke 13, 7. 34.

p. 67, l. 5 In Luke 3, 35. 39 f., he also avoids, with striking consistency, any violation of the Sabbath.

p. 67, l. 13 Sanh. 41 a; Aboda 8 b.

p. 67, l. 17 For Heliodorus, see 2 Macc. 3, 22 ff.; on Pilate, see Jos. *Jew. W.* 2, 9, 4.

p. 67, l. 28 Ber. 9, 5; cf. Jos. *Apion* 2, 7.

p. 69, l. 25 The identification of Sychar with Sichem is to be found as early as Jerome, and is supported by recent excavations. Simon Magus came from the same region; see Justin, *Apol.* 26, 2.

p. 69, l. 31 See John 4, 23. Cf. Stauffer, *Jerusalem und Rom* (Bern, 1957), chap. 8.

p. 71, l. 8 See E. von Dobschütz in *Z.N.W.,* Vol. 29 (1928), p. 344.

p. 72, l. 8 It may be asked whether the story of the temptation (Mark 1, 12 f.) should be inserted into this period. But the fast in the wilderness fits into the initial period of Jesus' ministry, immediately after his baptism at the edge of the desert of Judaea. See above, p. 64.

Notes

p. 72, l. 31 See Stauffer, *Jerusalem und Rom,* chaps. 1 and 6 ff.

p. 73, l. 11 H. G. Grünweller, *Palästinajüdisches in Johannes-evangelium* (Doctoral thesis, Erlangen, 1952), pp. 80, 161. Several of Jesus' sayings in John 5, 17–47, refer to the Feast of Tabernacles. Gustav Dalman, among others, wishes to refer John 5, 1, to a Passover because only in spring could there have been such an accumulation of rainwater as is assumed in John 5, 3 ff.; see Joachim Jeremias, *Die Wiederentdeckung von Bethesda* (Göttingen, 1949), p. 12. But the reference in John 5, 2 ff., can only be to spring water, not to rainwater.

p. 75, l. 22 Compare the 14 points in Stauffer, *Jerusalem und Rom,* chap. 4.

p. 78, l. 5 The penalties for the pseudo-prophet are extended and sharpened in the scrolls of the desert sect: "Every man who is under the control of the spirits of Belial shall be judged according to the law of necromancy and interpreters of signs" (Dmd. 12, 2 f.). Cf. above, note to page 9, line 20. According to this, Jesus would have been condemned to death in Qumran. For death sentences in the desert communities, see Dmd. 10, 1.

CHAPTER 5

P. 79, l. 5 Mark 1, 14 f. The chronological framework is derived from the Petrine tradition (see the Petrine formulae in Acts 10, 37, but see also Luke 23, 5); the kerygmatic contents include some material postdating Jesus.

p. 81, l. 10 For the time of sowing, see Mark 4, 1 ff. 26 ff. 30 ff.; for the time of storms, see Mark 4, 35 ff.

p. 82, l. 7 Mark 6, 16; Luke 9, 9; Jos. *Ant.* 18, 5, 2, 116.

p. 82, l. 10 See John 6, 14, and Test. Lev. 8, 15; 18, 11.

p. 82, l. 16 Cf. Jos. *Ant.* 14, 10, 8; Ber. 19 a; Tos. Yom Tob 1, 1.

p. 83, l. 6 See Ethelbert Stauffer, "*Zum apokalyptischen Festmahl in M 6, 34 ff.*" in *Z.N.W.,* Vol. 46 (1955), p. 264 ff.

p. 83, l. 9 Mark 6, 35 ff.; Matt. 14, 15 ff.; Luke 9, 12 ff.; Mark 8, 1 ff.; Matt. 15, 32 ff.

p. 84, l. 18 John 6, 60. 66. "*Sklēiros*" in John 6, 60, is a technical term in legal theology for the blasphemous words of an obdurate apostate; see Koh. r. 77 c; Epistle of Jude 15 and *passim.*

p. 84, l. 21 Mark 2, 13 ff.; cf. Philo, *Vit. Mos.* 2, 4. For Jesus' prosecution, see Stauffer, "*Neue Wege der Jesusforschung*" in *Wissenschaftliche Zeitschrift der Universität Halle* (1957), pp. 921–46.

p. 86, l. 7 John 6, 67; Luke 8, 1 ff.; cf. Luke 22, 28 ff.

p. 86, l. 20 See Mark 6, 2 f. 6 f.; Luke 4, 17 ff. 28 f.

p. 86, l. 27 Mark 15, 30 f. 36; Luke 23, 8 ff. 39; cf. *Toledoth Jeshu.*

p. 86, l. 28 Polemics in J Taan. 2, 1; Origen, *Cels.* 2, 9 and *passim.* Cf. Julian, *Contra Christianos,* ed. Carl Johannes Neumann, p. 130, on Luke 3, 8 ff.

p. 87, l. 4 On Luke 4, 30, see Tatian in *Ephraem.*

p. 87, l. 21 Luke 11, 49 ff.; 12, 51 ff.; 13, 22 ff.

p. 87, l. 29 The attitude of Herod Antipas toward Jesus appears vacillating and obscure (cf. Luke 13, 32). At one time Herod, either out of fear or benevolence, is seen offering the protection of a sovereign to his subject Jesus (see Mark 6, 16; Luke 23, 8; Sanh. 43 a, and above, note to page 9, line 20). Elsewhere we hear of Herod's spies and his plotting to destroy Jesus (see Mark 3, 6; 8, 15; 12, 13; Luke 13, 31; 23, 11 f.; Acts 4, 27). Herod I had already developed a brilliant spy system that was at least a match for the priests' system of secret witnesses. See Jos. *Ant.* 8, 4, 285; 15, 10, 4, 366 f.; *Jew W.* 1, 29, 1, 570; 1, 29, 2, 573.

p. 89, l. 16 Mark 9, 30 f.; John 7, 10; Luke 9, 51 ff.

CHAPTER 6

P. 90, l. 17 John 6, 14; 7, 40; cf. Test. Lev. 8, 15; 18, 5 ff.

p. 91, l. 8 Cf. Isa. 43, 10; Sukk. 53 a; see also above, chap. 8, 6. For the light thrown by legal history on John 8, 5, see *"Die Strafe für Ehebruch in Bibel und Halacha,"* in *Nov. Test.,* Vol 4 (1957), pp. 32–47.

p. 91, l. 19 John 8, 48.

p. 91, l. 23 Cf. Acts 8, 9 ff.; below, note to page 188, line 20.

p. 91, l. 29 John 8, 48. 52; cf. John 10, 20.

p. 91, l. 32 Shabb. 104 b; 17 a; 27 b; Tertullian, *De Spectaculis* 30.

p. 93, l. 21 The Shepherd Discourse of John 10, 1–8, employs several shepherd's words that are Semitic in language and style; see L. M. von Pakozdy, *"A Pasztor-Igek János Evangeliuma 10. Teszeben"* ("The Shepherd Sayings in John 10") in the periodical *Theologiai Szemle* (Debreczen, 1947), pp. 36–84.

p. 94, l. 20 Cf. Ethelbert Stauffer, *Jerusalem und Rom* (Bern, 1957), chap. 1.

p. 95, l. 1 Cf. 4 Ezra 12, 10 ff. 31 f., where the "eagle" appears as the symbol of the Roman imperial power, the "lion" as the symbol of the Messiah (see Rev. 5, 5).

p. 95, l. 13 Ps. 23, 1; 95, 7 f.; cf. Ezek. 34, 11 ff.; Isa. 40, 11.

Notes

p. 96, l. 14 Tos. Sanh. 10, 11; J Sanh. 7, 16. The western pilgrims' road from Galilee to Jerusalem passed through Lydda.

p. 98, l. 5 John 10, 40; 11, 8; Luke 13, 34.

p. 98, l. 7 Tos. Sanh. 10, 11; J Sanh. 7, 16; cf. John 10, 33.

p. 98, l. 8 See 2 Cor. 11, 25; Acts 14, 19 f. Note that John in 10, 39, uses the same verb for escape as does Luke in Acts 14, 20 (*exēilthen*). Underlying this is the Hebrew combination of *nimlat* (in Aramaic: *ithmelat*) and *min;* see 1 Sam. 23, 13; Ps. 124, 7; Jer. 34, 3; 41, 15; Pes. 118 and *passim.*

p. 99, l. 9 John 10, 41; Matt. 19, 2; Acts 10, 38; John 20, 30.

p. 99, l. 26 See Jos. *Ant.* 18, 7, 2, and Stauffer, *Jerusalem und Rom,* chap. 1.

p. 100, l. 1 See Luke 22, 5; Jos. *Ant.* 18, 5, 2; Tac. *Ann.* 6, 4 ff. and elsewhere.

p. 100, l. 9 Luke 13, 34; Mark 12, 1 ff.; Matt. 2, 29 ff.

p. 101, l. 17 See Pionius in the *Acta Sanctorum* for February 1, Vol. 1 (Paris, 1863), p. 45.

p. 102, l. 12 John 11, 48; cf. Jos. *Ant.* 18, 5, 2, 118.

p. 102, l. 19 See Tacitus, *Hist.* 5, 9: *"sub Tiberio quies."*

p. 102, l. 30 Sanh. 4, 2; Tos. Sanh. 3, 8; 7, 2 ff., etc.

p. 103, l. 14 See R. Travers Herford, *Christianity in Talmud and Midrash* . . . (1903), p. 83. From the context, *"pephanaw"* here means not "before him" but "beforehand."

p. 104, l. 21 According to an old variant reading (D), Jesus is supposed to have remained in hiding for a while in the vicinity of Sepphoris. Sepphoris was the famous headquarters of the Galilean resistance movement; it was three miles north of Nazareth, surrounded by hills with all sorts of hiding places.

p. 104, l. 22 *"Ezēitoun"* in John 11, 56, is an imperfect, just as it is in John 7, 11. This accords with the plural *"entolai"* in 11, 57, which indicates repeated proclamation of the order for capture, as required in Sanh. 43 a (40 days). For the police term *"mēinuein,"* see Jos. *Ant.* 15, 7, 10, 266; 15, 8, 4, 285.

p. 105, l. 18 We cannot yet exclude the possibility that the chronology of the Passion is confused by the juxtaposition of two completely different dates for the Passover.

p. 107, l. 28 John 12, 3 ff.; Mark 14, 3 ff.; Matt. 26, 7 ff.; cf. Luke 7, 37 ff.

p. 107, l. 31 See Deut. 15, 11.

p. 108, l. 1 We learn much concerning the validity of the Gospel tradition and its value as a historical source when we observe that the characters of Mary and Martha, the sisters of Lazarus, are given the same delineation in all the Gospels. Martha appears resolute, energetic, ready of tongue, used to giving orders, as eager to make suggestions as to reprove (Luke 10, 38. 40. 41; John 11, 20 ff. 28. 39 f.; 12, 2); Mary is hesitant, slow, quiet, easily moved, obedient, devoted (Mark 14, 3 ff.; Luke 10, 39. 42; John 11, 20. 29. 32 f.). Martha is a typical older sister, Mary a typical younger sister. These are persons of flesh and blood who obviously played a great part in the early community, each in her own fashion (cf. Mark 14, 9), and were known personally either to the Evangelists or to their informants.

CHAPTER 7

P. 110, l. 33 See Ethelbert Stauffer, *Nov. Test.,* Vol. 1 (1956), pp. 85 ff., 92 f.

p. 112, l. 4 See Stauffer, *Christ and the Caesars* (Philadelphia, 1955), pp. 112–37. Here also is an illustration of tribute money from a photograph by Kurt Lange.

p. 112, l. 18 Luke 22, 3 f.; cf. John 11, 48, and, on the problem of *quies publica,* once more Tac. *Hist.* 5, 9: *"sub Tiberio quies."*

p. 112, l. 22 John 9, 22; 16, 2.

p. 112, l. 25 Luke 22, 6; cf. Num. 30, 2 ff.; Acts 23, 14; Wilhelm Dittenberger, *Orientis Graeci Inscriptiones Selectae* (Leipzig, 1903), No. 532, 28 ff., and elsewhere.

p. 112, l. 30 A special study is in preparation.

p. 113, l. 7 This problem is handled a little too briefly in Joachim Jeremias's *The Eucharistic Words of Jesus* (Oxford, 1955). If Jesus, as Jeremias assumes, had a Passover lamb on the table at the Last Supper, why did he speak the interpretative words when the bread, and not the meat, was being eaten, especially if, as Jeremias holds, Jesus said: "This is my flesh"?

p. 113, l. 11 See 1 Cor. 5, 7; 11, 23; 15, 20; John 18, 28; Rev. 5, 6; Sanh. 43 a; 67 a.

p. 114, l. 18 See Mark 14, 50; Luke 22, 28; John 9, 22. 35; 16, 2; 18, 8.

p. 115, l. 3 The Passover meal was basically a family meal that women and children also attended. But at Jesus' last meal the Galilean women among the following of disciples were apparently absent, although they were in Jerusalem at the time (Mark 15, 40 f.; Luke 8, 2). Is there possibly a connection with the sacramental meals held by men alone among the desert sect and related groups? Cf. K. G. Kuhn, *"Über den ursprünglichen Sinn des Abendmahls*

Notes

und sein Verhältnis zu den Gemeinschaftsmahlen der Sektenschrift," *Ev. Theol.* (1950–1), p. 518.

p. 115, l. 9 See Stauffer, *Jerusalem und Rom* (Bern, 1957), chap. 4.

p. 115, l. 18 Mark 14, 17; Luke 22, 14; cf. Jub. 49, 10. 19.

p. 115, l. 19 Mark 14, 18; John 13, 4 ff. 23.

p. 115, l. 27 Luke 22, 17 f.; cf. Mark 14, 25; 1 Cor. 11, 26.

p. 115, l. 31 Mark 14, 18; cf. John 13, 21.

p. 116, l. 12 *"Ani hu welo acher";* see *The Passover Haggadah,* ed. Nahum Norbert Glatzer (New York, 1953), p. 36.

p. 116, l. 25 Ibid., p. 20.

p. 116, l. 33 Matt. 26, 26; Luke 22, 19; 1 Cor. 11, 24.

p. 117, l. 1 See Pes. 4, 4.

p. 117, l. 4 Luke 22, 20; 1 Cor. 10, 16; 11, 25.

p. 117, l. 15 Matt. 26, 27; Mark 14, 24; 1 Cor. 11, 25; Justin, *Apol.* 66, 3.

p. 117, l. 16 Mark 14, 26. The psalms in question are 113–18.

p. 117, l. 31 Mek. Ex. 12, 6, and elsewhere.

p. 118, l. 15 Tos. Keth. 55; cf. Luke 2, 46 f.; John 3, 1 ff.; 6, 59.

p. 118, l. 17 Cf. Luke 22, 21 ff.; John 13, 31 ff., and elsewhere.

p. 119, l. 12 John 18, 3: *"meta hoplōn";* cf. Jos. *Jew. W.* 5, 8, 244.

p. 119, l. 15 Cf. Mark 14, 44; Acts 5, 26; 23, 23 ff.

p. 120, l. 5 Mark 14, 43. 48; Matt. 26, 47. 55; Luke 22, 52.

p. 120, l. 12 Shabb. 8 ff.; cf. Jub. 2, 29; 50, 8.

p. 120, l. 27 R.H. 2, 9.

p. 121, l. 1 Luke 22, 53; John 18, 36.

p. 121, l. 21 The ancient Talmud lawyers speak of Jesus' religious trial only, and ignore the political trial. The crucial intervention of the Roman Procurator must have been embarrassing to them. H. Lietzmann, *"Der Prozess Jesu,"* in *Sitzungsberichte der Preussischen Akademie der Wissenschaften* (Berlin, 1931), p. 313 ff., paradoxically would accept only the trial before Pilate and eliminate the trial before Caiaphas. For an opposing viewpoint, see L. Wenger, *Die Quellen des römischen Rechts* (Vienna, 1953), p. 286 ff., and J. Blinzler, *Der Prozess Jesu* (2nd ed., Regensburg, 1955), p. 86 ff. But the correlation between the Gospel accounts of the religious trial and the legal provisions against heretics and the rules of procedure is far closer than Wenger and Blinzler suggest. Moreover, Wenger, Blinzler, and all other writers on the subject fail to deal adequately with the fact that the ecclesiastical trial was only the final act setting the seal on the preceding prosecution and can therefore be understood and evaluated correctly only in relation to the earlier part of the story.

p. 122, l. 23 John 18, 22 f.; cf. Ex. 22, 28; Acts 23, 2 ff. On John 18, 19, see E. Bammel, *Kaiphas* (forthcoming).

p. 122, l. 27 See Talmud W., Vol. 4, p. 299 b; Gustav Dalman, *Grammatik des jüdisch-palästinischen Aramäisch* (2nd ed., Leipzig, 1905), p. 161.

p. 123, l. 3 Tertullian, *De Spectaculis* 30: *"sabbati destructor."*

p. 123, l. 5 Mak. 1, 4; Sanh. 4, 5; 5, 1 f.

p. 123, l. 14 Mark 14, 58; 15, 29; Matt. 26, 61; 27, 40; Acts 6, 14; John 2, 19.

p. 124, l. 2 See J Sota 1, 16 d; B Sota 1, 4.

p. 124, l. 7 Cf. John 18, 23; 19, 10.

p. 124, l. 11 Deut. 19, 18 ff.; Mak. 1, 3 ff.

p. 124, l. 22 After the theophanic *"Ani hu,"* this saying about the Son of Man appears to be a moderating addendum, and sounds like a theological supplement by the church in the interests of popular eschatology. But at least three observations favor the authenticity of the *Logion* in this passage. (1) The words "and you will see . . ." in Mark 14, 62, can be understood not only as a moderating expansion, but also as a consistent development of the *"Ani hu"* (according to its meaning in John 8, 28); for it is characteristic of Jesus' "Son of Man" sayings that they presuppose the divine rank of the *huiŏs tou anthrōpou.* (2) In Mark 14, 62, no time for the coming of the Last Days is specified, as would be required by popular eschatology. The primitive church felt the lack and added an *"ap' arti"* (see Matt. 26, 64); it would appear, therefore, that Mark 14, 62, did not, after all, represent the theology of the church, but rather the words of Jesus. (3) Rabbi Eleazar, about A.D. 170, attacks a double-pronged saying of Jesus which, very much in the style of Mark 14, 62, speaks first of the theophany and then (without specifying time) of the Parousia; this *Logion* may well derive from the Jewish tradition of the trial of Jesus (see below, note to page 191, line 1).

p. 125, l. 10 Here, too, Caiaphas and all the councillors were obeying the rules of procedure; see 2 Kings 18, 37; Sanh. 7, 5; Sanh. 60 a; J Sanh. 7, 25 a; M.K. 25 b (Baraitha); Sifre Lev. 24, 11. But here, too, only Mark's report is entirely correct (14, 63: *"chitōnas"*); Matthew exaggerates (26, 65: *"himatïa"*). For the regulations allowed only the undergarments to be rent. Even the position and the length of the tear was prescribed. This was necessary in order that the prohibitions in Lev. 10, 6, and 21, 10, be observed.

p. 125, l. 25 Sanh. 4, 2; Sanh. 36 a; Git. 59 a.

p. 125, l. 26 Thus Mark 14, 64. Matt. 26, 66, is different, and is inconsistent with the situation.

Notes

p. 126, l. 1 Sanh. 5, 4; cf. 6, 1.

p. 126, l. 4 The two long Gospels have misunderstood and reshaped Jesus' wording of the theophany (Matt. 26, 64; Luke 22, 70). The Jewish tradition of Jesus, on the other hand, agrees with Mark's account and accepts Caiaphas' interpretation of Jesus' theophanic declaration. See below, note to page 191, line 1.

p. 126, l. 16 Mark 14, 65. The "some" are, of course, not councillors but the Levite police (see Luke 22, 63 f.). Matt. 26, 68, cannot be used, for it constructs a messianic legend which presupposes the messianic self-affirmation of Matt. 26, 63—and this is unhistorical. Justin, *Apol.* 35 is also unhistorical (a *testimonium;* see Isa. 58, 2.). The gospel of Peter 3, 7, is a compilation of messianic parodies and *testimonia,* and must therefore be left out altogether. Thus Mark 14, 65, and Luke 22, 63 f., remain the best evidence. They are supported by the fact that Jesus is mocked as a prophet, not as the Messiah. On the other hand, they are weakened by the accumulation of the accounts of mistreatment in the Passion story (cf. John 18, 22; Luke 23, 11; Mark 15, 16 ff.; Matt. 27, 27 ff.; John 19, 1 ff.). Further details in Lietzmann, op. cit., p. 317. J. Klausner, *Jesus* (London, 1947), also has doubts. Nevertheless, the mistreatment of Jesus in the courtyard of the High Priest's palace may be historical. The Levite police were alone with Jesus for hours, and for that reason alone may have taken all sorts of liberties. However, Jesus was the worst and most dangerous heretic who had ever appeared before a Jewish court of justice. The councillors therefore may have thought a dose of brutality, aside from the certain death penalty, to be quite in order. At the same time, the police may have acted spontaneously (cf. the semi-official torture and killing of Menahem in Jos. *Jew. W.* 2, 17, 9, 448), or they may have acted on official instructions from the court (the background and details of these instructions are in any case completely obliterated in Mark 14, 65). For, according to Tos. Shabb. 11, 15, and Shabb. 104 b, Jesus had violated Lev. 19, 28. The penalty for this, according to Mak. 3, 6, was scourging. For this purpose a condemned man was bound to a pillar (Mak. 3, 12; Sifre Deut. 25, 2; J Bikk. 64 a). The pilgrim of Bordeaux (circa A.D. 333) claimed to have seen in the palace of Caiaphas in Jerusalem the pillar to which Jesus was allegedly bound for his scourging by the Levite police (see F. Cabrol and H. Leclercq, *Dictionnaire d'archéologie chrétienne et de liturgie* [*Paris, 1923*], Vol. 5, p. 2, col. 1639, and further references there). Since the tenth century Christian art has also represented the "scourging at the pillar." But *Toledoth Jeshu* also report that the councillors had Jesus bound to a marble pillar and scourged; see

227

Samuel Krauss, *Das Leben Jesu nach jüdischen Quellen* (Berlin, 1902), p. 164 and *passim*.

p. 126, l. 24 Mark 15, 1; Matt. 27, 1; Luke 22, 66; 23, 1.

p. 126, l. 34 See Tos. Sanh. 9, 1 ff.; Sanh. 42 a, and elsewhere.

p. 127, l. 32 Sanh. 43 a; see above, p. 102.

p. 128, l. 5 See Sanh. 43 a; Rashi on Deut. 13, 9 f., and elsewhere. Recantation of a witness for the prosecution could not alter the verdict; see Appendix II, No. 71.

p. 128, l. 7 Acts 1, 16 ff.; Papias (according to a chain of proofs) in Erwin Preuschen, *Antilegomena* (2nd ed., Giessen, 1905), p. 97 f. This, of course, was early influenced by motives of scriptural theology and persecution legends.

p. 128, l. 10 See Acts 24, 1; Philo, *Legatio* 300; Jos. *Ant.* 18, 8, 4, and elsewhere.

p. 128, l. 15 John 18, 31. Here Lietzmann has extremely strong doubts; see op. cit., pp. 317–19. Against this, see Joachim Jeremias, *"Zur Geschichtlichkeit des Verhörs Jesu vor dem Hohen Rat,"* in *Z.N.W.*, Vol. 43 (1950–1), p. 145 ff.; L. Wenger, *"Über erste Berührungen des Christentums mit dem römischen Recht,"* in *Miscellanea Mercati*, Vol. 5 (Rome, 1946), p. 573 ff.

p. 129, l. 20 Luke 13, 1 ff.; cf. Philo, *Legatio* 300.

p. 129, l. 31 Cf. Matt. 4, 3; 26, 53; 27, 42.

p. 130, l. 5 See R. Delbrück, *"Antiquarisches zu den Verspottungen Jesu,"* in *Z.N.W.*, Vol. 41 (1942), p. 124 ff.

p. 130, l. 19 See Wenger, *Die Quellen des römischen Rechts* (Vienna, 1953), p. 288; Pes. 8, 6.

p. 131, l. 5 See Wenger, loc. cit.: "Certainly the subsequent scourging . . . could arouse doubts as to the trustworthiness of the account only in those who knew nothing of the Roman *coercitio*, of the *potestas* of the magistrates—without prejudice to the verdict, or even to the investigation—to apply means of chastisement which in the case of a non-Roman even included death."

p. 131, l. 9 Cf. Philo, *Flacc.* 5, 32 ff.

p. 131, l. 16 Luke 23, 32 f. Cf. Stauffer, *Jerusalem und Rom*, chap. 1.

p. 131, l. 27 See Stauffer, ibid.

p. 132, l. 8 Cf. Mark 15, 7, with Luke 13, 1.

p. 132, l. 16 Mark 15, 9. 12; Luke 23, 20; John 18, 39; 19, 4 f.

p. 132, l. 31 Tiberias on Lake Genesaret was the favorite residence of Herod Antipas.

p. 133, l. 13 See Philo, *Legatio* 302.

p. 133, l. 27 Suetonius, *Augustus* 66; Dio Cassius 53, 23, 5 ff.; 53, 24, 1; Jerome, *Chron., sub anno*.

Notes

p. 136, l. 6 Mark 15, 34; Matt. 27, 46; Luke 23, 34. 43. 46; John 19, 26. 28. 30.

p. 136, l. 10 J Git. 48 c; Tos. Git. 7, 1, and elsewhere.

p. 137, l. 1 The tradition of the text is trustworthy and attested by Marcion as well as by his opponent Irenaeus.

p. 137, l. 5 See Millar Burrows, *The Dead Sea Scrolls of St. Mark's Monastery* (New Haven, 1950), Pl. XLIV.

p. 137, l. 13 Acts 7, 60; Euseb. *H.E.* 2, 23, 16.

p. 138, l. 6 Cf. Deut. 21, 23, and Gal. 3, 13. Tertullian, *Adv. Jud.* 10 (at the beginning) testifies explicitly that the Jews based their attack on the Crucified on Deut. 21, 23.

p. 138, l. 17 Mark 15, 33; Matt. 27, 45; Luke 23, 44; John 19, 28 ff.

p. 138, l. 29 See Tamid 3, 2, and frequently.

p. 139, l. 21 See Pes. 5, 2 ff.; Gen. r. to 2, 2.

p. 139, l. 26 Mark 5, 35. 40; Luke 23, 49; John 19, 25. 35.

p. 139, l. 28 Mark 15, 44; Luke 23, 48 f.; John 19, 24.

p. 139, l. 34 Hodayoth, *Otsar* 39, 5 f. 12. 20, and elsewhere. Perhaps this psalm originated with More Hassadek himself; perhaps it merely follows his ideas and style. That question need not be settled here. For the question itself, cf. Test. Jos. 1, 6; John 8, 16. 29; 16, 32. In Hodayoth 39, 23, the author quotes Ps. 41, 10, in the sense of a passing danger. In John 13, 18, Jesus quotes the same verse in the sense of an inevitable catastrophe.

p. 140, l. 3 Cf. 1 Kings 18, 37; Isa. 26, 13; 1 Cor. 8, 4 ff.; Pesikta rabb. 36. ("The peoples of the world mock the martyred people of Israel and say, 'Where is your God? Why does He not save you?'")

p. 140, l. 23 Cf. Job 2, 9. Against this, Gen. 32, 37; Ps. 73, 23 a. In the Qumran psalms the word *Eli* is quite usual as a form of calling on God.

p. 141, l. 1 Ps. 22, 16; see Mark 15, 36; John 19, 28.

p. 141, l. 6 Cf. Pesikta rabb. 36. On the question of dating see Stauffer, *Nov. Test.*, Vol. 1 (1956), p. 86.

p. 141, l. 10 See Sifre on Lev. 24, 11.

p. 141, l. 32 John 19, 30; cf. John 5, 17; 13, 1; 17, 4.

p. 142, l. 9 Cf. Ep. Ar. 158 ff.; Ber. 5 a; 60 b; *Vita Adae* 45. 50; Apoc. Mos. 31. 42; Heb. Test. Naphthali 10, 9; Michael Sachs, *Tefillah* (Frankfurt am Main, 1939), p. 704 ff.; Ismar Elbogen, *Der jüdische Gottesdienst in seiner geschichtlichen Entwicklung* (3rd ed., Frankfurt am Main, 1929), p. 262. According to Deut. r. on 31, 14, Moses before his death also spoke some words of the evening prayer ("In thy hand are the souls of the living and the dead").

p. 142, l. 12 Luke 23, 46; cf. Sifre Deut. 6, 4; Tos. Ber. 1, 2.

p. 142, l. 14 Luke 23, 46: *"peratithemai tŏ pneuma"*; John 19, 30 b: *"paradŏken tŏ pneuma."*

p. 142, l. 23 Mark 15, 43; John 19, 38 ff. We would expect something entirely different; see especially Tos. Sanh. 9, 8. In such a case even the emperor cannot be buried with his ancestors.

p. 142, l. 25 Cf. Mark 6, 29; Acts 8, 2.

p. 142, l. 29 The terms *"planos"* and *"planēi"* in Matt. 27, 63 f., are probably the terms originally used in the Sanhedrin's polemics (cf. Sanh. 43 a).

p. 142, l. 31 See above, p. 119 f. Against the chronology of Mark 15, 8, see Pes. 8, 6.

p. 143, l. 3 John 18, 28; 19, 14. 31. 36. 42.

p. 143, l. 4 Rev. 5, 6 ff. Jesus equals the Passover lamb, surrounded by the twenty-four elders (i.e., heads of the twenty-four categories of priests) of the temple ritual.

p. 143, l. 4 In 1 Cor. 11, 23, Paul avoids the anachronistic designation "the night of the Passover" and instead speaks of "the night in which he was betrayed." In 1 Cor. 5, 7 (*"pascha"*) Paul gives 14 Nisan as the date of the crucifixion; in 1 Cor. 15, 20 (*"aparchēi"*) he assumes that the resurrection took place on 16 Nisan. It is clear that Paul's phraseology and symbolic language are based upon the same chronology of the Passion (which disagrees with the Synoptics).

p. 143, l. 4 Ev. Petri 2, 5: *"kai paredŏken autōn tō laō prŏ mias tōn azumōn, tēis heortēis autōn."*

p. 143, l. 5 Arab Tatian (ed. E. Preuschen), p. 221.

p. 143, l. 7 Sanh. 43 a; 67 a.

p. 143, l. 8 See Krauss, op. cit., p. 58 and elsewhere.

p. 143, l. 23 Cf. E. Enoch 51, 1 f.; 91, 10; 92, 3; Apoc. Mos. 41; 4 Ezra 7, 29 ff.; S. Bar. 50, 2 ff. and elsewhere.

p. 144, l. 8 Acts 2, 24; 3, 15; 4, 10; 5, 30; 10, 40.

p. 145, l. 4 Justin, *Dial.* 108; the transition into direct discourse may be a matter of style. In any case, it is characteristic of the rabbinical writings to ignore the trial before Pilate.

p. 145, l. 8 See Eusebius' Commentary on Isa. 18, 1: *"hiereis . . . grammata diacharaxantes eis panta diepempsantŏ ta ethnēi."* Cf. Acts 9, 2; 28, 21 f.

p. 145, l. 15 Tertullian, *De Spectaculis,* 30. The terrain around a grave was a source of much concern in ancient Palestine; this is proved by, for example, B. Bath. 6, 7.

p. 145, l. 19 See Krauss, op. cit., pp. 45, 58 f. and elsewhere; H. L. Strack, *Jesus, die Haeritiker und die Christen* (Leipzig, 1910), p. 15 ff.; H. von Campenhausen, *Der Ablauf der Osterereignisse und das Leere Grab* (Heidelberg, 1952), p. 29 ff. The oldest (but indirect) evidence on the *Toledoth* tradition of the empty tomb is to be found in the Chinese Life of Jesus of A.D. 641; see Stauffer, *Nov. Test.*, Vol. 1 (1956), p. 99.

p. 145, l. 27 Cf. the famous letters of Pliny the Younger to Trajan.

p. 146, l. 6 Euseb. *H.E.* 2, 2, 2 ff.

p. 146, l. 13 Euseb. *H.E.* 9, 5, 1. We find Justin, *Apol.* 35, 9, already mentioning *Acts of Pilate*, but presumably this was a Christian document.

p. 146, l. 31 Concerning the controversy over the "Inscription of Nazareth," see F. Cumont, *Revue historique*, Vol. 163 (1930), p. 241 ff.; J. Irmscher in *Z.N.W.*, Vol. 42 (1949), p. 172 ff.; S. F. de Visscher in *Archives d'histoire du droit orientale et Revue internationale des droits de l'antiquité*, Vol. 2 (1953), p. 285 ff.; Wenger, *Die Quellen des römischen Rechts*, p. 456 f. It has now been accepted that the inscription is genuine. Suggestions as to its date range between 55 B.C. and A.D. 137, but are becoming concentrated more and more on the period of Tiberius and Claudius (see Wenger, op. cit.). Attempts to explain it vary greatly. Each interpretation encounters difficulties. An interpretation in the light of Matt. 28, 15, seems to present the fewest problems. Thus, the explanation given above is reached, *per exclusionem,* having been considered by Cumont, recommended by Stephan Lösch, and defended by Wenger.

p. 147, l. 6 Jos. *Ant.* 3, 10, 5.

p. 147, l. 15 1 Cor. 15, 44; Col. 1, 18; 2, 12.

p. 147, l. 19 Cf. Luke 24, 24 ff.; John 20, 11 ff.

p. 148, l. 3 Luke 24, 34; 1 Cor. 15, 5; John 21, 15 ff.

p. 148, l. 9 John 21, 15 ff.; Luke 22, 31 f.; Matt. 16, 18 f.

p. 148, l. 18 Cf. Mark 14, 37. 72; Gal. 2, 11.

p. 148, l. 28 See E. Bammel in *Th.Z.*, Vol. 11 (1955), p. 401 ff. In the Apostolic Age there must have been many lists of witnesses more or less competing with one another; cf., e.g., the list of seven (including Nathanael) in John 21, 2.

p. 148, l. 30 The appearance to the Twelve (15, 5) is probably identical with the manifestation to all the apostles (15, 7).

p. 149, l. 10 Luke 24, 34; John 21, 15 ff.

p. 149, l. 15 Result in Jerome, *Vir. ill.* 2.

p. 149, l. 21 1 Cor. 15, 5 b = 1 Cor. 15, 7 b!

p. 150, l. 5 See Stauffer, *"Die Urkirche,"* in *Historia Mundi,* Vol. 4 (Munich, 1956), p. 299 ff.

p. 150, l. 29 1 Cor. 15, 8; 2 Cor. 5, 16; against this, John 1, 1 ff.

p. 151, l. 9 Luke 24, 11. 22 ff.; Mark 16, 11; cf. John 4, 42.

p. 151, l. 27 1 Cor. 15, 5. 7; Matt. 28, 9 ff.; Luke 24, 36 ff.; Acts 1, 3 ff.; John 20, 19 ff.; 21, 4 ff.; Mark 16, 14 ff.

p. 151, l. 29 John 20, 24 ff.; Luke 24, 13 ff.; Mark 16, 12; 1 Cor. 15, 6; John 20, 29.

p. 152, l. 17 Ps. Clem. *Rec.* 1, 42, 4; Sanh. 106 a; cf. 1 Sam. 28, 11 ff.; Deut. 12, 3.

p. 152, l. 19 Mart. Pionii *Act. Sanct.* for Feb. 1, Vol. 1 (Paris, 1863), p. 45: *"Dicunt Christum necromantiam exercuisse eiusque vi post crucem fuisse suscitatum."*

p. 152, l. 26 See Ign. Smyrn. 3, 2 and elsewhere.

p. 152, l. 28 Jerome, *Vir. ill.* 2.

p. 153, l. 2 Celsus, in Origen, *Cels.* 2, 55 ff.

p. 153, l. 6 Celsus, op. cit., 2, 63 and *passim.*

CHAPTER 8

P. 155, l. 1 See K. L. Schmidt in *Die Religion in Geschichte und Gegenwart* (2nd ed., Tübingen, 1929), Vol. 3, col. 147 f.: "Thus, insofar as individual sayings—for example, the 'But I say unto you . . .' [which Schmidt considers to be Jesus' own]—manifest a consciousness that runs counter to all human experience, the question must in all earnestness be asked whether these are not the words and actions of a fanatic who is enigmatic and mysterious, unsound and obscure. Thus a psychiatric study of the personality of Jesus becomes urgent."

p. 156, l. 9 See Ethelbert Stauffer, *Jerusalem und Rom* (Bern, 1957), chap. 7.

p. 156, l. 23 Luke 17, 21. We are concerned here with a variation, peculiar to Jesus, of the idea of the Messiah *incognitus.* See Stauffer, *"Agnostos Theos,"* in *The Background of the New Testament and Its Eschatology* (Cambridge, 1956), p. 181 ff.

p. 156, l. 28 Matt. 13, 17; Luke 4, 18 ff.; 16, 16.

p. 158, l. 4 Luke 24, 21; note the iterative imperfect *"ēilpizomen."*

p. 158, l. 8 Read with the Codex Sinaiticus and other texts, *"en tēi basileia."* The old variant *"eis tēin basileian"* is a subsequent (and partial) attempt to reconcile the criminal's question to Jesus' reply, and robs the dialogue of its decisive point.

Notes

p. 159, l. 2 1 Cor. 11, 26; 16, 23; Rom. 13, 11; Rev. 6, 10; Euseb. *H.E.* 3, 20, 4.

p. 159, l. 8 Mark 9, 1; 14, 62 b; Matt. 16, 28.

p. 159, l. 11 1 Thess. 4, 15; Mark 13, 30; John 21, 22.

p. 159, l. 13 See Papias in Euseb. *H.E.* 3, 39, 1, and on this S. Bar. 29, 5.

p. 159, l. 16 Matt. 23, 32 (cf. 24, 15 ff.). In my opinion, Albert Schweitzer rates the value of Matthew as a source too highly, and does not consider the counterevidence of the *Logia.* He bases his presentation of Jesus on a preference for such *dicta,* which in all likelihood postdate Jesus. (See, for example, *Leben-Jesu-Forschung,* pp. xi f. and 405.) Thus there came into being the "radically eschatological" picture of Jesus which M. Werner took over uncritically forty years later (*Die Entstehung des christlichen Dogmas* [Bern und Tübingen: 1st ed., 1941; 2nd ed., 1953]). In general, Werner seems to have greatly overestimated the crisis arising from the failure of the early church's eschatological expectations. Apocalyptic groups in the age of the New Testament had long been accustomed to such disappointments, and when the Last Things did not occur at the expected time, they postponed the final date without excessive crises of reorientation. This can be studied excellently in the *Oracula Sibyllina* and now also in the Qumran texts. For recent studies of Matthew, see E. von Dobschütz, *"Matt. als Rabbi und Katachet,"* in *Z.N.W.,* Vol. 27 (1928), p. 338 ff.; K. Stendhal, *The School of St. Matthew* (Uppsala, 1954); G. Bornkamm, *"Matt. als Interpret der Herrenworte,"* in *Th.L.Z.,* Vol. 79 (1954), col. 341 ff.; *"Enderwartung und Kirche im Matthäusevangelium,"* in *The Background of the New Testament and Its Eschatology,* pp. 220–60.

p. 159, l. 18 Matt. 23, 36; different in Luke 11, 51.

p. 159, l. 23 For message of the Baptist, see Matt. 3, 2; for message of Jesus, see Matt. 4, 17 (otherwise in Mark 1, 15, and also in Matt. 12, 28). Message of the Apostles, see Matt. 10, 7 (otherwise in Mark 13, 14 f.; Luke 9, 2; 10, 9).

p. 159, l. 28 Matt. 10, 23. The concept of the Son of Man is fused with that of the Messiah and becomes the central concept of eschatological expectation. Matt. 16, 13 ff. 28; differently, Mark 9, 1, and Luke 9, 27.

p. 160, l. 2 John 21, 23; cf. Acts 1, 7.

p. 160, l. 3 Rev. 22, 20.

p. 160, l. 4 *Yalkut Shimoni* 766 on Num. 23, 7; Euseb. *H. E.* 3, 20, 5.

p. 160, l. 11 All references for chap. 8, 2, in Stauffer, *"Messias oder*

Menschensohn?" in *Nov. Test.,* Vol. 1 (1956), pp. 81–102. If Jesus was *ex generatione* the son of Mary and thereby Ben Aaron (see note to page 45, line 4) and *ex adoptione* son of Joseph and thereby Ben David (see note to page 18, line 29), the christological conflict among the disciples is not hard to understand. Who is for Messiah ben Aaron, who for Messiah ben David? On this messianological debate cf. G. Friedrich, *Z.Th.K.* (1956), p. 265 ff.

p. 162, l. 8 Before about A.D. 500, Jewish discussions concerning Jesus are not based upon a polemical attitude toward the Gospels. Consequently, the Jewish sources on Jesus up to A.D. 500 can safely be considered as being independent of the Gospels. How greatly this material is colored by lack of knowledge, by confusion, by hearsay information, or by sheer fantasy is a question in itself, which need not be taken up here.

p. 162, l. 19 Note how carefully the cured man in John 9, 35 ff., avoids using the phrase "Son of Man."

p. 163, l. 6 "Son of Man" occurs outside the Gospels in Acts 7, 56; Rev. 1, 13; 14, 14; Hebr. 2, 6 ff. For the creeds in the primitive church, see Stauffer, *New Testament Theology* (New York, 1955), pp. 233 ff., 339 ff.

p. 163, l. 23 4 Ezra 13, 3 ff. 12. 25 ff. 51 f.

p. 164, l. 10 The history of the "Son of Man" tradition among Judaeo-Christians, the Baptist's circle, and the Mandaean groups is a problem in itself. Only a few references may be mentioned here: Jerome, *Vir. ill.* 2 (James); Euseb. *H.E.* 2, 23, 13 (James); John 1, 6 (probably a reshaping of a text from Enoch in accordance with the Baptist's doctrine); Ps. Clem. *Rec.* 1, 52, 3; 1, 60, 3; 2, 22, 4 f.; 3, 61, 1 f.; Ps. Clem. *Hom.* 3, 19 ff. (periodic reincarnation of the first man until the eschatological Son of Man); *Ginza,* Right-hand part, 1, 201 f.; *John Book* 76, 274 (reincarnations) and elsewhere. Apart from the two texts concerning James, Old Iranian, Jewish, and Gnostic traditions are only at some points intermixed with themes of Jesus; cf. also Job 15, 7 f.; E. Enoch 71, 14; Dmd. 20, 1; Philo, *Conf. Ling.* 146 and elsewhere.

p. 166, l. 6 See A. Erman, *Die Literatur der Ägypter* (Leipzig, 1923), p. 358 ff.

p. 166, l. 7 See C. Bartholomae, *Die Gathas des Avesta* (Strassburg, 1905).

p. 166, l. 33 Otsar, Pl. 38. Similar themes are also found in other hodayoth; thus, for example, in Otsar, Pl. 35, 21; 36, 13; 39, 25. Cf. *H.T.R.* (1953), p. 113 ff.

p. 167, l. 33 See Millar Burrows, *The Dead Sea Scrolls of St. Mark's Monastery,* Vol. 2 (1951), Pl. x f.

Notes

p. 168, l. 9 In accord with this are C. F. Burney's comments on language, style, and meter in *The Poetry of Our Lord* (Oxford, 1925), p. 171 f.

p. 169, l. 10 Matt. 11, 25-7; Luke 10, 21-2. For the history of the handing down of this *Logion,* see P. Winter, "Matt. 11, 27 and Luke 10, 22 from the First to the Fifth Century" in *Nov. Test.,* Vol. 1 (1956), pp. 112-48.

p. 169, l. 29 For the term *"rason"* in the Dead Sea scrolls, see C. H. Hunzinger, *"Neues Licht auf Lukas 2, 14,"* in *Z.N.W.,* Vol. 44 1952-3), p. 85 ff.

p. 169, l. 33 Luke 10, 18 ff. 21 a. 23 f.

p. 169, l. 35 The terms "father" and "son" in the religious usage of Judaism have a rich early history. But in the *Logia* of Jesus both terms are given a specific and exclusivistic meaning. See Mark 12, 6; 13, 32; Luke 23, 34, etc. Also Joachim Jeremias, *"Kennzeichen der ipsissima vox Jesu,"* in *Festschrift Wikenhauser* (Munich, 1953), p. 86 ff. See "Abba," *Th.L.Z.,* Vol. 79 (1954), col. 213: "Until the Middle Ages there is no evidence in Judaeo-Palestinian literature for the use of 'my Father' to address God." On Matt. 11, 27, see ibid., col. 214.

p. 171, l. 2 On the suffering Son of Man, see Stauffer, *Jerusalem und Rom,* chap. 3. On Jewish martyrological theology, see Stauffer, *New Testament Theology,* p. 331 ff.

p. 171, l. 24 Luke 12, 49 f.; cf. Mark 10, 38. The metaphor of plunging into the water of death was common in the ancient Orient.

p. 171, l. 27 John 12, 24. The doubling of the introductory *Amen* is Johannine; see Jeremias, op. cit., p. 89 ff. Nevertheless, the *Logion* itself probably is Jesus' own, for in the context of John 12 it is an isolated interpolation and has nothing in common with John's favorite metaphors, concepts, and ideas, or with the priestly tradition (see Hans Günter Grünweller, *Palästinajüdisches im Johannesevangelium* [Doctoral thesis, Erlangen, 1952], p. 106). On the other hand, it accords both in form and content with the authentic *Logia* of Jesus. The Eucharistic Words, which are in the style of a *mashal,* also belong here.

p. 172, l. 4 In the great Qumran scroll of Isaiah the reading in this passage is: "and for their sins he was stricken" (the consonantal text reads *"jphg"* without the *yod* of the *hiphil;* we vocalize it as *"juphga,"* the *"pual"*). Text. Benj. 4, 8, presupposes basically the same reading of the text: *"huper anomōn paradothēisetai (mianthēisetai) kai huper asebōn apothaneitai."* In the LXX Isa. 53, 12 reads: *"kai dia tas hamartias autōn paredothēi."* Paul (Rom. 4, 25; 1 Cor. 15, 3) and Justin (*Apol.* 51, 5) understand the text in the same way. No doubt this understanding influenced the Son-of-Man tradition of the Galilean Enoch circle (the atoning suffering of the Son of Man); again this image of the Son of Man seems to have been before Jesus' eyes in Mark 10, 45. In the Christology of the early church, scriptural proofs based on Isa. 53, 12, were of great importance (Paul, Justin, and elsewhere). In order to demolish this proof, the rabbinate, after Jamnia (around A.D. 90), recommended a new spelling (with the *yod* of the *hiphil*), vocalization, and interpretation of Isa. 53, 12. The Masoretic text reads: "and made intercession for the transgressors [*japhgia*]." The Targum paraphrases: "and on behalf of many guilty ones he will make intercession" [*jib'e*]. Aquila translates: *"occuret irridentibus."* The Vulgate is based on the Masora: *"et pro transgressoribus rogavit."* Luther relies on the Masora and the Vulgate: *"und hat für die Übeltäter gebeten."*

This may perhaps be taken as a sketch of the extremely complicated and much-debated history of the handing down of Isa. 53, 12 —a beautiful commentary on Matt. 5, 18. Editions of the text: Millar Burrows, op. cit.; Joseph Ziegler, *Isaias* (Göttingen, 1939); J. F. Stenning, *The Targum of Isaiah* (Oxford, 1949). For the discussion, see W. Zimmerli and J. Jeremias, "The Servant of God," in *S.B.T.,* Vol. 20 (1957), and E. Lohse, *Märtyrer und Gottesknecht* (Göttingen, 1955), p. 97 ff.

p. 172, l. 11 Luke 13, 32 f.

p. 172, l. 18 See Stauffer, *Jerusalem und Rom,* chap. 11.

p. 173, l. 12 Tehillim on Ps. 22, § 5, with allusions to Gen. 22, 4; 42, 17; Ex. 15, 22; 2 Kings 20, 5; Isa. 2, 16; Jonah 2, 1; Hos. 6, 2.

p. 174, l. 7 The most important material will be found in J. Richter, *Ani Hu und Ego eimi; Die Offenbarungsformel "Ich bin es" in der biblischen Welt und Umwelt* (Doctoral thesis, Erlangen, 1956). I have given here only a brief sketch, with some additions and modifications.

p. 174, l. 23 Deut. 5, 1 ff.; 31, 10; Neh. 8, 1, etc. On the theophanic theme, see L. I. Pap, *Das israelitische Neujahrsfest* (Kampen, 1933), pp. 43, 80, and elsewhere.

p. 174, l. 24 See Jer. 33, 11; P. Volz, *Das Neujahrsfest Jahves* (Tübingen, 1912), pp. 33, 42; A. Weiser, *Psalmen* (Göttingen, 1950), pp. 470 f., 474. For the post-Exile period, see Ezra 3, 10 f.; 1 Chron. 16, 8 ff.; B. Jacob, *Z.A.W.,* Vol. 16 (1896), p. 167.

p. 175, l. 9 On the three Psalms 46, 50, and 81, see R. Kittel, *Die Psalmen* (Leipzig, 1929); H. Schmidt, *Die Psalmen* (Tübingen, 1934); and Weiser, loc. cit. Ps. 46 was perhaps prompted by the delivery of Jerusalem in the year 701. In Ps. 81, 4, *"hag"* is probably the Feast of Tabernacles. For the post-Exilic period see A. Büchler, *Z.A.W.*, Vol. 20 (1900), p. 98 ff.; Volz, op. cit., pp. 43, 60.

p. 175, l. 20 Cf. Isa. 43, 1 ff. 5. 10.

p. 175, l. 24 Cf. Isa. 43, 10 ff., and Deut. 6, 4.

p. 175, l. 31 On this also cf. Isa. 43, 10 ff., and Deut. 6, 4.

p. 176, l. 2 For the pre-Exilic origin of all the psalms (except Ps. 137) see I. Engnell, *Studies in Divine Kingship in the Ancient Near East* (Uppsala, 1943), p. 176. For the post-Exilic origin of Psalms 46, 50, and 81, see, e.g., H. J. Krauss, *Königsherrschaft Gottes* (Tübingen, 1951), pp. 114, 131; partly also H. Gunkel and T. Begrich, *Einleitung in die Psalmen* (Göttingen, 1933), p. 379 ff.; E. Selling and L. Rost, *Einleitung in das Alte Testament* (8th ed., Heidelberg, 1950), p. 152 f. For the post-Exilic origin of the Hallel psalms, see H. Gunkel; partly also Kittel, loc. cit., and Selling-Rost, op. cit., p. 153.

p. 176, l. 20 Isa. 43, 10: *"ki ani huah"*; MT reads: *"ani hu"*; Targum: *"ana hu"*; LXX: *"ego eimi."*

p. 176, l. 22 For this the Targum paraphrases: "I am [*ana hu*] He since the day was, the ages of the ages are mine, and beside me there is no God." This same formula is already found in Targ. Isa. 41, 4, and again in Targ. Isa. 44, 6; 48, 12.

p. 176, l. 23 Isa. 43, 11: *"Anochi, anochi Yahwe."* Targum: "Ana, ana Yahwe." LXX v. 1: *"Ego eimi, ego eimi Kuriōs."*

p. 176, l. 25 Isa. 43, 12: *"anochi higgadthi"*; LXX v. 1. has *"ego anēingeila."* See the emphatic *"Ani"* in Isa. 46, 4; 48, 15, and frequently. The Targum inserts "Abraham" here: "I declared unto Abraham what was to come." The same interpolation of the figure of Abraham is found in the Targ. Isa. 46, 11, and 48, 15 f.

p. 176, l. 27 Isa. 43, 12: *"Ani el."* The Masoretic text writes *"waani el"* and by this addition (*"waw"*) spoils the construction, style, and meaning.

p. 176, l. 28 Isa. 43, 13: *"miiyom ani huah."* LXX v. 1: *"ap' archēis ego eimi."* Targum: *"min alma ana hu,"* "from Eternity, I am."

p. 176, l. 34 Isa. 43, 25 Targum: *"Ana, ana hu."* LXX v. 1: *"ego eimi, ego eimi hŏ exaleiphōn."* C. H. Dodd in *The Interpretation of the Fourth Gospel* (Cambridge, 1953), p. 94, quite boldly translates: "I am I AM who erases your iniquities."

p. 177, l. 11 Isa. 41, 4. 10. 13 f. 17; 42, 6. 8 f.; 44, 6. 24; 45, 2 f. 5 f. 7. 12 f. 18 f. 21 f.; 46, 4. 9; 48, 12 f. 15. 18. 23; 51, 12. 15; 52, 6; 54, 16.

p. 177, l. 14 Isa. 41, 4; 46, 4; 48, 12.

p. 177, l. 5 See Isa. 43, 10 ff. 25; 45, 3. 6. 18. 21 ff.; 46, 4. 9; 49, 18. 23. 26 and elsewhere.

p. 177, l. 8 Cf. Deut. 4, 35. 39; 7. 9; 1 Kings 18, 39. For the older and different wording of Ex. 3, 14, see E. Schild, "I Am That I Am" in *V.T.,* Vol. 4 (1954), p. 296 ff.

p. 177, l. 11 In the LXX, see Isa. 41, 15; 44, 2 f.; 45, 7. 12. 19; 46, 4; Ezek. 34, 15; (Zeph. 2, 15); etc. In the Targumim see, e.g., Isa. 45, 21; 49, 8; Deut. 32, 39: "I am [*ana hu*] that I am and that I was, and I am [*waana hu*] that I shall be."

p. 177, l. 15 Aleph is the first letter of *Elohim* and also of *Amen;* thus in D.S.M. 10, 1 (cf. Rev. 3, 14!). The four points replace the four letters of the Tetragrammaton, which is often also used in ancient Hebrew writing.

p. 177, l. 19. God = *"huah"* in D.S.M. 3, 25; 4, 25; 10, 18. The emphatic "He" is derived from Isa. 43, 25; 51, 12, and elsewhere, and from the point of view of sheer grammar can be dispensed with here exactly as the emphatic "I" is in Isa. 43, 12; 46, 4; 48, 15; 51, 12 and elsewhere. God = *"howe olam"* in D.S.M. 11, 4. Cf. with this Isa. 43, 14 and elsewhere.

p. 178, l. 30 See W. H. Brownlee, A. M. Habermann, H. Bardtke, and others on this.

p. 179, l. 5 Apoc. Abrah., ed. Bonwetsch, 8 f. Cf. Isa. 43, 1 ff., and frequently. Explanatory "I" formulae are attached, as in Isa. 46, 4, and often. Moreover, the affinity with the Targum Isa. is noticeable here. See Isa. 43, 12 (revelation to Abraham); 43, 13 (*"min alma"*); 43, 10 (ages). Similar speeches stressing the "I" are already to be found in Jub. 24, 22; E. Enoch 108, 12, etc.

p. 179, l. 7 See M. Buttenwieser, *Die hebräische Eliasapokalypse* (Leipzig, 1897), 8. Also Isa. 43, 10; Deut. 32, 39; and elsewhere.

p. 179, l. 13 See H. Bardtke, *"Die Parascheneinteilung der Jesaiarolle I,"* in *Festschrift Dornseiff* (1953), p. 62 and frequently. For the use of Isa. 40–55 in the divine service, see L. Venetianer, *"Ursprung und Bedeutung der Prophetenlektionen," Z.D.M.G.,* Vol. 63 (1909), p. 153 ff. On Isa. 43, 7 ff., see A. Büchler, "The Triennial Reading of the Law and Prophets," *J.Q.R.,* Vol. 6 (1894), p. 59 ff.

p. 179, l. 20 See Rosh Hashana 31 a and elsewhere; also Büchler, *Z.A.W.* (1900), p. 102 ff.

p. 179, l. 30 Sukk. 53 a Baraitha.

p. 179, l. 31 Lazarus Goldschmidt, *Das babylonische Talmud (editio maior* and *minor),* recognizes the ambiguity of Hillel's saying, but does not perceive that it is meant to be a *mashal.* Hillel was fond of enigmatic "I" sayings. See Aboth 1, 4: "If I am not for myself who is for me? And being for my own self what am I? And if not now when?" Cf. also J. Sukk. 5, 55 b.

p. 180, l. 1 Thus Tos. Sukk. 4, 3; Mek. Ex. 20, 24; Aboth de R. Nathan 12. Similarly Rashi de Troyes (*c.* 1100) in Billerbeck, Vol. 2, p. 807, and Moses de Leon (*c.* 1300): "If the *Shekinah* [= *Ani*] is here, all is here." (See *Auszug aus dem Buche Sohar* [Berlin, 1852], p. 10 f.) Similarly, Wilhelm Bacher, *Agada der Tannaiten* (Strassburg, 1903), Vol. 1, p. 5; Talmud W., Vol. 1, p. 110; G. Klein, *Der älteste christliche Katechismus* (Berlin, 1909), p. 46.

p. 180, l. 6 Thus the non-Jewish scholars P. Billerbeck (Vol. 2, p. 807) and E. L. Dietrich (*Z.R.G.G.,* Vol. 4 [1952], p. 306)—both failing to consider the historical problems of the form and the old and rich *Ani* tradition in Jewish theology and liturgy.

p. 180, l. 21 Sukk. 4, 5. For the history of exegesis, see H. Bornhäuser, *Sukka* (Berlin, 1935); Billerbeck, Vol. 2, pp. 793, 797; M. Jastrow, *Dictionary of the Targumim, etc.* (New York, 1950), *"Ani."* On Arabic "I" formulae, see G. Widengren, *Muhammad, The Apostle of God and His Ascension* (1955), pp. 48–54.

p. 180, l. 24 A classical example of this is provided by the ancient formulae and cries of the Roman Salians; see R. Civilli, *Les Prêtres danseurs de Rome* (Paris, 1913), p. 177 etc.

p. 181, l. 7 Talmud W., Vol. 1, pp. 110, 456. Moses de Leon explains: *Ani we Hu* = God and the Shekinah (see *Auszug aus dem Buche Sohar,* p. 19).

p. 181, l. 11 Cf. Mark 11, 9 f.; 14, 26; Matt. 21, 15, and elsewhere.

p. 181, l. 23 See E. D. Goldschmidt, *Die Pesachhaggada* (Berlin, 1936), p. 54 f. For the interpretation and early date, see D. Daube, *The New Testament and Rabbinic Judaism* (London, 1956), p. 325 ff.

p. 181, l. 24 See Isa. 43, 10 f.; 45, 22; 46, 9.

p. 181, l. 29 M. Glatzer, *The Passover Haggadah* (New York, 1953), p. 98 ff.; cf. Ps. 115, 9 ff.

p. 181, l. 34 See Mid. 4, 2; Ber. 104 a; Pesikta rabb. 104 a on Isa. 42, 8; Ex. r. and Rashi on Ex. 2, 6; Talmud W., Vol. 1, p. 456. Cf. Djelaleddin Rumi in G. Hölscher, *Die Profeten* (Leipzig, 1914), p. 23 (8 times *Allah hu*). R. Paret of Tübingen has kindly pointed out to me that invocations such as *Huwa* (*He = God*), *Hu,* and *Allahu* are frequent in Islamic texts.

p. 182, l. 6 Mek. Ex. 15, 3. See Deut. 32, 39 f., and Isa. 41, 4. The same formulae are in Mek. Ex. 20, 2 (with an allusion to Deut. 32, 39 f.); Isa. 41, 4; 44, 6; 46, 4, and elsewhere.

p. 182, l. 11 See Ex. r. on 20, 2.

p. 182, l. 18 See Ex. r. on 20, 2; Gen. r. on 48, 21. In the tractate Sopherim 4, 1, the formula of revelation *"ehejeh asher ehejeh"* ("I will be he who I will be") appears among the substitute names for Yahweh; see *Machsor Vitry,* ed. Hurwitz (Nuremberg, 1923), p. 692. Rashi on Ex. 3, 14, considers this a saying guaranteeing redemption.

p. 182, l. 27 See Ex. r. on 3, 12; Pesikta rabb. 104 a.

p. 183, l. 26 Echoes of this controversy are in the *Toledoth Jeshu;* see Samuel Krauss, *Das Leben Jesu nach jüdischen Quellen* (Berlin, 1902), p. 54 and elsewhere.

p. 183, l. 29 See Luke 24, 36 ff.; John 21, 1 ff.; 1 Cor. 15, 5 ff.

p. 184, l. 11 A favorite theme of the Hallel psalms (see Ps. 114, 3 ff.), of the Exodus *haggadah* at the Passover table, and of numerous Passover hymns. But see also Mark 4, 35 ff. For the association of the "I" formula with the theme of controlling the sea, see, e.g., Isa. 43, 1 ff.

p. 184, l. 15 For "Have no fear," etc., in association with "I" formulae, see, e.g., Isa. 41, 4 ff. 13 ff.; 43, 1 ff.; 44, 2 ff.; 51, 9 ff.; in the *Hallel* psalms, e.g., Ps. 115, 9 ff.; 118, 5 f.

p. 185, l. 5 The *Ascension of Isaiah* is a Christian devotional book of around A.D. 300 which contains divers pieces of pre-Christian and early Christian tradition; it is preserved most completely in Ethiopic. See R. H. Charles, *The Ascension of Isaiah* (London, 1900).

p. 185, l. 12 The execution of Peter in the course of Nero's persecution of the Christians in August A.D. 64. Paul and his martyrdom are ignored. This suggests the Judaeo-Christian origin of the pamphlet. The note on the flight into the desert also points to the same origin. The oracle probably arose in Palestine or Syria.

p. 185, l. 14 The two initial words of the Ethiopic self-affirmation, *"Ana usetu,"* formed from *Ana hu, Ana huatu,* correspond exactly with the Aramaic "I" formulae. See C. Brockelmann, *Grundriss der vergleichenden Grammatik der semitischen Sprachen* (Berlin, 1908), Vol. 1, p. 302 f.

p. 185, l. 22 The number (1,335 days) comes from Dan. 12, 12. If the beginning of these 1,335 days is set at the end of August A.D. 64 (martyrdom of Peter), then the expiration date will be the end of April 68. Nero, however, lived and reigned until June 9, 68. Accordingly, the prediction should have been published by April 68 at the latest. But the same pamphlet mentions the flight to the desert of those who remained faithful to Christ, probably the flight of the Christian community of Jerusalem to Pella early in 68. Therefore the prediction cannot have been made before January 68. It follows that this pamphlet was probably composed in the spring of 68, during a period full of political as well as apocalyptic excitement. Then, when Nero did not go down to hell on the set date and Jesus Christ's longed-for Parousia also failed to materialize in June 68, the prediction was redated, reshaped, and reinterpreted in rough-and-ready fashion to apply to the returning Nero (see, e.g., Sib. 5, 28 ff.). In this form it was then worked into the *Ascension of Isaiah*. Concerning the controversy over the chronology of *Asc. Isa.* 3, 13 ff., see O. Cullmann, *Petrus* (Zürich, 1952), p. 122 f.

p. 186, l. 2 Cf. Sib. 5, 34: "*isazōn thĕō hauton.*"

p. 186, l. 31 On John 17, 3, see Stauffer, *Nov. Test.*, Vol. 1 (1956), p. 93.

p. 187, l. 2 Isa. 40, 21; 41, 22 f. 26; 42, 9 ff.; 43, 9. 12 (see above, p. 176); 44, 7 f.; 46, 10; 48, 3. 14.

p. 187, l. 7 See Millar Burrows, op. cit., Vol. 1 (1950), Pl. XLIII: "*lachen veda ammi shemi bayyom hahuah ḳi ana huah hamedabber hinneni.*" After "*shemi*" there is no "*lachen.*" The Masuretic text must be corrected accordingly. After "*hinneni*" there is a gap (part of a blank line). Accordingly, the Septuagint text (diverging from Rahlfs and Ziegler) should be read with the following punctuation: "*dia toutŏ gnōsetai hŏ laŏs mou tŏ onoma mou en tēi hēimera ekeinēi, oti ego eimi autos hŏ lalōn; pareimi*" (Euseb.: "*idou eimi*"). The same caesura also occurs in the Targum at this point.

p. 187, l. 12 See Epiphanius, *Haer.* 23, 5, 5; 41, 3, 2; 66, 42, 8, and *Ancor* 53, 4. For Isa. 52, 6, as a proleptic *dictum* of the pre-existent *logos*, see in Pseudo-Cyprian, *De Jud. incred.* (ed. Hartel), Vol. 4, p. 124: "*ipse qui loquebar veni.*" Compare with this the interpolation of the *Memra* in the Targum on Isa. 52, 6, and throughout in the Targum paraphrase of Isa. 40–55.

p. 188, l. 20 Here a few references to Pseudo-Clement must suffice. See Ps. Clem. *Hom.* 2, 24; *Rec.* 1, 72, 3; 2, 15, 2; 3, 46 f. Perhaps in Mark 13, 6, Mark is thinking of Simon Magus (in Rome)? A critical analysis of this and similar remarks, with a study of the sources, their tendencies, and their place in the history of religion, is sorely needed.

p. 189, l. 18 See Isa. 43, 12; 46, 11; 48, 15; and above, note to page 176, line 25.

p. 190, l. 7 The thrice-repeated "*ego eimi*" in John 18, 5 ff., in spite of its overwhelming effect, is probably to be understood merely as a simple introduction of himself; see 18, 8. (The antithesis is: "I—the others," not: "God—man.") Similarly, C. K. Barrett, *St. John*

(London, 1955), p. 434, with a reference to John 9, 9, but not without a "reminiscence" of John 13, 9.

p. 190, l. 12 Instead, we find in the Johannine Farewell Discourses an accumulation of manifestation-like promises in the style of Isa. 40–55: ". . . and you also are witnesses, because you have been with me from the beginning" (John 15, 27; cf. Isa. 44, 8). "In that day you will know that I am in my Father . . ." (John 14, 20; cf. Isa. 52, 6 ff.). "And now I have told you before it takes place, so that when it does take place, you may believe" (John 14, 29; cf. Isa. 43, 9 f.). "But I have said these things to you, that when their hour comes you may remember that I told you of them" (John 16, 4; cf. Isa. 43, 12).

p. 190, l. 22 John 8, 24 ff. 58 f.; Mark 13, 6; John 13,19; Mark 14, 62.

p. 191, l. 1 Yalkut Shimoni, § 766 on Num. 23. Also Mek. Ex. 20, 1, combats "heretical 'I' sayings" (cf. Daube, op. cit., p. 327). This polemic intent appears to be even more obvious in a hitherto unknown text of the Mekilta which E. Bammel has discovered and will publish.

p. 191, l. 12 J Taan. 2, 1. The three self-revelatory sayings are: *"Ani el"; "Ben Adam Ani"; "Ani oleh lashshamayim."* The word "regret" here has nothing to do with a change of heart (cf. Num. 23, 19) or penitence (as in Sanh. 107 b), but refers to the inevitable end of a blasphemer, the death penalty. See J Sanh. 10, 29 a: "His end will be that he will be strangled."

p. 191, l. 30 John 4, 26; Mark 6, 50; John 6, 20; Mark 13, 6; John 13, 19.

p. 192, l. 7 See Matt. 27, 63; Justin, *Dial.* 108; Sanh. 43 a; and elsewhere.

p. 192, l. 11 See Matt. 28, 15; Acts 28, 22; Justin, *Dial.* 17; 108; Euseb. on Isa. 18, 1.

p. 192, l. 32 The recorded tradition here is the same as in the case of the "Son of Man" of *"amēin legō humin."* These phrases, too, surely go back to Jesus; but not all the *logia* in which they occur are authentic.

p. 192, l. 33 In the Septuagint *"Ego eimi"* is the prevailing translation of the Hebrew "I" formula *"Ani hu,"* which in the Targum of Isaiah appears in the Aramaic form *"Ana hu."* Accordingly, the self-revelatory formula *"ego eimi"* in the Gospels may be regarded as the translation of *"Ani hu"* or *"Ana hu"* spoken by Jesus. Delitzsch's retranslation (*"Ani hu"*) agrees with this and, above all, with the Palestinian Syriac (*"Ana hu"*). See Matt. 14, 27; John 6, 20; 8, 24. 28 and frequently.

Notes

p. *193, l. 17* Mark 14, 62; cf. John 8, 28, etc.

p. *193, l. 28* Mark 14, 62, states without specifying any time: *"kai opsesthe katheimenon kai erchomenon."* This is the genuine style of Jesus. Matt. (26, 64) notices the absence of what counted most to him and his friends, the imminence of the appointed day, and adds on his own accord: *"ap' arti opsesthe katheimenon kai erchomenon."* Luke (22, 69) omits *"opsesthe"* and *"erchomenon"* and writes, in keeping with his own Christology: *"apo tou nun estai katheimenos"* (cf. Luke 22, 43; Acts 7, 56). The spurious ending in Mark combines Matthew and Luke, and expresses itself as though Jesus had ascended the throne by an actually visible process: Mark 16, 19.

p. *194, l. 2* See Mark 2, 10. 28; 14, 62; Luke 19, 10 (the description of God in Ezek. 34, 16, appears here as a description of the Son of Man); John 5, 27. The Son of Man in E. Enoch already appears frequently in the dignity of God.

p. *194, l. 30* The most characteristic expression of this claim is Jesus' formula of announcement: *"Amēin legō humin,"* which takes the place of God's oath in the Old Testament; cf. Ez. 14, 16 ff., and Origen on Ez. 14, 20. Moreover, it should be noticed how the Palestinian Syriac translates the formula: *"amen amer ana lachun"* (similarly Delitzsch). According to this, in Jesus' mother tongue a personal pronoun was used here which is omitted in the Greek. Consequently, the emphatic *Ana* was on Jesus' lips far more frequently than has been assumed hitherto from the wording of the Greek Gospels (Matt. 5, 21 ff., is hardly Jesus' own wording).

A NOTE ON THE AUTHOR

ETHELBERT STAUFFER, Professor at the University of Erlangen, has achieved international reputation as the author of *Christ and the Caesars* and *New Testament Theology* (both 1955).

He was born in 1902 in the Rhineland, and received his education at the universities of Halle-Wittenberg, Berlin, and Tübingen. He taught at Halle and Tübingen before assuming his present position at Erlangen Divinity School, where he also conducts the *Seminar für Geschichte des Urchristentums* (Seminar for the History of Primitive Christianity). He is one of the editors of the international quarterly *Novum Testamentum*, published in Leiden, Holland.

Professor Stauffer lives with his wife and his four children in a suburb of Erlangen.

A NOTE ON THE TYPE

THIS BOOK is set on the Linotype in Granjon, a type named in compliment to Robert Granjon, but neither a copy of a classic face nor an entirely original creation. The design is based upon the type used by Claude Garamond (1510–61) in his beautiful French books, and more closely resembles Garamond's own than do any of the various types that bear his name.

Robert Granjon began his career as type-cutter in 1523. The boldest and most original designer of his time, he was one of the first to practice the trade of type-founder apart from that of printer. Between 1557 and 1562 Granjon printed about twenty books in types designed by himself, following after the fashion of the day, the cursive handwriting of the time. These types, usually known as "caractères de civilité," he himself called "lettres françaises," as especially appropriate to his own country.

This book was composed, printed, and bound by Kingsport Press, Inc., Kingsport, Tenn. Paper manufactured by P. H. Glatfelter Company, Spring Grove, Pennsylvania. Typography and binding design by Guy Fleming.